PRAXIS
PHYSICAL EDUCATION 091

By: Sharon Wynne, M.S.

Contributing author: Carrie Harper

XAMonline, INC.
Boston

To obtain permission(s) to use the material from this work for any purpose including workshops or seminars, please submit a written request to:

XAMonline, Inc.
25 First Street, Suite 106
Cambridge, MA 02141
Toll Free 1-800-509-4128
Email: info@xamonline.com
Web: www.xamonline.com
Fax: 1-617-583-5552

Library of Congress Cataloging-in-Publication Data

Wynne, Sharon A.
    PRAXIS Physical Education 091 / Sharon A. Wynne. 3rd ed
    ISBN 978-1-60787-071-5
    1. Physical Education
    2. Study Guides
    3. PRAXIS
    4. Teachers' Certification & Licensure
    5. Careers

Disclaimer:

The opinions expressed in this publication are the sole works of XAMonline and were created independently from the National Education Association, Educational Testing Service, or any State Department of Education, National Evaluation Systems or other testing affiliates.

Between the time of publication and printing, state specific standards as well as testing formats and Web site information may change and therefore would not be included in part or in whole within this product. Sample test questions are developed by XAMonline and reflect content similar to that on real tests; however, they are not former test questions. XAMonline assembles content that aligns with state standards but makes no claims nor guarantees teacher candidates a passing score. Numerical scores are determined by testing companies such as NES or ETS and then are compared with individual state standards. A passing score varies from state to state.

Printed in the United States of America   œ-1

PRAXIS Physical Education 091
ISBN: 978-1-60787-071-5

Table of Contents

DOMAIN II
MANAGEMENT, MOTIVATION, AND COMMUNICATION 65

COMPETENCY 3
MANAGEMENT AND MOTIVATION 67

COMPETENCY 4
COMMUNICATION 74

DOMAIN III
PLANNING, INSTRUCTION, AND STUDENT ASSESSMENT 79

COMPETENCY 5
PLANNING AND INSTRUCTION 81

COMPETENCY 6

DOMAIN IV

COMPETENCY 7

PRAXIS
PHYSICAL EDUCATION 091

SECTION 1
ABOUT XAMONLINE

XAMonline—A Specialty Teacher Certification Company

Created in 1996, XAMonline was the first company to publish study guides for state-specific teacher certification examinations. Founder Sharon Wynne found it frustrating that materials were not available for teacher certification preparation and decided to create the first single, state-specific guide. XAMonline has grown into a company of over 1,800 contributors and writers and offers over 300 titles for the entire PRAXIS series and every state examination. No matter what state you plan on teaching in, XAMonline has a unique teacher certification study guide just for you.

XAMonline—Value and Innovation

We are committed to providing value and innovation. Our print-on-demand technology allows us to be the first in the market to reflect changes in test standards and user feedback as they occur. Our guides are written by experienced teachers who are experts in their fields. And our content reflects the highest standards of quality. Comprehensive practice tests with varied levels of rigor means that your study experience will closely match the actual in-test experience.

To date, XAMonline has helped nearly 600,000 teachers pass their certification or licensing exams. Our commitment to preparation exceeds simply providing the proper material for study—it extends to helping teachers **gain mastery** of the subject matter, giving them the **tools** to become the most effective classroom leaders possible, and ushering today's students toward a **successful future**.

SECTION 2
ABOUT THIS STUDY GUIDE

Purpose of This Guide

Is there a little voice inside of you saying, "Am I ready?" Our goal is to replace that little voice and remove all doubt with a new voice that says, "I AM READY. **Bring it on!**" by offering the highest quality of teacher certification study guides.

Organization of Content

You will see that while every test may start with overlapping general topics, each is very unique in the skills they wish to test. Only XAMonline presents custom content that analyzes deeper than a title, a subarea, or an objective. Only XAMonline presents content and sample test assessments along with **focus statements**, the deepest-level rationale and interpretation of the skills that are unique to the exam.

Title and field number of test

→Each exam has its own name and number. XAMonline's guides are written to give you the content you need to know for the specific exam you are taking. You can be confident when you buy our guide that it contains the information you need to study for the specific test you are taking.

Subareas

→These are the major content categories found on the exam. XAMonline's guides are written to cover all of the subareas found in the test frameworks developed for the exam.

Objectives

→These are standards that are unique to the exam and represent the main subcategories of the subareas/content categories. XAMonline's guides are written to address every specific objective required to pass the exam.

Focus statements

→These are examples and interpretations of the objectives. You find them in parenthesis directly following the objective. They provide detailed examples of the range, type, and level of content that appear on the test questions. **Only XAMonline's guides drill down to this level.**

How Do We Compare with Our Competitors?

XAMonline—drills down to the focus statement level.
CliffsNotes and REA—organized at the objective level
Kaplan—provides only links to content
MoMedia—content not specific to the state test

Each subarea is divided into manageable sections that cover the specific skill areas. Explanations are easy to understand and thorough. You'll find that every test answer contains a rejoinder so if you need a refresher or further review after taking the test, you'll know exactly to which section you must return.

How to Use This Book

Our informal polls show that most people begin studying up to eight weeks prior to the test date, so start early. Then ask yourself some questions: How much do you really know? Are you coming to the test straight from your teacher-education program or are you having to review subjects you haven't considered in ten years? Either way, take a **diagnostic or assessment test** first. Also, spend time on sample tests so that you become accustomed to the way the actual test will appear.

This guide comes with an online diagnostic test of 30 questions found online at *www.XAMonline.com*. It is a little boot camp to get you up for the task and reveal things about your compendium of knowledge in general. Although this guide is structured to follow the order of the test, you are not required to study in that order. By finding a time-management and study plan that fits your life you will be more effective. The results of your diagnostic or self-assessment test can be a guide for how to manage your time and point you toward an area that needs more attention.

After taking the diagnostic exam, fill out the **Personalized Study Plan** page at the beginning of each chapter. Review the competencies and skills covered in that chapter and check the boxes that apply to your study needs. If there are sections you already know you can skip, check the "skip it" box. Taking this step will give you a study plan for each chapter.

Week	Activity
8 weeks prior to test	Take a diagnostic test found at www.XAMonline.com
7 weeks prior to test	Build your Personalized Study Plan for each chapter. Check the "skip it" box for sections you feel you are already strong in. ✗ **SKIP IT** ☐
6-3 weeks prior to test	For each of these four weeks, choose a content area to study. You don't have to go in the order of the book. It may be that you start with the content that needs the most review. Alternately, you may want to ease yourself into plan by starting with the most familiar material.
2 weeks prior to test	Take the sample test, score it, and create a review plan for the final week before the test.
1 week prior to test	Following your plan (which will likely be aligned with the areas that need the most review) go back and study the sections that align with the questions you may have gotten wrong. Then go back and study the sections related to the questions you answered correctly. If need be, create flashcards and drill yourself on any area that you makes you anxious.

SECTION 3
ABOUT THE PRAXIS EXAMS

What Is PRAXIS?

PRAXIS II tests measure the knowledge of specific content areas in K-12 education. The test is a way of insuring that educators are prepared to not only teach in a particular subject area, but also have the necessary teaching skills to be effective. The Educational Testing Service administers the test in most states and has worked with the states to develop the material so that it is appropriate for state standards.

PRAXIS Points

1. The PRAXIS Series comprises more than 140 different tests in over 70 different subject areas.

2. Over 90% of the PRAXIS tests measure subject area knowledge.

3. The purpose of the test is to measure whether the teacher candidate possesses a sufficient level of knowledge and skills to perform job duties effectively and responsibly.

4. Your state sets the acceptable passing score.

5. Any candidate, whether from a traditional teaching-preparation path or an alternative route, can seek to enter the teaching profession by taking a PRAXIS test.

6. PRAXIS tests are updated regularly to ensure current content.

Often **your own state's requirements** determine whether or not you should take any particular test. The most reliable source of information regarding this is your state's Department of Education. This resource should have a complete list of testing centers and dates. Test dates vary by subject area and not all test dates necessarily include your particular test, so be sure to check carefully.

If you are in a teacher-education program, check with the Education Department or the Certification Officer for specific information for testing and testing timelines. The Certification Office should have most of the information you need.

If you choose an alternative route to certification you can either rely on our website at *www.XAMonline.com* or on the resources provided by an alternative certification program. Many states now have specific agencies devoted to alternative certification and there are some national organizations as well, for example:

National Association for Alternative Certification
http://www.alt-teachercert.org/index.asp

Interpreting Test Results

Contrary to what you may have heard, the results of a PRAXIS test are not based on time. More accurately, you will be scored on the raw number of points you earn in relation to the raw number of points available. Each question is worth one raw point. It is likely to your benefit to complete as many questions in the time allotted, but it will not necessarily work to your advantage if you hurry through the test.

Follow the guidelines provided by ETS for interpreting your score. The web site offers a sample test score sheet and clearly explains how the scores are scaled and what to expect if you have an essay portion on your test.

Scores are usually available by phone within a month of the test date and scores will be sent to your chosen institution(s) within six weeks. Additionally, ETS now makes online, downloadable reports available for 45 days from the reporting date.

It is **critical** that you be aware of your own state's passing score. Your raw score may qualify you to teach in some states, but not all. ETS administers the test and assigns a score, but the states make their own interpretations and, in some cases, consider combined scores if you are testing in more than one area.

What's on the Test?

The Praxis Physical Education: Content Knowledge 091 exam lasts 2 hours and consists of 120 multiple-choice questions. The breakdown of the questions is as follows:

Category	Approximate Number of Questions	Approximate Percentage of the Test
I: Content Knowledge and Student Growth and Development	36	30%
II: Management, Motivation, and Communication	30	25%

Continued on next page

| III: Planning, Instruction, and Student Assessment | 30 | 25% |
| IV: Collaboration, Reflections, and Technology | 24 | 20% |

Question Types

You're probably thinking, enough already, I want to study! Indulge us a little longer while we explain that there is actually more than one type of multiple-choice question. You can thank us later after you realize how well prepared you are for your exam.

1. **Complete the Statement.** The name says it all. In this question type you'll be asked to choose the correct completion of a given statement. For example:

> **The Dolch Basic Sight Words consist of a relatively short list of words that children should be able to:**
>
> A. Sound out
>
> B. Know the meaning of
>
> C. Recognize on sight
>
> D. Use in a sentence

The correct answer is C. In order to check your answer, test out the statement by adding the choices to the end of it.

2. **Which of the Following.** One way to test your answer choice for this type of question is to replace the phrase "which of the following" with your selection. Use this example:

> **Which of the following words is one of the twelve most frequently used in children's reading texts:**
>
> A. There
>
> B. This
>
> C. The
>
> D. An

Don't look! Test your answer. _____ is one of the twelve most frequently used in children's reading texts. Did you guess C? Then you guessed correctly.

3. **Roman Numeral Choices.** This question type is used when there is more than one possible correct answer. For example:

> **Which of the following two arguments accurately supports the use of cooperative learning as an effective method of instruction?**
> I.   Cooperative learning groups facilitate healthy competition between individuals in the group.
> II. Cooperative learning groups allow academic achievers to carry or cover for academic underachievers.
> III. Cooperative learning groups make each student in the group accountable for the success of the group.
> IV. Cooperative learning groups make it possible for students to reward other group members for achieving.
>
> A. I and II
>
> B. II and III
>
> C. I and III
>
> D. III and IV

Notice that the question states there are **two** possible answers. It's best to read all the possibilities first before looking at the answer choices. In this case, the correct answer is D.

4. **Negative Questions.** This type of question contains words such as "not," "least," and "except." Each correct answer will be the statement that does **not** fit the situation described in the question. Such as:

> **Multicultural education is not**
>
> A. An idea or concept
>
> B. A "tack-on" to the school curriculum
>
> C. An educational reform movement
>
> D. A process

Think to yourself that the statement could be anything but the correct answer. This question form is more open to interpretation than other types, so read carefully and don't forget that you're answering a negative statement.

5. Questions that Include Graphs, Tables, or Reading Passages. As always, read the question carefully. It likely asks for a very specific answer and not a broad interpretation of the visual. Here is a simple (though not statistically accurate) example of a graph question:

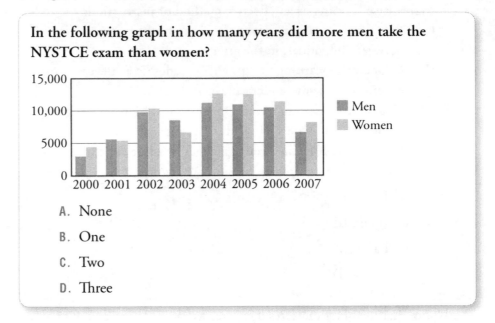

In the following graph in how many years did more men take the NYSTCE exam than women?

A. None

B. One

C. Two

D. Three

It may help you to simply circle the two years that answer the question. Make sure you've read the question thoroughly and once you've made your determination, double check your work. The correct answer is C.

SECTION 4
HELPFUL HINTS

Study Tips

1. You are what you eat. Certain foods aid the learning process by releasing natural memory enhancers called CCKs (cholecystokinin) composed of tryptophan, choline, and phenylalanine. All of these chemicals enhance the neurotransmitters associated with memory and certain foods release memory

enhancing chemicals. A light meal or snacks of one of the following foods fall into this category:

- Milk
- Rice
- Eggs
- Fish
- Nuts and seeds
- Oats
- Turkey

The better the connections, the more you comprehend!

2. See the forest for the trees. In other words, get the concept before you look at the details. One way to do this is to take notes as you read, paraphrasing or summarizing in your own words. Putting the concept in terms that are comfortable and familiar may increase retention.

3. Question authority. Ask why, why, why? Pull apart written material paragraph by paragraph and don't forget the captions under the illustrations. For example, if a heading reads *Stream Erosion* put it in the form of a question (Why do streams erode? What is stream erosion?) then find the answer within the material. If you train your mind to think in this manner you will learn more and prepare yourself for answering test questions.

4. Play mind games. Using your brain for reading or puzzles keeps it flexible. Even with a limited amount of time your brain can take in data (much like a computer) and store it for later use. In ten minutes you can: read two paragraphs (at least), quiz yourself with flash cards, or review notes. Even if you don't fully understand something on the first pass, your mind stores it for recall, which is why frequent reading or review increases chances of retention and comprehension.

5. Get pointed in the right direction. Use arrows to point to important passages or pieces of information. It's easier to read than a page full of yellow highlights. Highlighting can be used sparingly, but add an arrow to the margin to call attention to it.

6. Place yourself in exile and set the mood. Set aside a particular place and time to study that best suits your personal needs and biorhythms. If you're a night person, burn the midnight oil. If you're a morning person set yourself up with some coffee and get to it. Make your study time and place as free from distraction as possible and surround yourself with what you need, be it silence or music. Studies have shown that music can aid in concentration, absorption, and retrieval of information. Not all music, though. Classical music is said to work best

7. **The pen is mightier than the sword.** Learn to take great notes. A by-product of our modern culture is that we have grown accustomed to getting our information in short doses. We've subconsciously trained ourselves to assimilate information into neat little packages. Messy notes fragment the flow of information. Your notes can be much clearer with proper formatting. *The Cornell Method* is one such format. This method was popularized in *How to Study in College*, Ninth Edition, by Walter Pauk. You can benefit from the method without purchasing an additional book by simply looking up the method online. Below is a sample of how *The Cornell Method* can be adapted for use with this guide.

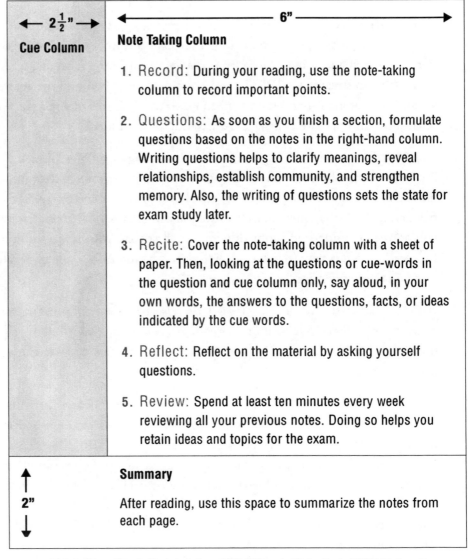

← 2½" → **Cue Column**	← 6" → **Note Taking Column** 1. Record: During your reading, use the note-taking column to record important points. 2. Questions: As soon as you finish a section, formulate questions based on the notes in the right-hand column. Writing questions helps to clarify meanings, reveal relationships, establish community, and strengthen memory. Also, the writing of questions sets the state for exam study later. 3. Recite: Cover the note-taking column with a sheet of paper. Then, looking at the questions or cue-words in the question and cue column only, say aloud, in your own words, the answers to the questions, facts, or ideas indicated by the cue words. 4. Reflect: Reflect on the material by asking yourself questions. 5. Review: Spend at least ten minutes every week reviewing all your previous notes. Doing so helps you retain ideas and topics for the exam.
↑ 2" ↓	**Summary** After reading, use this space to summarize the notes from each page.

*Adapted from How to Study in College, Ninth Edition, by Walter Pauk, ©2008 Wadsworth

8. **Check your budget.** You should at least review all the content material before your test, but allocate the most amount of time to the areas that need the most refreshing. It sounds obvious, but it's easy to forget. You can use the study rubric above to balance your study budget.

The proctor will write the start time where it can be seen and then, later, provide the time remaining, typically fifteen minutes before the end of the test.

Testing Tips

1. **Get smart, play dumb.** Sometimes a question is just a question. No one is out to trick you, so don't assume that the test writer is looking for something other than what was asked. Stick to the question as written and don't overanalyze.

2. **Do a double take.** Read test questions and answer choices at least twice because it's easy to miss something, to transpose a word or some letters. If you have no idea what the correct answer is, skip it and come back later if there's time. If you're still clueless, it's okay to guess. Remember, you're scored on the number of questions you answer correctly and you're not penalized for wrong answers. The worst case scenario is that you miss a point from a good guess.

3. **Turn it on its ear.** The syntax of a question can often provide a clue, so make things interesting and turn the question into a statement to see if it changes the meaning or relates better (or worse) to the answer choices.

4. **Get out your magnifying glass.** Look for hidden clues in the questions because it's difficult to write a multiple-choice question without giving away part of the answer in the options presented. In most questions you can readily eliminate one or two potential answers, increasing your chances of answering correctly to 50/50, which will help out if you've skipped a question and gone back to it (see tip #2).

5. **Call it intuition.** Often your first instinct is correct. If you've been studying the content you've likely absorbed something and have subconsciously retained the knowledge. On questions you're not sure about trust your instincts because a first impression is usually correct.

6. **Graffiti.** Sometimes it's a good idea to mark your answers directly on the test booklet and go back to fill in the optical scan sheet later. You don't get extra points for perfectly blackened ovals. If you choose to manage your test this way, be sure not to mismark your answers when you transcribe to the scan sheet.

7. Become a clock-watcher. You have a set amount of time to answer the questions. Don't get bogged down laboring over a question you're not sure about when there are ten others you could answer more readily. If you choose to follow the advice of tip #6, be sure you leave time near the end to go back and fill in the scan sheet.

Do the Drill

No matter how prepared you feel it's sometimes a good idea to apply Murphy's Law. So the following tips might seem silly, mundane, or obvious, but we're including them anyway.

1. Remember, you are what you eat, so bring a snack. Choose from the list of energizing foods that appear earlier in the introduction.

2. You're not too sexy for your test. Wear comfortable clothes. You'll be distracted if your belt is too tight or if you're too cold or too hot.

3. Lie to yourself. Even if you think you're a prompt person, pretend you're not and leave plenty of time to get to the testing center. Map it out ahead of time and do a dry run if you have to. There's no need to add road rage to your list of anxieties.

4. Bring sharp number 2 pencils. It may seem impossible to forget this need from your school days, but you might. And make sure the erasers are intact, too.

5. No ticket, no test. Bring your admission ticket as well as **two** forms of identification, including one with a picture and signature. You will not be admitted to the test without these things.

6. You can't take it with you. Leave any study aids, dictionaries, notebooks, computers, and the like at home. Certain tests **do** allow a scientific or four-function calculator, so check ahead of time to see if your test does.

7. Prepare for the desert. Any time spent on a bathroom break **cannot** be made up later, so use your judgment on the amount you eat or drink.

8. Quiet, Please! Keeping your own time is a good idea, but not with a timepiece that has a loud ticker. If you use a watch, take it off and place it nearby but not so that it distracts you. And **silence your cell phone**.

To the best of our ability, we have compiled the content you need to know in this book and in the accompanying online resources. The rest is up to you. You can use the study and testing tips or you can follow your own methods. Either way, you can be confident that there aren't any missing pieces of information and there shouldn't be any surprises in the content on the test.

If you have questions about test fees, registration, electronic testing, or other content verification issues please visit *www.ets.org*.

Good luck!

Sharon Wynne
Founder, XAMonline

DOMAIN I
CONTENT KNOWLEDGE AND STUDENT GROWTH AND DEVELOPMENT

PERSONALIZED STUDY PLAN

KNOWN MATERIAL/ SKIP IT

PAGE	COMPETENCY AND SKILL	
3	**1: Core concepts**	☐
	1.1: Terminology, principles, concepts, and applications of the basic sciences as related to motor skills and movement activities	☐
	1.2: Principles of biomechanics and kinesiology as they relate to motor skills and movement patterns	☐
	1.3: Movement concepts	☐
	1.4: Exercise physiology	☐
	1.5: Anatomy and physiology	☐
	1.6: Current and historical trends, issues, and developments in physical education	☐
	1.7: Understanding of the rules, strategies, skills, techniques, and concepts associated with a variety of movement activities and games across the age and grade spectra	☐
	1.8: Liability and legal consideration pertaining to the use of equipment, class organization, supervision, and program selection	☐
	1.9: Effects of substance abuse on student performance, health, and behavior	☐
58	**2: Student growth and development**	☐
	2.1: Appropriate learning and practice opportunities based on growth and motor development stages, individual characteristics and individual needs of students, learning environment, and task	☐
	2.2: Monitoring of performance in order to design safe instruction that meets students' developmental needs in the psychomotor, cognitive, and affective domains	☐
	2.3: Developmental readiness to learn and refine motor skills and movement patterns	☐
	2.4: Perception in motor development	☐
	2.5: Appropriate and effective instruction related to students' cultures and ethnicities, personal values, family structures, home environments, and community values	☐
	2.6: Use of appropriate professional support services and resources to meet students' needs	☐

COMPETENCY 1
CORE CONCEPTS

SKILL 1.1 **Terminology, principles, concepts, and applications of the basic sciences as related to motor skills and movement activities** *(e.g., anatomy and physiology, exercise physiology, biomechanics and kinesiology, motor development and motor learning)*

Health-Related Components of Physical Fitness

There are five health-related components of physical fitness: cardiorespiratory or cardiovascular endurance, muscle strength, muscle endurance, flexibility, and body composition.

Components of fitness

- **Cardiovascular endurance:** The ability of the body to sustain aerobic activities (activities requiring oxygen utilization) for extended periods.

- **Muscle strength:** The ability of muscle groups to contract and support a given amount of weight.

- **Muscle endurance:** The ability of muscle groups to contract continually over a period of time and support a given amount of weight.

- **Flexibility:** The ability of muscle groups to stretch and bend.

- **Body composition:** The body is composed of many types of tissue, including bone, muscle, organ tissue, and fat. Lean body mass (LBM) is the non-fat tissue. Of the tissue tested via calipers, hydrostatic weighing, or another method, the key is that lean body mass is the majority and fatty tissue is the minority of the body. The two times in a person's life that the body is supposed to gain fat cells are during gestation/infancy and, for females, during puberty. Teachers of young students are not encouraged to dwell on body fat percentage, and measuring children could send the wrong message. As girls and boys pass puberty and are looking toward a healthy life, tread lightly when testing body fat. In certain classes, like an independent fitness and weight loss class, teaching the students about testing body fat might be important in the curriculum. If body fat is tested, it should be done at the beginning and the end of the semester class. For teen boys, obesity is defined as a body fat percentage of 25% or greater. For teen girls, it is 32% or greater.

> *There are five health-related components of physical fitness: cardiorespiratory or cardiovascular endurance, muscle strength, muscle endurance, flexibility, and body composition.*

Body mass index

Body Mass Index (BMI) is used by doctors and insurance companies as an easy way to test for obesity. It is a flawed test because it relies only on height and weight. Someone who is not fat but extremely fit and muscular could be considered obese by this test. It is, however, a reality that employers and insurance companies—as well as some standards for excellence in fitness education awards and grants—use this formula, so the teacher should know what BMI is and how to check it.

BMI = (weight in pounds) × 703/height in inches.

Below is the general chart that doctors and insurance companies use.

Category	Number Range
Underweight	18.5
Normal	18.5–24.9
Overweight	25–29.9
Obese	30+

In an independent fitness class or a class focused on lifestyle change, it would be a good project to calculate BMI and LBM and compare the two. Do both tests have the same result, or is the student considered healthy by one and not healthy by the other? Explain the differences in the tests. This is also a good cross-curricular mathematics project.

Wellness

Wellness has two major components: Understanding the basic human body functions and knowing how to establish for and maintain personal fitness. Wellness includes developing awareness and knowledge of how certain everyday factors, stress, and personal decisions can affect one's health. Teaching fitness needs to go along with skill and activity instruction. Life-long fitness and the benefits of a healthy lifestyle need to be part of every PE teacher's curriculum. Cross-discipline teaching and teaching thematically with other subject matter in classrooms would be the ideal method to teach health to adolescents.

Wellness for overall health is the main concern of modern physical education in public schools. No longer are we just training the athletes to perform; we are also teaching the entire population of students to maintain a sense of wellness and health for life. We are lifestyle trainers, not just physical trainers.

> BMI = (weight in pounds) × 703/height in inches.

Major Muscles and Bones; Functional Movement

Muscles

Shoulders

- Deltoids: Move the arm from rotator cuff; triangular-shaped muscles that cover the shoulders and move the arm in all directions.

Arms

- Biceps brachii (front of upper arm): Control the eccentric movement of arm (bends the elbow)

- Triceps brachii (back of upper arm): Control the concentric movement of arm (extends the upper arm)

Legs

- Quadriceps (front of upper leg): Control the eccentric movement of the thigh (extends the leg from knee to hip).

- Hamstrings (back of upper leg): Control the concentric movement of thigh (aids in bending the knee from the rear of the leg).

- Gastrocnemius (back of lower leg—calves): Aids in ankle and knee movement.

- Gluteus maximus (buttocks): The main gluteal muscle aiding in hip movement. Other hip-moving muscles include gluteus medius, gluteus minimus, and sacro iliac.

Chest

- Pectoralis major: Aids in deltoid and latissimus dorsi movement; main chest muscle; protects the ribcage and major organs.

Back

- Latissimus dorsi: A large back muscle; aids in deltoid and pectoralis movement as well as core movement; protects the rib cage from the back.

Waist

- Rectus abdominis: The largest stomach muscle, stretching from ribs to hips. This muscle aids in all waist movement, stability, and protection of abdominal organs. Other abdominals include obliques (sides) and transverse (wraps the lower abdominals). All abdominals work together to aid in all body movement.

Motor development

Development of motor skills begins as the human body begins to move in utero. Infancy and toddlerhood in normal development show beginnings of movement and development of muscles for proper function of the body. As the child gets older, the muscles should begin to develop. For example, a child will go from crawling to walking to running to jumping to leaping to skipping to jumping rope. Each person is different, and each child's development will go at a different pace. However, early childhood (from toddlerhood to kindergarten) is a vital phase to introduce the major movements of the body so that the child can continue to work on his or her development.

Movement is controlled by the frontal lobe of the brain. Delay in this part of the brain will impact the child's development of basic movement patterns. Muscles are designed to work in the specific functions listed earlier in this section, so a child's practice of functional movement will impact the development of each specific muscle group. Also, an injury to a bone or muscle as an infant or toddler could delay function of a specific muscle group or could show imbalance in pairs or groups of muscles. For example, a child who breaks a leg bone at the time when he or she is learning major muscle function might learn an alternate way to move, which could lead to larger muscles on one side of the body and atrophy of the other side.

Whereas fitness classes used to focus on straight squats and walking lunges for the leg muscles, now fitness classes should use bending and lifting, lateral movement, and stretching and reaching to develop the system of muscles used to do specific tasks.

Modern exercise focuses more on the natural way the body moves, or the function of the musculoskeletal system. Modern school fitness programs should address the way the muscles are designed to move and coordinate programs around everyday use of the muscles. Of course, all exercises should be done with attention to safety: Children should never lift beyond their capabilities, and they should never twist in a way that would endanger ligaments or tendons (such as the delicate knee area). In previous years, injury was a problem because students were not taught the true functions of the muscles. Now, programs should be in place to teach true functional movement to greatly reduce any chance of injury in and out of the classroom.

> ### SKILL 1.2 Principles of biomechanics and kinesiology as they relate to motor skills and movement patterns *(e.g., summation of forces, center of gravity, force/speed relations, torque)*

Summation of Forces

Many muscles and muscle systems work together to create one simple movement at the right time. For example, when watching a baseball pitcher throw the ball, his movement includes his abdominals pulling in, leg muscles contracting and releasing to move his foot, pectoralis and latissimus dorsi muscles to begin arm movement, elbow flexion to pull the arm in, deltoid muscles to move the shoulder, and all arm muscles in conjunction with chest, back, and abdominal muscles to release the ball. All of this has to occur at a given time and space for the ball to be thrown the way the pitcher wants it to be thrown.

Center of Gravity

If we did not feel centered in our own bodies, we would be pulled easily to the ground by the force of Earth's gravity. With every movement, the body must adjust its center (mainly the core and lower back) to keep us upright or in our desired position.

Force/Speed Relations

The amount of force our muscles use for a given movement directly or indirectly relates to the speed of that movement. Going back to the baseball pitcher example, the speed of his muscle contractions in his leg, chest, back, arm, and abdominals will directly impact the speed of the final movement, which directly impacts the speed of the release of the ball and the ball's speed over the plate.

Torque

TORQUE is rotational force. The amount of force a person uses to rotate a muscle group will impact the output of force. Using the pitcher as an example, he uses rotator muscles (abdominals and back muscles) to turn his body and then the rotator cuff of his shoulder to release the pitch.

TORQUE: rotational force

SKILL 1.3 **Movement concepts** *(e.g., body awareness, spatial awareness, effort, relationship)*

Concept of Body Awareness Applied to Physical Education Activities

BODY AWARENESS is a person's understanding of his or her own body parts and the capability of their movements.

Instructors can assess body awareness by watching students play a game of "Simon Says" and asking the students to touch different body parts. You can also instruct students to form their bodies into various shapes, such as moving from straight to round or twisted, and to fit into differently sized spaces.

BODY AWARENESS: a person's understanding of his or her own body parts and the capability of their movements

In addition, you can instruct children to touch one part of their bodies with another. Also, they could be asked to use various body parts to do activities like stamping their feet, twisting their necks, clapping their hands, nodding their heads, wiggling their noses, snapping their fingers, opening their mouths, shrugging their shoulders, bending their knees, closing their eyes, bending their elbows, or wiggling their toes.

Concept of Spatial Awareness Applied to Physical Education Activities

SPATIAL AWARENESS:
the ability to make decisions about an object's positional changes in space

SPATIAL AWARENESS is the ability to make decisions about an object's positional changes in space. In short, it is the awareness of three-dimensional position changes in space.

Developing spatial awareness requires two sequential phases:

1. Identifying the location of objects in relation to one's own body in space

2. Locating more than one object in relation to each other

Concept of Effort Qualities Applied to Physical Education

EFFORT QUALITIES:
the qualities of movement that apply the mechanical principles of balance, time, and force

EFFORT QUALITIES are the qualities of movement that apply the mechanical principles of balance, time, and force. Effort awareness is the application of this knowledge.

- Balance: Activities for balance include having children move on their hands and feet, lean, move on lines, and balance and hold shapes while moving. Modern equipment, such as balance balls, is effective in training to balance on unstable surfaces.

- Time: Activities illustrating the concept of time can include having children move as fast as they can and as slow as they can in specified, timed movement patterns.

- Force: Activities illustrating the concept of force can include having students use their bodies to produce enough force to move them through space. They can also paddle balls against walls and jump over objects of various heights.

SKILL
1.4 **Exercise physiology** *(e.g., components of health-related fitness; components of skill-related fitness; fitness guidelines such as frequency, intensity, time/ duration, type/mode; principles of exercise such as specificity, overload, progression; roles of body systems in exercise; short-term and long-term effects of physical training; nutrition as related to exercise; fitness; metabolic response to exercise)*

Functions of Excercise

In general, exercise is used for two functions: health and skill. In health-related fitness, the person is concerned with metabolic function, cardiorespiratory benefit of the exercise, and/or muscle development or hypertrophy. In skill-related exercise, the exerciser is more concerned with learning a muscle-memory skill in a particular sport or activity.

Types of exercise

- Cardiorespiratory: Strengthens heart and lungs
- Body Composition: Increases LBM and/or decreases fatty tissue
- Agility: Skill-related for functional movement; the ability to change the direction of the body rapidly and with ease
- Coordination: Skill-related to train muscles to work together
- Balance: Trains muscles to keep body in alignment
- Muscle strength: Increases fast-twitch muscle tissue
- Muscle endurance: Increases slow-twitch muscle tissue
- Flexibility: Trains muscle to lengthen
- Power: Trains explosive movement

Role of Exercise in Health Maintenance

The health risk factors improved by physical activity include cholesterol levels, blood pressure, stress-related disorders, heart diseases, weight and obesity disorders, early death, certain types of cancer, musculoskeletal problems, mental health, and susceptibility to infectious diseases. The following chart is a list of physical activities that can reduce some of these health risks.

ACTIVITY	HEALTH-RELATED COMPONENTS OF FITNESS	SKILL-RELATED COMPONENTS OF FITNESS
Aerobic Dance	Cardiorespiratory, body composition	Agility, coordination
Bicycling	Cardiorespiratory, muscle strength, muscle endurance, body composition	Balance
Calisthenics	Cardiorespiratory, muscle strength, muscle endurance, flexibility, body composition	Agility
Circuit Training	Cardiorespiratory, muscle strength, muscle endurance, body composition	Power
Cross Country Skiing	Cardiorespiratory, muscle strength, muscle endurance, body composition	Agility, coordination, power
Jogging/Running	Cardiorespiratory, body composition	
Rope Jumping	Cardiorespiratory, body composition	Agility, coordination, reaction time, speed
Rowing	Cardiorespiratory, muscle strength, muscle endurance, body composition	Agility, coordination, power
Skating	Cardiorespiratory, body composition	Agility, balance, coordination, speed

OVERLOAD PRINCIPLE: involves exercising at an above-normal level to improve physical or physiological capacity

SPECIFICITY PRINCIPLE: overloading a particular fitness component

Basic Training Principles

The OVERLOAD PRINCIPLE involves exercising at an above-normal level to improve physical or physiological capacity (a higher than normal workload).

The SPECIFICITY PRINCIPLE is overloading a particular fitness component. In order to improve a component of fitness, you must isolate and specifically work on a single component. Metabolic and physiological adaptations depend on the type of overload; hence, specific exercise produces specific adaptations, creating specific training effects. Specificity does not mean that a person can spot train, that is, lose body fat on a particular spot on the body.

The PROGRESSION PRINCIPLE states that once the body adapts to the original load/stress, no further improvement of a component of fitness will occur without an additional load.

There is also a REVERSIBILITY-OF-TRAINING PRINCIPLE, which states that all gains in fitness are lost with the discontinuance of a training program.

Modifications of Overload

We can modify overload by varying frequency, intensity, and time. Frequency is the number of times we implement a training program in a given period (e.g., three days per week). Intensity is the amount of effort put forth or the amount of stress placed on the body. Time is the duration of each training session. A modern study shows that increasing frequency and intensity reduces the need to overload the muscle with heavy weights. When used properly, functional exercise and minimal equipment show muscular results equivalent to overloading and may be more acceptable in physical education environments.[1]

Target Heart Rate Zone

The target heart rate (THR) zone is a common measure of aerobic exercise intensity. Participants find their THR and attempt to raise their heart rates to the desired level for a certain period of time. There are three ways to calculate the target heart rate:

1. Maximum oxygen uptake, which is 60% to 90% of functional capacity.

2. Karvonean formula = [Maximum heart rate (MHR) − resting heart rate (RHR)] × intensity + RHR.

   MHR= 220 − age.

   Intensity = Target heart range (which is 60% − 80% of MHR − RHR + RHR).

   THR = (MHR − RHR) × 0.60 + RHR to (MHR − RHR) × 0.80 + RHR

3. Cooper's formula: THR = (220 − age) × 0.60 to (220 − age) × 0.80.

The important part about heart rate is that no two people are alike. A teacher cannot assume that the formula will work for all students, especially when students have different chemical make-ups, fitness levels, sizes, and energy levels. The rate of perceived exertion (RPE) level is very important in physical exercise. The teacher needs to spend some time talking about what different zones feel like.

- Level 1–2: Do you feel like you are sitting still and totally relaxed?

- Level 3–4: Do you feel like you are taking a stroll?

- Level 5–6: Is your heart pumping, but you are not breathless?

- Level 7–8: Do you feel like you are working your hardest without feeling out of control?

- Level 9–10: Do you feel like you cannot talk because you cannot get enough air?

In a physical fitness class, students should feel like they are at levels 1–2 when they are sitting still, listening to instructions. They should feel that they are warming up or getting energized in levels 3–4. Most of their work is in levels 5–8, depending on the activity. Students should not feel levels 9–10 in a PE class. If they do, they should be directed to reduce intensity slowly, but not to stop suddenly, as this can cause syncope (that is, loss of consciousness).

It is possible for highly trained athletes who are working to improve their skills to feel levels 9–10 in a very high-intensity sport activity, but the 9–10 feeling should be no more than 30 seconds at a time and should be done in intervals. Appropriate interval training greatly increases endurance in very fit athletes. This kind of training is not for burning fat and calories, but for increasing their threshold of comfort and ability. This type of training is *not* for the public school physical education class.

Principles of Overload, Progression, and Specificity Applied to Improvement of Health-Related Components of Fitness

Cardiorespiratory fitness

- Overloading for cardiorespiratory fitness:

  - Frequency = minimum of 3 days/week

  - Intensity = exercising in target heart rate zone

  - Time = minimum of 30 minutes

- Progression for cardiovascular fitness:

  - Begin at a frequency of 3 days/week and work up to no more than 6 days/week

  - Begin at an intensity near THR threshold and work up to 80% of THR

  - Begin at 30 minutes and work up

- Specificity for cardiovascular fitness:

  - To develop cardiovascular fitness, you must perform aerobic (with oxygen) activities for at least fifteen minutes without developing an oxygen debt. Aerobic activities include, but are not limited to, brisk walking, jogging, bicycling, and swimming.

Muscle strength and endurance

- Overloading for muscle strength:

  - Frequency = every 48 hours for each trained muscle group (avoiding working the same muscle group 2 days in a row to avoid fatigue). Working a muscle group in a general way, not to fatigue or high intensity, is acceptable on a daily basis.

  - Intensity = 60% to 90% of assessed muscle strength.

  - Time = 3 sets of 8–15 reps, or one set to fatigue per exercise.

- Progression for muscle strength:

  - Every other day per trained muscle group. Strength training can occur every day, but a fatigued muscle group must take 24 days off to recover and rebuild.

  - Begin near 60% of determined muscle strength and work up to no more than 90% of muscle strength.

  - Begin with 1 set with 10–15 reps and work to multiple sets or reduce to one set of fatiguing the muscle.

- Specificity for muscle strength:

  - To increase muscle strength for a specific part or parts of the body, you must target that or those part or parts of the body.

Flexibility

- Overloading for flexibility:

  - Frequency = after each day of exercise, after fatigue of a muscle or muscle group, or during exercise in a mind–body exercise segment, such as yoga or Pilates skills

  - Intensity = stretch muscle to comfort, not to pain or to stress other muscles

  - Time = truly stretching a muscle takes more time than we have in a day, but brief (8 second) stretches can be effective in relieving muscle tightness and in keeping the muscle from cramping or shortening

- Progression for flexibility:
  - Sfter daily exercise
  - Begin stretching with slow movement as far as possible without pain, holding at the end of the range of motion (ROM) and work up to stretching no more than 10% beyond the normal ROM; breathe into deeper stretches
  - Begin with 1 set with 1 rep, holding stretches for 8 seconds
- Overloading to improve body composition
  - Frequency = daily aerobic exercise
  - Intensity = depends on the fitness ability of the student
  - Time = 30–90 minutes per day
- Progression to improve body composition:
  - Begin daily
  - Begin a low aerobic intensity and work up to a longer duration (see cardiorespiratory progression)
  - Begin low-intensity aerobic exercise for 30 minutes and work up to 90 minutes
- Specificity to improve body composition:
  - Increase aerobic exercise and decrease caloric intake

Principles and Activities for Developing Aerobic Endurance

The term AEROBIC refers to conditioning or exercise that requires the use of oxygen to derive energy. Aerobic conditioning is essential for fat loss, energy production, and effective functioning of the cardiovascular system. Aerobic exercise is difficult to perform for many people, and participants must follow certain principles and activities in order to develop aerobic endurance.

When a person is breathless, he or she has moved into the anaerobic threshold. Anaerobic activity changes the way the body processes energy and is not used for weight loss. Anaerobic activity, when used with a trained professional, can help the exerciser improve cardiovascular and respiratory strength. However, most typical students should not be allowed to be in this zone for more than a few seconds because their bodies cannot recover quickly. A high-endurance athlete would be able to handle the anaerobic threshold in short bursts (30 seconds) and need to be advised and guided by a professional.

AEROBIC: conditioning or exercise that requires the use of oxygen to derive energy

Tips that aid in developing and building aerobic endurance include working out for extended periods at the target heart rate, slowly increasing aerobic exercises, exercising for three or four times per week, and taking adequate rest to help the body recover.

Relationship Between Human Growth and Development and Appropriate Physical Activity

Understanding the rate of the developmental growth process that occurs during adolescence will help educators understand growth and development norms. It will help them identify early-maturing or late-maturing students. The age when the puberty growth spurt occurs and the speed with which adolescents experience puberty vary greatly within each gender. This can affect participation in physical activity and sports. If the instructor pays attention to the varying body sizes and maturity stages of the students, forming teams in co-educational classes can easily accommodate the needs of both genders' changing maturities.

Starting in middle school and continuing into high school, it is perfectly acceptable for boys and girls to participate in non-contact physical activities together. These activities rely on lower-body strength and agility (e.g. capture the flag, ultimate Frisbee, running). In more physical activities that require upper body strength, coaches should form teams based on individual skill levels to prevent injury. Matching teams evenly based on skill and maturity is important. This ensures that individual skill level deficiencies are not as apparent and the activity remains fun for all participants. Teachers need to monitor and adjust physical activities as necessary to ensure a positive, competitive experience. Appropriate activities would include individual or partner badminton or tennis matches and team competitions such as flag football.

Biological and Environmental Influences on Gender Differences in Motor Performance

The differences in motor performance between males and females result from certain biological and environmental influences. Generally, people perceive males as stronger, faster, and more active than females. This higher activity level can stem from childhood behaviors influenced by certain environmental factors. The superior motor performance results largely from the biological makeup of males versus females.

In most cases, the male body contains less fat mass and more muscle mass than the female body. In addition, the percentage of different types of muscle differs between males and females. Males have more fast-twitch muscle fibers, allowing for more short duration, explosive movements, such as jumping and sprinting. Hormones and natural high-twitch muscle fibers make the male muscles develop differently from the female muscles, which is why the sexes are generally separated in sports.

Hormones and natural high-twitch muscle fibers make the male muscles develop differently from the female muscles, which is why the sexes are generally separated in sports.

Slow-twitch muscle fibers that are more common in girls and young boys make endurance activities easier. Long distance running, aerobic dance, and isometric body work are generally easier for girls. Girls' bodies change through puberty; their hips become wider and some fatty tissues increase. Girls should be encouraged, not discouraged, to exerciseat this time as body consciousness becomes an issue.

Certain environmental factors also contribute to the gender differences in motor performance. As children, boys tend to be more physically active. Society expects boys to participate in different sports and activities from girls. When not exposed to certain activities early on, many children lose the chance to try certain things. This is why male ballet dancers and female football players are very rare.

> SKILL 1.5 **Anatomy and physiology** (e.g., skeletal, muscular, nervous, circulatory, and respiratory systems)

Musculoskeletal System

See specific muscles in Skill 1.1

BONES	
Skull	• Composed of cranium (head) and facial bones
Vertebral column—backbone	• Seven cervical vertebrae (neck) • Twelve thoracic vertebrae (middle back) • Five lumbar vertebrae (lower back)
Shoulder	• Clavicle – collarbone • Scapula – shoulder socket located on this bone
Thorax	• Sternum – breastbone • Ribs – twelve pairs, each attaching to the twelve thoracic vertebrae
Arm	• Humerus – upper arm; attaches to scapula to form shoulder joint • Ulna and radius – forearm

Continued on next page

Legs	• Femur – upper leg; largest bone in body
	• Tibia and fibula – lower leg
	• Patella – knee
Hip	• Ilium, ischium, and pubis

Structures, Locations, and Functions of the Three Types of Muscular Tissue

The main function of the muscular system is movement. There are three types of muscle tissue: skeletal, cardiac, and smooth.

SKELETAL MUSCLE is voluntary. These muscles are attached to bones and are responsible for their movement. Skeletal muscle consists of long fibers and is striated due to the repeating patterns of the myofilaments (made of the proteins actin and myosin) that make up the fibers.

CARDIAC MUSCLE is found in the heart. Cardiac muscle is striated like skeletal muscle. It differs from skeletal muscle in that the plasma membrane of the cardiac muscle causes the muscle to beat even when away from the heart. The action potentials of cardiac and skeletal muscles also differ.

SMOOTH MUSCLE is involuntary. It is found in organs and enables functions such as digestion and respiration. Unlike skeletal and cardiac muscle, smooth muscle is not striated. Smooth muscle has less myosin and does not generate as much tension as skeletal muscle.

Mechanism of skeletal muscle contraction

A nerve impulse strikes a muscle fiber. This causes calcium ions to flood the sarcomere. Calcium ions allow adenosine triphosphatel (ATP) to expend energy. The myosin fibers creep along the actin, causing the muscle to contract. Once the nerve impulse has passed, calcium is pumped out and the contraction ends.

Movement of body joints

The axial skeleton consists of the bones of the skull and vertebrae. The appendicular skeleton consists of the bones of the legs, arms and tail, and shoulder girdle. Bone is a connective tissue. Parts of the bone include compact bone, wich gives strength; spongy bone, wich contains red marrow to make blood cells and yellow marrow in the center of long bones to store fat cells; and the periosteum, wich is the protective covering on the outside of the bone.

> **SKELETAL MUSCLE:** voluntary muscles that are attached to bones and are responsible for their movement

> **CARDIAC MUSCLE:** muscle found only in the heart

> **SMOOTH MUSCLE:** involuntary muscle that is found in organs and enables functions such as digestion and respiration

JOINT: a place where two bones meet

A **JOINT** is a place where two bones meet. Joints enable movement. Ligaments attach bone to bone. Tendons attach bone to muscle. Joints allow great flexibility in movement. There are three types of joints:

1. Ball-and-socket: Allows for rotational movement. An example is the joint between the shoulder and the humerus. Ball-and-socket joints allow humans to move their arms and legs in different ways.

2. Hinge: Movement is restricted to a single plane. An example is the joint between the humerus and the ulna.

3. Pivot: Allows for the rotation of the forearm at the elbow and the hand at the wrist.

Body Systems

Muscular system

The function of the muscular system is to provide optimal movement for the parts of the human body. The specific functions of each muscle depend on its location. In all cases, however, muscle action is the result of the action of individual muscle cells. Muscle cells are unique in that they are the only cells in the body that have the property of contractility. This gives muscle cells the ability to shorten and develop tension. This is extremely important for human movement.

Muscles are classified in three categories:

1. Skeletal: Muscles that attach to the bone

2. Smooth (visceral): Muscles that are associated with an internal body structure

3. Cardiac: Muscles that form the wall of the heart

Skeletal muscles are the only voluntary muscles, meaning they contract as initiated by the will of a person.

Smooth (visceral) and cardiac muscles are both involuntary muscles, meaning they are governed by nerve impulses found in the autonomic nervous system.

Skeletal and cardiac muscles are striated, or band-like, whereas visceral muscles are smooth.

Skeletal system

The skeletal system has several functions:

1. Support: The skeleton acts as the framework of the body. It gives support to the soft tissues and provides points of attachment for the majority of the muscles.

2. Movement: The majority of muscles attach to the skeleton and many of the bones meet (or articulate) in moveable joints, wich means that the skeleton plays an important role in determining the extent and kind of movements of which the body is capable.

3. Protection: Clearly, the skeleton protects internal organs from injury; this includes the brain, spinal cord, thoracic organs, bladder, and reproductive organs.

4. Mineral reservoir: Vital minerals are stored in the bones of the skeleton. Some examples are calcium, phosphorus, sodium, and potassium.

5. Hemopoiesis, or blood-cell formation: After a mother gives birth, the red marrow in specific bones produces the blood cells found in the circulatory system.

The human skeletal system is composed of 206 individual bones that are held in position by strong fibrous ligaments. These bones can be grouped into two categories:

1. Axial skeleton: 80 bones total (skull, vertebral column, thorax)

2. Appendicular skeleton: 126 bones total (pectoral, upper limbs, pelvic, lower limbs)

Endocrine system

The endocrine system is not a clearly defined anatomical system, but rather is composed of various glands that are located throughout the body. The main function of this system is to aid in the regulation of body activities by producing chemical substances known as hormones. Through a complicated regulation system, the bloodstream distributes hormones throughout the body. Each hormone affects only specific targeted organs.

The primary endocrine glands are the pituitary, thyroid, parathyroids, adrenals, pancreas, and gonads. Additionally, the kidneys, gastrointestinal organs, and placenta exhibit endocrine activity, but to a lesser extent than the primary glands.

> *The endocrine system is not a clearly defined anatomical system, but rather is composed of various glands that are located throughout the body.*

The hormones produced by the endocrine system do not fall into an easily defined class of chemical substances. Some are steroids (such as cortisol), others are proteins (such as insulin), and still others are polypeptides and amino acids (such as parathyroid hormone and epinephrine).

Regardless of the specific chemical substance, the hormones produced by the endocrine system play a critical role in aiding the regulation and integration of the body processes.

Immune system

The immune system's function is to defend the human body against infectious organisms and other attacking forces, such as bacteria, microbes, viruses, toxins, and parasites. Simply put, the immune system strives every day to keep human beings healthy and free of disease and illness.

White blood cells are considered to be the most important part of the immune system.

The immune system is made up of two main fluid systems: the blood stream and the lymph system. They are intertwined throughout the body and are responsible for transporting the agents of the immune system. White blood cells are considered to be the most important part of the immune system.

Different types/names of white blood cells are:

- Leukocytes (this is often used as the primary term for white blood cells)
- Lymphocyte
- Monocytes
- Granulocytes
- B-cells
- Killer T-cells
- Suppressor T-cells
- Natural killer cells
- Neutrophils
- Eosinophils

ANTIGEN: a foreign substance that invades the body

A foreign substance that invades the body is referred to as an ANTIGEN. When an antigen is detected, the immune system goes into action immediately. Several types of cells start working together. These initial cells try to recognize and respond to the antigen, thereby triggering white blood cells to release antibodies. Antigens and antibodies have been referred to throughout the scientific community as fitting like a "key and a lock." Once these antibodies have been produced in the body, they stay in the body; if the same antigen enters the body again, the body is immune and protected.

VACCINES: antigens given in very small amounts

VACCINES are antigens given in very small amounts. They stimulate both humoral and cell-mediated responses. After vaccination, memory cells recognize future exposure to the antigen so the body can produce antibodies much more quickly.

There are three types of immunity:

1. **Innate immunity:** The immunity with which everyone is born

2. **Adaptive immunity:** Immunity that develops throughout our lives (i.e., antibodies) as we are exposed to diseases and illnesses

3. **Passive immunity:** An immunity that comes from outside us (i.e., outside antibiotics)

There are two defense mechanisms in the immune system: non-specific and specific.

The **non-specific immune mechanism** has two lines of defense. The first line of defense is the physical barriers of the body. These include the skin and the mucous membranes. The skin prevents the penetration of bacteria and viruses as long as there are no abrasions on the skin. Mucous membranes form a protective barrier around the digestive, respiratory, and genitourinary tracts. In addition, the pH of the skin and the mucous membranes inhibits the growth of many microbes. Mucous secretions (tears and saliva) wash away many microbes and contain lysozyme, which kills microbes.

The second line of defense includes white blood cells and the inflammatory response. **Phagocytosis** is the ingestion of foreign particles. Neutrophils make up about seventy percent of all white blood cells. Monocytes mature to become macrophages, which are the largest phagocytic cells. Eosinophils are also phagocytic. Natural killer cells destroy the body's own infected cells instead of invading the microbe directly.

The other part of the second line of defense is the inflammatory response. The blood supply to the injured area increases, causing redness and heat. Swelling also typically occurs with inflammation. Basophils and mast cells release histamine in response to cell injury. This triggers the inflammatory response.

The **specific immune mechanism** recognizes specific foreign material and responds by destroying the invader. These mechanisms are specific and diverse. They are able to recognize individual pathogens.

Circulatory system

The function of the closed circulatory system (cardiovascular system) is to carry oxygenated blood and nutrients to all cells of the body and return carbon dioxide waste to the lungs for expulsion. Put another way, the function of the circulatory system is to transport blood leaving the heart to all parts of the body, permitting the exchange of certain substances between the blood and body fluids, and ultimately returning the blood to the heart.

ARTERIES: carry blood away from the heart

VEINS: return blood to the heart

CAPILLARIES: allow for the exchange of substances between the blood and the cells of the body

The circulatory system is composed of veins, arteries and capillaries. ARTERIES carry blood away from the heart, VEINS return blood to the heart, and CAPILLARIES allow for the exchange of substances between the blood and the cells of the body. Capillaries are the most important vessels of the blood vascular system. Arteries must be able to withstand great pressure, and veins are the largest vessels of the system.

The heart, blood vessels, and blood make up the cardiovascular system, which is closely related to the circulatory system.

The following diagram shows the structure of the heart, noting the specific arteries and veins:

Heart

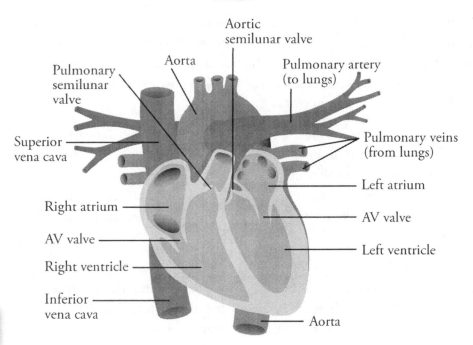

We are able to speak, sing, and laugh by varying the tension of the vocal cords as exhaled air passes over them.

TIDAL VOLUME: the volume of air inhaled and exhaled

VITAL CAPACITY: the maximum volume the lungs can inhale and exhale

Respiratory system

The primary function of the respiratory system is the intake of oxygen brought into the body through normal breathing or aerobic activity and the removal of carbon dioxide with the assistance of the circulatory system. The respiratory system also makes vocalization possible.

The lungs are the respiratory surface of the human respiratory system. A dense net of capillaries contained just beneath the epithelium forms the respiratory surface. The surface area of the epithelium is about 100 m² in humans. The volume of air inhaled and exhaled is the TIDAL VOLUME. This is normally about 500 mL in adults. VITAL CAPACITY is the maximum volume the lungs can inhale and exhale. This is usually around 3.4 mL.

To describe the respiratory system more thoroughly, air enters the mouth and nose, where it is warmed, moistened, and filtered of dust and particles. Cilia in the trachea trap and expel unwanted material in the mucus. The trachea splits into two bronchial tubes, and the bronchial tubes divide into smaller and smaller bronchioles in the lungs. The internal surface of the lung is composed of alveoli, which are thin-walled air sacs. These allow for a large surface area for gas exchange. Capillaries line the alveoli. Oxygen diffuses into the bloodstream, and carbon dioxide diffuses out of the capillaries and is exhaled from the lungs due to partial pressure. Hemoglobin, a protein containing iron, carries the oxygenated blood to the heart and all parts of the body.

The thoracic cavity holds the lungs. The diaphragm muscle below the lungs is an adaptation that makes inhalation possible. As the volume of the thoracic cavity increases, the diaphragm muscle flattens out and inhalation occurs. When the diaphragm relaxes, exhalation occurs.

Digestive system

The function of the digestive system is to break food down into nutrients, absorb them into the blood stream, and deliver them to all cells of the body for use in cellular respiration. Every cell in the body requires a constant source of energy in order to perform its particular function(s). The digestive system breaks down or alters ingested food by mechanical and chemical processes so that it can ultimately cross the wall of the gastrointestinal tract and enter the blood vascular and lymphatic (circulatory) systems.

The digestive system consists of a tube called the gastrointestinal tract (alimentary canal) that extends from the mouth to the anus. As long as food remains in the gastrointestinal tract, it is considered to be outside the body. To "enter" the body, it must cross the wall of the digestive tract. Emptying into the digestive tube are the secretions of the salivary glands, gastric glands, intestinal glands, liver, and pancreas, all of which assist in the digestion of food. These regions include the mouth, esophagus, stomach, and small and large intestines.

Activities of the digestive system can be divided into six parts:

1. Ingestion of food into the mouth

2. Movement of food along the digestive tract

3. Mechanical preparation of food for digestion

4. Chemical digestion of food

5. Absorption of digested food into the circulatory and lymphatic systems

6. Elimination of indigestible substances and waste products from the body by defecation

Reproductive system

The reproductive system differs greatly from the other organ systems of the body in that it does not contribute to the survival or homeostasis of a human being. Instead, the organs of the reproductive system ensure the continuance of the species.

The reproductive system produces gametes (germ cells). Through sexual intercourse, the male gamete (sperm) joins with a female gamete (ovum). This joining is called FERTILIZATION. The organs of the female reproductive system provide a suitable environment in which the fertilized ovum (zygote) can develop into a stage in which it is capable of surviving outside the mother's body.

The organs that produce the gametes are referred to as the primary or essential sex organs. Specifically, these are the gonads (testes) in the male and the ovaries in the female. Additionally, the organs that produce the gametes are also responsible for producing hormones that influence the development of secondary sex characteristics and regulation of the reproductive system. In the male, specialized cells in the testes produce androgen hormones. The most active of these is testosterone. In the female, the ovaries produce estrogen and progesterone.

The structures that transport, protect, and nourish the gametes in both the male and female are referred to as accessory sex organs. In the male, these include:

- The epididymis
- The prostate gland
- The ductus deferens
- The scrotum
- The seminal vesicles
- The penis

Female accessory sex organs include:

- The uterine tubes
- The vagina
- The uterus
- The vulva

Neurophysiology of Motor Control

The nervous system plays a vital role in motor control. It allows for effective use of the skeletal muscles and coordinates with the brain, skeleton, and joints.

Before looking at the function of the nervous system, we must first examine the basic anatomy. First, a muscle consists of a group of muscle fibers. At least one motor nerve, which consists of fibrous extensions (axons) of a group of motor

---

> The reproductive system differs greatly from the other organ systems of the body in that it does not contribute to the survival or homeostasis of a human being.

> **FERTILIZATION:** when a male gamete (sperm) joins with a female gamete (ovum)

neurons, controls every muscle fiber in the body. As axons enter the muscles, they branch off into terminals, forming a neuromuscular junction with a single muscle fiber. A motor neuron together with the muscle fibers it supplies is known as a motor unit.

Muscular contraction occurs when a motor neuron transmits an electrical impulse. The number of muscle fibers per motor unit varies between four and several hundred. The muscles controlling very fine movements (e.g., fingers and eyes) have very small motor units. Examples of movements controlled by small motor units include writing, sewing, and tying shoelaces. These types of motor skills are generally not present in the early stages of life and are called fine motor skills. Larger muscles (e.g., hips and legs) controlling less precise movements have large motor units. Examples of such movements include walking, throwing objects, and performing sit-ups. These movements are present even in the earliest stages of life and are called gross motor skills.

> Proper development and function of the nervous system does not always occur. Improper development results in various diseases that affect motor control, including cerebral palsy, dyspraxia, multiple sclerosis, and Parkinson's disease.

SKILL 1.6 Current and historical trends, issues, and developments in physical education (e.g., laws, teaching methods, theories, concepts, techniques)

The History of Physical Education in the United States

Germany, Sweden, and England greatly influenced the early development of physical education, particularly from the late 1700s to the mid-1800s. Turner Societies were introduced to the states by German immigrants. Turner Societies advocated a system of gymnastics training that employed or utilized heavy equipment (e.g., horizontal and parallel bars, side horse) in their pursuit of fitness. In contrast, the Swedish preferred attaining and maintaining fitness through the use of light equipment. Their system of exercise to promote health was through systematic movements through the use of light equipment (e.g., ropes, climbing, and wands). The English brought sports and games to America. The type of sports and games that the English brought emphasized moral development through participation in physical activities.

> Germany, Sweden, and England greatly influenced the early development of physical education, particularly from the late 1700s to the mid-1800s.

In 1823, the first school to include physical education as a requirement in its curriculum was the Round Hill School, a private school in Northampton, Massachusetts. Throughout the 1800s, the inclusion of physical education in schools across the United States became prominent. In 1824, Catherine Beecher was the "first American to design a program of exercise for American children" (Lumpkin, Angela. 1994. *Physical Education and Sport: A contemporary Introduction*, 3rd edition. St. Louis: Mosby. pg. 202). Beecher was the founder of the Hartford Female Seminary. The curriculum of physical education that Beecher designed consisted of what we would refer to today as calisthenics. She was also an extremely active advocate for including physical education in the public schools curriculum. It took until 1855 for this to happen, when Cincinnati, Ohio, became the first public school system to offer physical education to its students.

In 1866, California became the first state to pass a law, that required two periods of exercise a day in its public schools. From 1855 to 1900, Beecher and her contemporaries—Edward Hitchcock, Dudley Allen Sargent, and Dio Lewis—were the leaders in physical education. Debates abounded as to whether it was best to use the system they had established in America, or if it would be better to use the German, Swedish, or English system to provide a national physical education program for America. These debates were referred to as the "Battle of Systems."

Throughout the 1890s, during this great period of debate, John Dewey challenged the traditional education system. Dewey and his colleagues were responsible for expanding the education system in America based on the "three Rs" to include physical education. It was also during this time that many higher education schools began to offer training for physical education teachers. Because of the strong emphasis on the sciences, including courses in physiology and anatomy, many of the professors of these students held medical degrees.

In 1983, Thomas Wood stated that "the great thought of physical education is not the education of the physical nature, but the relation of physical training to complete education, and then the effort to make the physical training contribute its full share to the life of the individual." (National Education Association. 1893. NEA Proceedings 32:621. pg.621.) This was the beginning of a change in thinking about the importance of physical education in regard to the overall education of the country's children. Many early twentieth-century educational psychologists, including John Dewey, Edward Thorndike, and Stanley Hall, supported Wood's ideas and the important role of children's play in furthering their ability to learn. As a result, in 1927, *The New Physical Education* was published by Wood and Rosalind Cassidy, who was a strong advocate of education through physical activity.

Charles McCloy supported Wood's and Cassidy's line of thinking in his published work. He believed that physical education did more than just contribute to the overall well-being and learning of children. He held that physical education's primary objective was the development of skills as well as the maintenance of the body. The testing of motor skills was a significant part of McCloy's contribution to physical education. Additionally, his philosophy of testing motor skills paralleled the scientific movement in education during this time period.

In the early 1920s, many states passed legislation that required physical education in the schools. This trend continued until the 1950s, when all states eventually required physical education in their schools. The curriculum of physical education changed as a result of significant historical events. For example, during World War II, the emphasis in physical education shifted from games to physical conditioning. In 1953, the President's Council on Physical Fitness was established when it was noted through the Kraus-Weber study that American children were far less fit than children in European countries. The council was established to assist the falling fitness levels of America's children and youth.

In the early 1920s, many states passed legislation that required physical education in the schools. This trend continued until the 1950s, when all states eventually required physical education in their schools.

Current Trends

As American society becomes more sedentary, health issues become more widespread. There is much concern over the statistics of overweight and obese children in this country, as well as kids with serious health-related illnesses such as Type II Diabetes. Because of this, the national and state governments have stepped in to create standards and specifications for physical education in the schools.

The U.S. Department of Health and Human Services has the following guidelines for youth and fitness:

1. Children and adolescents should perform 60 minutes of aerobic exercise daily.

2. Children and adolescents should include strengthening exercises at least three of those days every week.

3. Children should include bone-strengthening activities at least three days per week. (Studies show that stressing bones, as when jumping and leaping, strengthens them.)

4. Children should be encouraged to do something enjoyable to create a lifelong appreciation for exercise.[2]

According to the National Association for Sport and Physical Education (NASPE), which is a national accreditation program for physical education, these are the current standards for school physical education:

1. Children should demonstrate competency in basic motor skills.

2. Children should understand general movement that they apply to learning an activity or sport.

3. Children should participate in some sort of physical activity regularly.

4. Children should achieve and maintain a healthy standard of fitness.

5. Children should show respect for others in activity and sports settings.

6. Children should value physical activity in terms of health, enjoyment, and creativity.[3]

NASPE also lists the four components of a high-quality physical education.

All children should have:

1. The opportunity to learn

2. Meaningful content

3. Appropriate instruction

4. Student and program assessment[4]

> **NASPE has ideas and methods for appropriate assessment on its website:**
>
> www.aahperd.org/naspe/

A tool now available to physical education departments and to families is the Cooper Institute Fitnessgram, which is a guided journal of fitness and individual development in personal fitness. *See http://www.cooperinstitute.org/ourkidshealth /index.cfm*

> **Most states have specific standards for physical education classes. State standards can be found at:**
>
> www.aahperd.org/naspe /standards/stateStandards/

There are many state laws also mandating the amount of time a child should be in physical education classes or organized fitness classes. Some states also have recess laws, or laws mandating how much free play time should be allowed for children. These laws are to protect children's rights to a public education in fitness because in recent years, schools have reduced physical education time due to their demands in academics.

An example of state mandated physical education is the Texas Education Code-Section 28.002 Required Curriculum, passed in 2007. This law states that all children through eighth grade in Texas should have thirty minutes per day of organized physical education.[5]

The History of Physical Education

Contributions of early societies to the profession

Games often had a practical, educational aim, like playing house. In addition, games such as gladiatorial games had political aims. Economic games included fishing and hunting. Families played board games. There were ceremonial reasons for games found in dances. Finally, ball games provided an opportunity for socialization.

- Early society: The common activities performed in early societies included war-like games, chariot racing, boating and fishing, equestrian games, hunting, music and dancing, boxing and wrestling, bow and arrow activities, dice, and knucklebones.

- Egyptian: The common activities performed in Egypt were acrobatics, gymnastics, tug of war, hoop and kick games, ball and stick games, juggling, knife-throwing games of chance, board games, and guessing games (e.g., how many fingers are concealed).

- Bronze Age: The activities performed during the Bronze Age (3000 to 1000 BCE) were bullfights, dancing, boxing, hunting, archery, running, and board games.

- Greek Age: The Greeks are best known for the Olympic Games. Their other contributions were the pentathlon, which included the jump, the discus, and the javelin. The pankration was a combination of boxing and wrestling. The Greeks also played on seesaws and enjoyed swinging, hand guessing games, blind man's bluff, dice games (losers had to carry their partners pick-a-back), and hoop and board games. Funeral games are described in *The Iliad*.

- Romans: The Romans kept slaves and were advocates of "blood sports." Their philosophy was to die well. There were unemployment games. Roman baths were popular, as were ball games, stuffed feathers, pila trigonalis, follis, and balloon or bladder ball. The Capitoline games were held in 86 CE. These union guild athletes were paid for their activities, which included artificial fly-fishing. The games that were popular during this period were top spinning, odds and evens, riding a long stick, knucklebones, and hide and seek.

- Chinese: The Chinese contributed the following: jujitsu, fighting cocks, dog racing, and football. In Korea, Japan, and China, children played with toys and lanterns. Common activities included building snowmen, playing with dolls, making/playing with shadows, flying kites, and fighting kites. Children enjoyed rope walker toys, windmills, turnip lanterns, ring puzzles, and playing horse. Noblemen engaged in hopping, jumping, leapfrog, jump rope, seesaw, and drawing.

Major events in the history of physical education and the historical relationship of physical education to health and fitness

- Egypt: Sport dancing among the nobility, physical skills among the masses, and physical training for wars.

- Cretans: Learned to swim.

- Spartan and Greeks: Emphasized severe physical training and NOT competitive sport.

- Athenians: Believed in the harmonious development of the body, mind, and spirit.

- Roman Empire: The Romans established the worth of physical education. During the Dark Ages, children learned fitness and horsemanship. The squires learned how to become knights by boxing and fencing. Swimming was also popular. During the Renaissance, people developed the body for health reasons. The Romans combined the physical and mental aspects of exercise in their daily routines.

- 1349-1428: Physical education was necessary for a person's total education and also as a means of recreation.

- 1546: Martin Luther saw physical activities as a substitute for vice and evil.

- Sweden: In 1839, Ling strove to make PE a science.

- Colonial period: Religion denounced play. Pleasure was either banned or frowned upon.

- National period: Began in 1823. Games and sports were available as after-school activities. There was an introduction of gymnastics and calisthenics.

- Civil War (1860): This period saw gymnastics and non-military use of PE. Physical education became organized. PE became part of the school curriculum and held a respectable status among other subjects. YMCA was founded. Gulick was the Director of PE in New York City; Dudley Allen Sargent was teaching physical education at Harvard University.

- Great Depression of the 1930s: Physical fitness movement. Bowling was the number one activity. Dance, gymnastics, and sports were popular. The Heisman Trophy was awarded in 1935. After WWII, many Americans had access to outdoor pools.

Major trends since WWII influencing physical education

- WWII: Selective Service examinations revealed the poor physical fitness of the country's youth. Thus, physical education classes focused on physical conditioning.

- 1942: President Roosevelt established the Division of Physical Fitness, run by John B. Kelly (who alerted Roosevelt about the poor fitness levels of the youth). This division was dissolved and placed under the Federal Security Agency (FSA) with numerous organizations promoting fitness. Under the FSA, Frank Lloyd was Chief of the Physical Fitness Division, William Hughs was Chief Consultant, and Dorothy LaSalle was head of the work for women and children.

- 1953: Kraus-Webber tests: Of the 4,264 participants from the United States, 57% failed a general muscular fitness test. Only 8.7% of Europeans failed.

After WWII ended, the eagerness for fitness waned.

Again, John Kelly alerted the president (Eisenhower) of the need for a fitness movement. Eisenhower ordered a special conference that was held in June 1956.

- 1956: AAHPERD Fitness Conference established the President's Council on Youth Fitness and a President's Citizens Advisory Committee on the Fitness of American Youth.

During the 1950s, modern dance gave way to the contemporary. Gymnastics had new equipment, including a higher balance beam, trampolines, and uneven bars. The Swedish gymnastics boom was over, and ropes and ladders, wands, dumbbells, and Indian clubs were no longer fashionable. Core sports for boys were football, baseball, basketball, and track and field. Core sports for women were basketball and volleyball.

- 1972: Passage of TITLE IX OF THE EDUCATIONAL AMENDMENTS ACT ensured that girls and women receive the same rights as boys and men for educational programs, including physical education and athletics.

- 1970 to present: Emphasized preventative medicine, wellness, physical fitness, and education that is more scholarly, more specialized, and more applicable to all segments of population, such as the elderly, handicapped persons, and those out of organizations (non-school sports): AAU (mid-twentieth century controlled amateur sports); Little League; North American Baseball Association.

- International amateur sports: Olympic Governing Committee.

- Intercollegiate sports: National Collegiate Athletic Association (NCAA scholarship in 1954); National Association of Intercollegiate Athletics (NAIA); National Junior College Athletic Association (NJCAA).

- Interscholastic sports: National Federation of State High School Athletic Associations.

- Organizations for girls' and women's sports: Athletic and Recreation Federation of College Women (ARFCW); the Women's Board of the U.S. Olympic Committee; National Section of Women's Athletics (NSWA; promoted intercollegiate sports such as US Field Hockey and Women's International Bowling and established special committees). The Women's Division of NAAF merged its interests in the NSWA of AAHPERD, changing its name to National Section for Girls and Women's Sports (NSGWS). Mel Lockes, chairperson of NSGWS in 1956, was against intercollegiate athletics for women. In 1957, NSGWS changed its name to Division of Girls and Women's Sports (DGWS), still a division of AAHPERD. A lack of funds hurt DGWS.

John Fitzgerald Kennedy changed the name of the President's Citizens Advisory Committee of Fitness of American Youth to the President's Council on Physical Fitness. Lyndon Baines Johnson changed the name to President's Council on Physical Fitness and Sports.

TITLE IX OF THE EDUCATIONAL AMENDMENTS ACT: ensured that girls and women receive the same rights as boys and men for educational programs, including physical education and athletics

Philosophies of Education

The various philosophies of education greatly influence the goals and values of physical education.

Important educational philosophies related to physical education are idealism, realism, pragmatism, naturalism, existentialism, humanism, and eclecticism.

Idealism: The mind, developed through the acquisition of knowledge, is of the highest importance. Values exist independent of individuals. Fitness and strength activities contribute to the development of one's personality. Horace Mann, Wadsworth, Kant, Plato, and Descartes were idealists.

Realism: The physical world is real. A realist believes in the laws of nature, the scientific method, and mind and body harmony. Religion and philosophy coexist. Physical fitness results in greater productivity, physical drills are important to the learning process, athletic programs lead to desired social behavior, and play and recreation help life adjustment. Aristotle was a realist.

Pragmatism: Experience is the key to life. Dynamic experience shapes individuals' truth. Education is child-centered. Varied activities present experiences that are more meaningful. Activities promote socializing. Problem-solving accomplishes learning. John Dewy and Charles Pierce were pragmatists.

Naturalism: This philosophy is materialistic. Things that actually exist are found only within the physical realm of nature. Nature is valuable. The individual is more important than society. Self-activities accomplish learning and activities are more than physical in nature. Naturalists promote play and discourage high levels of competition. Physical education takes a holistic approach.

Existentialism: The chief concern is individualism. Existentialists do not want the individual to conform to society. They promote freedom of choice and a variety of interests. Individuals need to have their own system of values. Playing develops creativity and the discovery of the "inner self." Sartre, Soren, and Kierkegaard were existentialists.

Humanism and eclecticism: These are the modern philosophies of physical education that most schools follow today. The humanistic philosophy is based on development of individual talents and total fulfillment that encourages total involvement and participation in one's environment. Humanists encourage self-actualization and self-fulfillment. Curriculums based on the humanistic approach are more student-centered. The eclectic approach combines beliefs from different philosophies and does not resemble any single philosophy. When blended skillfully, the eclectic approach affords a sound philosophy for an individual.

Philosophies of education applied to physical education goals

- Physical/organic development goal (realism philosophy): Activities build physical power by strengthening the body's systems, resulting in the ability to sustain adaptive effort, shorten recovery time, and develop resistance to fatigue. The core values are individual health, greater activity, and better performance by an adequately developed and properly functioning body.

- Motor/neuromuscular development goal (realism philosophy): Develops body awareness producing movement that is proficient and graceful and uses as little energy as possible. Students develop as many skills as possible so their interests are wide and varied to allow more enjoyment and better adjustment to group situations. Varied motor development skills affect health by influencing how leisure time is spent. Values include reducing energy expenditure, building confidence, bringing recognition, enhancing physical and mental health, making participation safer, and contributing to aesthetic sense.

- Cognitive development goal (idealism philosophy): Deals with acquiring knowledge and the ability to think and interpret knowledge. Scientific principles explain time, space, and flow of movement. Learning physical activities requires thinking and coordination of movements and mastering and adapting to one's environment. Individuals should also acquire knowledge of rules, techniques, and strategies of activities. Cognitive values include healthy attitudes and habits, such as body awareness, personal hygiene, disease prevention, exercise, proper nutrition, and knowledge of health service providers.

- Social/emotional/affective development goal (existentialism philosophy): Deals with helping individuals make adjustments—personal, group, and societal—by positively influencing human behavior. Performance defines success, and success develops self-confidence. Wholesome attitudes throughout the various growth stages promote the development of an appropriate self-concept, which is very important. Values include meeting basic social needs (sense of belonging, recognition, self-respect, and love) that produce a socially well-adjusted individual.

Relationship between Teaching and Coaching

Both teachers and coaches must be able to identify students' mistakes and deficiencies and devise plans that will produce improvement. In addition, teachers and coaches must work effectively with students of different personality types, ability levels, and learning styles. Finally, teachers and coaches must be able to

Teaching and athletic coaching share many similarities and a few key differences.

communicate well with their students and develop a relationship of trust that produces a positive learning environment.

Teaching and athletic coaching differ in two important ways. First, while teaching is always a long-term process with long-term achievement goals, coaching can involve either a long-term or short-term coach-student relationship. For example, a beginning tennis player might desire a coach that will mold her game over many years (long-term relationship), while a more advanced player might seek a coach to help fix a particular stroke (short-term relationship).

The second key difference is that coaching requires different motivational tactics. Athletic coaches must often convince students that they need to change a particular technique or strategy and motivate students through periods of skill regression when they implement changes. Although teachers must motivate students to learn, they most likely do not have to sell students on a particular method of learning.

Accountability

The declining status of physical education in school curricula is attributable, in part, to a lack of accountability for teachers, students, and schools.

Accountability is a major issue in physical education. The importance placed on academic testing has caused schools to decrease the time spent on physical education. In addition, schools often fail to hold physical education instructors to the same achievement standards as academic teachers. Instructors often do not assess and monitor student progress and development in athletic skill and fitness. To regain its position as an important part of the learning environment, physical education must increase accountability. Well-trained and qualified instructors must implement lesson plans and assessments that help students develop skill and fitness. Instructors and school officials should base student assessments on personal progress, not generic achievement standards.

Roles, Benefits, and Effects of Competition

Competition is the ultimate test of athletic skill, fitness, and performance. Competitive athletic events help assess a student's skill level, mental toughness, desire, and effort. Competition also provides many life lessons that benefit participants physically, personally, and socially.

The physical benefits of competitive sports are many. Participation in sports provides fitness maintenance, stress relief, satisfaction derived from mastering skills, and exposure to healthy lifestyle habits.

Competitive sports also teach life lessons that benefit participants on many personal levels. Competition demonstrates the value of preparation and hard work. In addition, participants learn teamwork, time management, and leadership skills. Finally, participants in competitive sports learn resilience from dealing with injuries, losses, setbacks, and adversity.

Competitive sports are also an excellent social activity. Participants build relationships, interact with others with similar interests, and learn to recognize the value of diversity.

While the effects of competition are largely positive, negative experiences in competitive sports can be very damaging. Overzealous coaches and parents, overly competitive and hostile teammates and opponents, and unnecessary pressure and expectations are common problems in youth athletics. Coaches, parents, and youth league officials must closely monitor competitive situations to ensure that all participants have a positive experience.

Coaches, parents, and youth league officials must closely monitor competitive situations to ensure that all participants have a positive experience.

SKILL 1.7 **Understanding of the rules, strategies, skills, techniques, and concepts associated with a variety of movement activities and games across the age and grade spectra; emphasis predominately on softball, soccer, swimming, tennis, track and field, and volleyball, with questions based on possibly other sports and activities commonly used in physical education settings**

Rules, Regulations, Strategies and Skills of Commonly Taught Sports and Activities

Soccer

Offenses and fouls
The following are direct free-kick offenses:

- Hand or arm contact with the ball
- Using hands to hold an opponent
- Pushing an opponent
- Striking/kicking/tripping or attempting to strike/kick/trip an opponent
- Goalie using the ball to strike an opponent
- Jumping at or charging an opponent
- Kneeing an opponent
- Any contact fouls

The following are indirect free-kick offenses:

- Same player playing the ball twice at the kickoff, on a throw-in, on a goal kick, on a free kick, or on a corner kick

- The goalie delaying the game by holding the ball or carrying the ball more than four steps

- Failure to notify the referee of substitutions/re-substitutions, and that player then handling the ball in the penalty area

- Any person who is not a player entering playing field without a referee's permission

- Unsportsmanlike actions or words in reference to a referee's decision

- Dangerously lowering the head or raising the foot too high to make a play

- A player resuming play after being ordered off the field

- Offsides: An offensive player must have two defenders between him and the goal when a teammate passes the ball to him.

- Attempting to kick the ball when the goalkeeper has possession or interference with the goalkeeper to hinder him or her from releasing the ball

- Illegal charging

- Leaving the playing field without referee's permission while the ball is in play

Strategies

- **Heading:** Using the head to pass, to shoot, or to clear the ball
- **Tackling:** Attempting to take possession of the ball from an opponent
- **Passing:** Successful play requires knowledgeable utilization of space

Terminology

- **Center:** Passing from the outside of the field near the sideline into the center
- **Charge:** Illegal or legal body contact between opponents
- **Chip:** Lofting the ball into the air using the instep kick technique; contacting the ball very low, causing it to loft quickly with backspin
- **Clear:** Attempting to move the ball out of danger by playing the ball a great distance
- **Corner kick:** A direct free kick from the corner arc awarded to the attacking player when the defending team last played the ball over their own end line

- Cross: A pass from the outside of the field near the end line to a position in front of the goal
- Dead ball situation: The organized restarting of the game after a stop in play
- Direct free kick: A free kick whereby the kicker may score from the initial contact
- Dribble: The technique of a player self-propelling the ball with the feet in order to maintain control of the ball while moving from one spot to another
- Drop ball: The method used to restart the game after temporary suspension of play when the ball is still in play
- Goal area: The rectangular area in front of the goal where the ball is placed for a goal kick
- Half volley: Contacting the ball just as it hits the ground after being airborne
- Head: Playing the ball with the head
- Indirect free kick: A free kick from which a player other than the kicker must contact the ball before a goal can be scored
- Kickoff: The free kick starting play at the beginning of the game, after each period, or after a score
- Obstruction: Illegally using the body to prevent an opponent from reaching the ball
- One-touch: Immediately passing or shooting a received ball without stopping it
- Penalty area: The large rectangular area in front of the goal where the goalkeeper is allowed to use his hands to play the ball
- Penalty kick: A direct free kick awarded in the penalty area against the defending team for a direct free kick foul
- Settle: Taking a ball out of the air and settling it on the ground so that it is rolling and no longer bouncing
- Square pass: A pass directed towards the side of a player
- Tackle: A technique to take the ball away from the opponents
- Through pass: A pass penetrating between and past the defenders
- Throw-in: The technique to restart the game when the ball goes out of play over the sideline

- **Touchline**: The side line of the field
- **Trap**: The technique used for receiving the ball and bringing it under control
- **Two-touch receiving**: Trapping and immediately re-passing the ball

Softball

Basic rules

- Each team plays nine players in the field (sometimes 10 for slow pitch)
- Field positions are one pitcher, one catcher, four infielders, and three outfielders (four outfielders in ten-player formats)
- The four bases are 60 feet apart
- Any ball hit outside of the first or third base line is a foul ball (i.e., runners cannot advance and the pitch counts as a strike against the batter)
- If a batter receives three strikes (i.e., failed attempts at hitting the ball) in a single at bat, that player strikes out
- The pitcher must start with both feet on the pitcher's rubber and can only take one step forward when delivering the underhand pitch
- A base runner is out if:
  - The opposition tags him with the ball before he reaches a base
  - The ball reaches first base before he does
  - He runs outside the base path to avoid a tag
  - A batted ball strikes him in fair territory
- A team must maintain the same batting order throughout the game
- Runners cannot lead off and base stealing is illegal
- Runners may overrun first base, but can be tagged out if off any other base

Tennis

A player loses a point when

- The ball bounces twice on her side of the net
- The player returns the ball to any place outside the designated areas
- The player stops or touches the ball in the air before it lands out-of-bounds
- The player intentionally strikes the ball twice with the racket

- The ball strikes any part of a player or racket after initial attempt to hit the ball

- A player reaches over the net to hit the ball

- A player throws his racket at the ball

- The ball strikes any permanent fixture that is out of bounds (other than the net)

- A ball touching the net and landing inside the boundary lines is in play (except on the serve, where a ball contacting the net results in a "let," or replay of the point)

- A player fails, on two consecutive attempts, to serve the ball into the designated area (i.e., double fault)

Strategies

- Lobbing: Using a high, lob shot for defense, giving the player more time to get back into position

- Identifying opponent's weaknesses and attacking them; recognizing and protecting one's own weaknesses

- Outrunning and out-thinking an opponent

- Using change of pace, lobs, spins, approaching the net, and deception at the correct times

- Hitting cross-court (from corner to corner of the court) for maximum safety and opportunity to regain position

- Directing the ball away from the opponent

Terminology

- Ace: A serve that is untouched by the opponent's racket

- Advantage (Ad): A scoring term; the next point won after the score is "deuce"

- Alley: The 4.5-foot strip on either side of the singles court that is used to enlarge the court for doubles

- Approach shot: A shot hit inside the baseline while approaching the net

- Backcourt: The area between the service line and the baseline

- Backhand: Strokes hit on the left side of a right-handed player

- Backspin: Spin placed on a ball that causes the ball to bounce back towards the hitter

- **Back swing:** The beginning of all ground strokes and service motion requiring a back swing to gather energy for the forward swing
- **Baseline:** The end line of a tennis court
- **Break:** Winning a game when the opponent serves
- **Center mark:** A short mark bisecting the baseline
- **Center service line:** The line perpendicular to the net dividing the two service courts in halves
- **Center strap:** The strap at the center of the net anchored to the court to facilitate a constant 3-foot height for the net at its center
- **Center stripe:** Another term for the center service line
- **Chip:** A short chopping motion of the racket against the back and bottom side of the ball, imparting backspin
- **Chop:** Placing backspin on the ball with a short, high-to-low forward swing
- **Cross-court:** A shot hit diagonally from one corner of the court over the net into the opposite corner of the court
- **Cut off the angle:** Moving forward quickly against an opponent's cross-court shot, allowing the player to hit the ball near the center of the court rather than near the sidelines
- **Deep (depth):** A shot bouncing near the baseline on ground strokes and near the service line on serves
- **Default:** A player who forfeits his or her position in a tournament by not playing a scheduled match
- **Deuce:** A term used when the game score is 40-40
- **Dink:** A ball hit very softly and relatively high to ensure its safe landing
- **Double fault:** Two consecutive out-of-bounds serves on the same point, resulting in loss of the point
- **Doubles lines:** The outside sidelines on a court used only for doubles
- **Down-the-line:** A shot hit near a sideline traveling close to, and parallel to, the same line from which the shot was initially hit
- **Drive:** An offensive shot hit with extra force
- **Drop shot:** A ground stroke hit so that it drops just over the net with little or no forward bounce
- **Drop volley:** A volley hit in such a manner that it drops just over the net with little or no forward bounce

- **Error:** A mistake made by a player during competition
- **Flat shot:** A ball hit so there is no rotation or spin when traveling through the air
- **Foot fault:** Illegal foot movement before service, penalized by losing that particular serve; common foot faults are stepping on or ahead of the baseline before the ball has been contacted and running along the baseline before serving
- **Forecourt:** The area between the net and the service line
- **Forehand:** The stroke hit on the right side of a right-handed player
- **Frame:** The rim of the racket head plus the handle of the racket
- **Game:** Scoring term when a player wins 4 points before an opponent while holding a minimum 2-point lead
- **Grip:** The portion of the racket that is grasped in the player's hand
- **Groundstroke:** Any ball hit after it has bounced
- **Half volley:** A ball hit inches away from the court's surface after the ball has bounced
- **Hold serve:** Winning your own serve; if you lose your own serve, your serve has been "broken"
- **Let (ball):** A point replayed because of some kind of interference
- **Let serve:** A serve that touches the net tape, falls into the proper square, and is played over
- **Linesman:** A match official who calls balls "in" or "out"
- **Lob:** A ball hit with sufficient height to pass over the out-stretched arm of a net player
- **Lob volley:** A shot hit high into the air from a volleying position
- **Love:** A scoring term that means zero points or games
- **Match:** A contest between two or four opponents
- **Match point:** The point prior to the final point of a match
- **Midcourt:** The area in front of the baseline or behind the service line of the playing court
- **Net ball:** A ball that hits the net, falling on the same side as the hitter
- **No man's land:** A general area within the baseline and proper net position area. When caught in this area, the player must volley or hit ground strokes near his or her feet.

- **Offensive lob:** A ball hit just above the racket reach of an opposing net player
- **Open face racket:** A racket whose face is moving under the ball; a wide-open racket face is parallel to the court surface
- **Overhead:** A shot hit from a position higher than the player's head
- **Over-hitting:** Hitting shots with too much force; over-hitting usually results in errors
- **Pace:** The speed of the ball
- **Passing shot:** A shot passing beyond the reach of the net player landing inbounds
- **Poach:** To cross over into your partner's territory in doubles in an attempt to intercept the ball
- **Racket face:** The racket's hitting surface
- **Racket head:** The top portion of the racket frame that includes the strings
- **Rally:** Opponents hitting balls back and forth across the net
- **Receiver:** The player about to return the opponent's serve
- **Server:** The player initiating play
- **Service line:** The line at the end of the service courts parallel to the net
- **Set:** A scoring term meaning the first player to win six games with a minimum two-game lead
- **Set point:** The point, if won, which will give the player the set
- **Sidespin:** A ball hit rotating on a horizontal plane
- **Signals in doubles:** Signaling your partner that you are going to poach at the net
- **Singles line:** The sideline closest to the center mark that runs the entire length of the court
- **Slice:** The motion of the racket head going around the side of the ball, producing a horizontal spin on the ball
- **Tape:** The band of cloth or plastic running across the top of the net
- **Telegraphing the play:** Indicating the direction of one's intended target before hitting the ball
- **Topspin:** Forward rotation of the ball

- Touch: The ability to make delicate, soft shots from several positions on the court
- Twist: A special rotation applied to the ball during the serve, causing the ball to jump to the left (of right-handed server)
- Umpire: The official that calls lines
- Under spin: A counterclockwise spin placed on the ball (i.e., backspin)
- Volley: Hitting the ball in the air before it bounces on the court

Track and field

Common track and field events

- Sprint races: 100, 200, 400 meter dash; 110, 400 meter hurdles
- Distance races: One-mile, 5000 and 10000 meter foot races
- Jumping events: High jump, long jump, broad jump, triple jump, pole vault
- Relay races: Team sprint or distance foot races
- Throwing events: Hammer, discus, javelin, shot put

Rules of track and field events

- In all sprint races, runners must stay in their lane on the track, and the first person to cross the finish line wins. Any runner who goes outside his or her lane is disqualified.
- Depending on local rules, one or two "false starts" (running before the start signal) results in disqualification.
- In all jumping events, participants must take off on or before a designated "foul line," and the person with the longest jump wins.
- "Foul" jumps do not receive a score.
- In all relay races, teams must pass a baton within a designated transition area, and the first team to cross the finish line with the baton wins.
- Failed baton exchanges result in disqualification.
- In all throwing events, participants must release the object within a specified area, and the person with the longest throw wins.
- Releasing the object outside the designated area is a "foul," and foul throws do not receive a measurement.

Volleyball

The following infractions by the receiving team result in a point awarded to the serving side; an infraction by the serving team results in side-out:

- Illegal serves or serving out of turn

- Illegal returns or catching or holding the ball

- Dribbling or a player touching the ball twice in succession

- Contact with the net (two opposing players making contact with the net at the same time results in a replay of the point)

- Touching the ball after it has been played three times without passing over the net

- A player's foot completely touching the floor over the centerline

- Reaching under the net and touching a player or the ball while the ball is in play

- The players changing positions prior to the serve

Strategies

- Using forearm passes (bumps, digs, or passes) to play balls below the waist, to play balls that are driven hard, to pass the serve, and to contact balls distant from a player

Terminology

- Attack: Returning the ball across the net in an attempt to put the opponents at a disadvantage

- Ball handling: Executing any passing fundamental

- Block: Intercepting the ball just before or as it crosses the net

- Bump: See *forearm pass*

- Court coverage: A defensive player's court assignment

- Dig: An emergency pass usually used to defend a hard-driven attack

- Dink: A soft shot off the fingertips to lob the ball over a block

- Double foul: Infraction of rules by both teams during the same play

- Drive: An attacking shot contacted in the center that attempts to hit the ball off the blocker's hands

- Fault: Any infraction of the rules

- **Forearm pass:** A pass made off the forearms that is used to play served balls, hard-driven spikes, or any low ball
- **Free ball:** A ball returned by the opponent that is easily handled
- **Frontcourt:** The playing area where it is legal to block or attack
- **Held ball:** A ball that is simultaneously contacted above the net by opponents and momentarily held upon contact
- **Kill:** An attack that cannot be returned
- **Lob:** A soft attack contacted on the back bottom-quarter of the ball, causing an upward trajectory
- **Overhand pass:** A pass made by contacting the ball above the head with the fingers
- **Overlap:** An illegal foot position when the ball is dead, with an adjacent player putting another out of position
- **Play over:** Replaying the rally because of a held ball or the official prematurely suspending play; the server re-serves with no point awarded
- **Point:** A point is scored when the receiving team fails to legally return the ball to the opponents' court
- **Rotation:** Clockwise movement of the players upon gaining the ball from the opposing team
- **Serve:** Putting the ball in play over the net by striking it with the hand
- **Set:** Placing the ball near the net to facilitate attacking
- **Setter:** The player assigned to set the ball
- **Side out:** Side is out when the serving team fails to win a point or plays the ball illegally.
- **Spike:** A ball hit with top spin and with a strong downward force into the opponents' court
- **Spiker:** The player assigned to attack the ball
- **Spike-roll:** An attack that first takes an upward trajectory using the spiking action (with or without jumping)
- **Topspin (Overspin):** Applying forward spin to the ball during the serve, spike, or spike roll

Basketball

Fouls and penalties

- A player touching the floor on or outside the boundary line is out-of-bounds

- The ball is out of bounds if it touches anything (a player, the floor, an object, or any person) that is on or outside the boundary line

- An offensive player remaining in the three-second zone of the free-throw lane for more than three seconds is a violation

- A ball firmly held by two opposing players results in a jump ball

- A throw-in is awarded to the opposing team of the last player touching a ball that goes out-of-bounds

Strategies

Use a Zone Defense	• To prevent drive-ins for easy lay-up shots • When playing area is small • When team is in foul trouble • To keep an excellent rebounder near opponent's basket • When opponents' outside shooting is weak • When opponents have an advantage in height • When opponents have an exceptional offensive player, or when the best defenders cannot handle one-on-one defense
Offensive Strategies against Zone Defense	• Using quick, sharp passes to penetrate zone, forcing opposing player out of assigned position • Overloading and mismatching
Offensive Strategies against One-On-One Defense	• Using the "pick-and-roll" and the "give-and-go" to screen defensive players so as to open up offensive players for shot attempts • Teams may use free-lancing (spontaneous one-one-one offense), but more commonly they use "sets" of plays

Terminology

- Backcourt players (guards): Players who set up a team's offensive pattern and bring the ball up the court

- Backdoor: An offensive maneuver in which a player cuts towards the baseline to the basket, behind the defenders, and receives a ball for a field goal attempt

- Baseline: The end line of the court

- Blocking/boxing out: A term used when a player is positioned under the backboard to prevent an opposing player from achieving a good rebounding position

- Charging: Personal contact by a player with the ball against the body of a defensive opponent

- Corner players (forwards): Tall players that make up the sides of the offensive set-up who are responsible for the rebounding and shooting phases of the team's offense

- Cut: A quick, offensive move by a player attempting to get free for a pass

- Denial defense: Aggressive individual defense to keep an offensive player from receiving a pass

- Double foul: Two opponents committing personal fouls against each other simultaneously

- Dribble: Ball movement by a player in control who throws or taps the ball in the air or onto the floor and then touches it; the dribble ends when the dribbler touches the ball with both hands simultaneously, loses control, or permits the ball to come to rest while in contact with it

- Drive: An aggressive move by a player with the ball towards the basket

- Fake (feint): Using a deceptive move with the ball pulling the defensive player out of position

- Fast break: Quickly moving the ball down court to score before the defense has a chance to set up

- Field goal: A basket scored from the field

- Freelance: No structure or set plays in the offense

- Free throw: The right given to a player to score one or two points by unhindered shots for a basket from within the free throw circle and behind the free throw line

- Give-and-go: A maneuver when the offensive player passes to a teammate and then immediately cuts in toward the basket for a return pass

- Held ball: Occurs when two opponents have one or both hands firmly on the ball and neither can gain possession without undue roughness

- **Inside player (center, post, pivot):** This player is usually the tallest player in the team who is situated near the basket, around the three-second lane area, and is responsible for rebounding and close-range shooting

- **Jump ball:** A method of putting the ball into play to start the game or any overtime periods by tossing it up between two opponents in the center circle

- **Outlet pass:** A term used to designate a direct pass from a rebounder to a teammate (the main objective is starting a fast break)

- **Overtime period:** An additional period of playing time when the score is tied at the end of the regulation game

- **Personal foul:** A player foul that involves contact with an opponent while the ball is alive or after the ball is in possession of a player for a throw-in

- **Pick:** A special type of screen where a player stands so that the defensive player slides to make contact to free an offensive teammate for a shot or drive

- **Pivot:** Occurs when a player who is holding the ball steps once or more than once in any direction with the same foot while the other foot, called the pivot foot, remains at its point of contact with the floor; also another term for the inside player

- **Posting up:** A player cutting to the three-second lane area, pausing, and anticipating a pass

- **Rebound:** When the ball bounces off the backboard or basket

- **Restraining circles:** Three circles with a six-foot radius; one is located in the center of the court, and the others are located at each of the free-throw lines

- **Running time:** Not stopping the clock for fouls or violations

- **Screen:** An offensive maneuver positioning a player between the defender and a teammate to free the teammate for an uncontested shot

- **Switching:** Defensive guards reversing their guarding assignments

- **Technical foul:** A non-contact foul by a player, team, or coach for unsportsmanlike behavior or failing to abide by rules regarding submission of lineups, uniform numbering, or substitution procedures

- **Telegraphing a pass:** A look or signal to indicate where the ball is going to be passed

- **Throw-in:** A method of putting the ball in play from out-of-bounds

- **Traveling:** Illegal movement, in any direction, of a player in possession of the ball within bounds; moving with the ball without dribbling

- Violation: An infraction of the rules resulting in a throw-in from out-of-bounds

> **SKILL 1.8 Liability and legal consideration pertaining to the use of equipment, class organization, supervision, and program selection**

Physical Education Supervision and Management

Strategies for injury prevention

1. Participant screenings: Evaluate injury history, anticipate and prevent potential injuries, watch for hidden injuries and reoccurrence of an injury, and maintain communication.

2. Standards and discipline: Ensure that athletes obey rules of sportsmanship, supervision, and biomechanics.

3. Education and knowledge: Stay current with the knowledge of first aid, sports medicine, sport technique, and injury prevention through clinics, workshops, and communication with staff and trainers.

4. Conditioning: Programs should be year-long and participants should have access to conditioning facilities both in and out of season. This will produce more fit and knowledgeable athletes who are less prone to injury.

5. Equipment: Perform regular inspections; ensure proper fit and proper use. Always make sure students are wearing clothing appropriate for the activity.

6. Facilities: Maintain standards and use safe equipment.

7. Field care: Establish emergency procedures for serious injury.

8. Rehabilitation: Use objective measures, such as power output on an isokinetic dynamometer.

9. Weather Conditions: Use common sense and always err on the side of caution in extreme heat/cold or possible stormy weather conditions.

Prevention of common athletic injuries

- Foot: Start with good footwear, foot exercises.
- Ankle: Use high-top shoes and tape support; strengthen plantar (calf), dorsiflexor (shin), and ankle eversion (ankle outward).

- Shin splints: Strengthen ankle dorsiflexors and tibialis anterior by doing calf raises.

- Achilles tendon: Stretch dorsiflexion and strengthen plantar flexion (heel raises).

- Knee: Increase strength and flexibility of calf and thigh muscles.

- Back: Use proper body mechanics.

- Tennis elbow: Lateral epicondylitis caused by bent elbow, hitting late, not stepping into the ball, heavy rackets, and rackets that are strung too tight.

- Head and neck injuries: Avoid dangerous techniques (e.g., grabbing face mask or horse collar) and carefully supervise dangerous activities like the trampoline. Helmets are absolutely vital in any sport that could result in a hit to the head or a fall on the head. More and more research has shown that slight concussions at an early age cause serious mental and physical problems as the person gets older. Any sign of concussion (confusion, dizziness, unconsciousness) after a blow to the head or fall should result in immediate referral to a doctor or emergency room.[6]

> *School officials and instructors should base equipment selection on quality and safety; goals of physical education and athletics; participants' interests, age, sex, skills, and limitations; and trends in athletic equipment and uniforms.*

Knowledgeable personnel should select the equipment and should keep continuous service and replacement considerations in mind (i.e., what's best in year of selection may not be best the following year). One final consideration is the possibility of reconditioning versus the purchase of new equipment. When selecting and updating weight machines, keep in mind the size of the students, and also keep the girls in mind if they are going to use those machines. Their bodies are shaped differently from the boys' bodies. After purchasing equipment, make sure all students know how to adjust the settings for their bodies.

Harmful Exercise Techniques and Environmental Conditions

Instructors and participants should make safety and injury prevention top priority in exercise activities. There are a number of potential risks associated with physical activity, and instructors must be familiar with all the risks to prevent an emergency situation.

Equipment

Exercise equipment in poor condition has the potential for malfunction. Instructors should perform weekly checks to ensure all equipment is in proper working order. If it is not, the instructor or maintenance staff must repair the equipment before students use it. Placement of exercise equipment is also important. There should be adequate space between machines and benches to ensure a safe environment. Students who have not gone through the initial training on the equipment by a professional should not be allowed to use it.

Technique

Instructors should stress proper exercise technique at all times, especially with beginners, to prevent development of bad habits. Whether it's weightlifting, running, or stretching, participants should not force any body part beyond the normal range of motion. Pain is a good indicator of overextension. Living by the phrase "no pain, no gain" is potentially dangerous. Participants should use slow and controlled movements. In addition, participants must engage in proper warm-up and cool-down before and after exercise.

When lifting weights, lifters should always have a partner. A spotter can help correct the lifter's technique and help lift the weight to safety if the lifter is unable to do so. A partner can also offer encouragement and motivation. Flexibility is an often overlooked, yet important, part of exercise that can play a key role in injury prevention. Participants should perform stretching exercises after each workout session.

Environment

Environmental conditions can be very dangerous and potentially life threatening. Be cautious when exercising in extremely hot, cold, and/or humid conditions. High humidity can slow the body's release of heat, increasing the chances of heat-related illnesses. Hydration in hot environments is very important. Drink two cups of water two hours before exercise, and hydrate regularly during exercise at the same rate at which the sweat is lost. While performing exercise lasting a long period of time, it is possible to drink too much water, resulting in a condition known as hyponutremia, or low sodium content in the body. Water cannot replace sodium and other electrolytes lost through sweat. Drinking sports drinks can solve this problem.

Many states and school districts have specific rules governing when students and athletes can exercise or train outside. Heat can cause quick dehydration, heat stroke, or heat exhaustion. A student who feels sick should be taken to a cool, indoor area immediately. Any sign of unconsciousness should result in a referral to the emergency room. Vomiting or extreme fatigue should be treated with a release to a doctor or emergency room. Sunburn is also dangerous. Students exercising outside should be advised to wear sunscreen and reapply during breaks. Sun poisoning is a very dangerous condition caused by a serious sunburn, and any sunburn could eventually cause cancer.

Cold environments can also be a problem when exercising. The human body works more efficiently at its normal temperature. Wear many layers of clothing

> *Instructors should stress proper exercise technique at all times, especially with beginners, to prevent development of bad habits.*

to prevent cold-related illnesses such as frostbite and hypothermia. In the case of students suffering from asthma, wearing a cloth over the mouth during exercise increases the moisture of the air breathed in and can help prevent an attack. Asthmatic students should have their inhalers or other breathing treatments or medicines available in case of emergency.

Identifying Exercise Equipment as Either Sound or Unsound Using Physiological Principles

Rolling machines, vibrating belts, vibrating tables and pillows, massaging devices, electrical muscle stimulators, weighted belts, motor-driven cycles and rowing machines, saunas, and plastic or rubberized sweat and sauna suits are all ineffective exercise equipment because they produce PASSIVE MOVEMENT, that is, movement with no voluntary muscle contractions.

Sound exercise equipment produces ACTIVE MOVEMENT resulting from the participant initiating the movement of the equipment or the participant voluntarily producing muscle contractions.

Exercise equipment has not been under much scrutiny until recent years, and many unsafe products have been on the market. Now, the American Society of Testing Materials (ASTM) is involved in testing and releasing documentation on exercise equipment. Generally speaking, simple is better. Free weights, medicine balls, stability balls, exercise bands and mats, punching bags, and general cardio equipment are inexpensive and effective for a school environment.[7]

> **PASSIVE MOVEMENT:** movement with no voluntary muscle contractions

> **ACTIVE MOVEMENT:** movement produced by voluntary muscle contractions

> *Poor or unsafe equipment can be removed from the marketplace based on the ASTM standards of safety.*

Equipment and Facility Selection and Maintenance

Additional guidelines for selection of equipment

- Follow purchasing policies
- Relate purchasing to program, budget, and finances
- Consider maintenance
- Abide by legal regulations
- Recognize administrative considerations (good working relationships at all personnel levels)
- Determine best value for money spent
- Ensure that participants have own equipment and supplies when necessary
- Purchase from reputable manufacturers and distributors
- Follow competitive purchasing regulations

- Use school forms with clearly identified brand, trademark, and catalog specifications

Equipment maintenance procedures

- Inspect supplies and equipment upon delivery
- Label supplies and equipment with organization's identification
- Create consistent policies for issuing and returning supplies and equipment
- Keep equipment in perfect operating condition
- Store equipment properly
- Properly clean and care for equipment (including garments)

Facility selection considerations

- Bond issues for construction
- Accessibility to girls, women, minorities, and the handicapped
- Energy costs and conservation
- Community involvement
- Convertibility (movable walls/partitions)
- Environment must be safe, attractive, clean, comfortable, practical, and adaptable to individual needs
- Compliance with public health codes
- Effective disease control

Facility maintenance procedures

- Custodial staff, participants, and the physical education and athletic staffs must work together to properly maintain the facility
- Pools need daily monitoring of water temperature, hydrogen ion concentration, and chlorine
- Gymnasium play areas must be free from dust and dirt
- Showers and drying areas need daily cleaning and disinfecting
- Participants' clothing should meet health standards to prevent odor and bacterial growth
- Outdoor playing fields must be clear of rocks and free of holes and uneven surfaces

- Disinfect and clean drinking fountains, sinks, urinals, and toilets daily
- Air out and sanitize lockers frequently

Establishment of Curriculum Frameworks and Student Performance Standards

A **CURRICULUM FRAMEWORK** is a set of broad guidelines that aids educational personnel in producing specific instructional plans for a given subject or study area. The legislative intent of a curriculum framework is to promote a degree of uniformity and instructional consistency in curriculum offerings.

CURRICULUM FRAME-WORK: a set of broad guidelines that aids educational personnel in producing specific instructional plans for a given subject or study area

Federal legislation

The Department of Health and Human Services recommended legislative changes, including those for education. Title IX prohibits sex discrimination in educational programs, and PL 94-142 requires schools to provide educational services for handicapped students.

Adapted Physical Education National Standards, revised in 2008, gives physical education teachers fifteen national standards regarding children with special needs.

1. Human development: Understanding knowledge and skills of children based on their families and home lives

2. Motor behavior: Understanding average motor development and principles of motor development, and relating this to individual needs and challenges

3. Exercise science: Understanding the physiological and developmental challenges of children with disabilities

4. Measurement and evaluation: Compliance with federal and state laws regarding students with special needs and appropriate evaluation

5. History and philosophy: Knowing the law and its factors as applicable to modern education

6. Unique attributes of learners: Understanding and using individualized instruction

7. Curriculum theory and development: Selecting goals and assessments based on individual needs

8. Assessment: Measuring and evaluating with regard to individual development

9. Instructional design and planning: Applying human and motor development when organizing unit plans

10. Teaching: Considering human and motor development in the approach for teaching the individual

11. Consultation and staff development: Staff development should be available to address these standards

12. Student and program evaluation: Adapted physical education should be included in overall evaluation of a student's education

13. Continuing education: The teacher should try to stay updated on standards and methods of teaching students with individual needs

14. Ethics: All children are to be treated fairly

15. Communication: The teacher should communicate properly with staff, administration, and parents

State legislation

State governments (Departments of Education) are primarily responsible for education. Departments of Education establish policies for course curriculum, number of class days and class time, and the number of credits required for graduation. Most states now have mandated time dedicated to organized physical activity. To see what is required for your state, see *http:www.aahperd.org/naspe /standards/stateStandards/.*

Impact of education reforms

Enrollment in public schools is up, and there is renewed administrative, parental, and student support. Additional impacts include coeducational classes, separate teams for boys and girls and men and women (otherwise the school must create a coeducational team), equal opportunities for both sexes (facilities, equipment and supplies, practice and games, medical and training services, academic tutoring, coaching, travel and per diem allowances, and dining and housing facilities), and equitable expenditure of funds for both genders.

Title IX takes precedence over all conflicting state and local laws and conference regulations. Federal aid (even aid not related to physical education or athletics) must comply with Title IX. Title IX prohibits discrimination in personnel standards and scholarships selection.

Liability Concerns in Physical Education

Historically, common-law rules stated that individuals could not sue government agencies without the consent of the agencies. However, federal and state courts have begun to allow individuals to sue both federal and state governments. Thus, public schools and school districts are now subject to liability lawsuits.

Compulsory elements of the school curriculum, such as physical education, prompt courts to decide based on what is in the best interests of the public.

Although school districts still have immunity in many states, teachers do not have such immunity. Whether employed by a private person or a municipal corporation, every employee has a duty not to injure another by a negligent act of commission.

The following is a list of common legal terms and conditions applicable to physical education.

- **Tort:** A legal wrong resulting in a direct or indirect injury; includes omissions and acts intended or unintended to cause harm

- **Negligence:** Failing to fulfill a legal duty according to common reasoning; includes instruction and facility maintenance; instructors must consider sex, size, and skill of participants when planning activities and grouping students.

- **In loco parentis:** Acting in the place of the parent in relation to a child

- **Sports product liability:** Liability of the manufacturer to the person using the manufacturer's product who sustains injury/damage from using the product

- **Violence and legal liability** (intentional injury in sports contests): Harmful, illegal contact of one person by another (referred to as battery)

- **Physical education classes held off campus and legal liability:** Primary concern is providing due care, which is the responsibility of management and staff members of sponsoring organization; failing to observe "due care" can result in findings of negligence

- **Attractive nuisance:** An object that results in physical injury that the responsible party should have foreseen

Actions that help avoid lawsuits

- Knowing the health status of each person in the program

- Considering the ability and skill level of participants when planning new activities

- Grouping students to equalize competitive levels

- Using safe equipment and facilities

- Properly organizing and supervising classes

- Never leaving a class or allowing students to use any school equipment without supervision at all times

- Knowing first aid (do not diagnose or prescribe)

- Keeping accident records

- Giving instruction prior to dangerous activities

- Being sure that injured students get medical attention and examination

- Getting exculpatory agreements (parental consent forms)

- Having a planned, written disposition for students who suffer injuries or become ill

- Providing a detailed accident report if one occurs

- Joining your local school district union—unions provide liability insurance and legal representation, should the need arise

---

SKILL 1.9 Effects of substance abuse on student performance, health, and behavior

Any substance affecting the normal functions of the body, illegal or not, is potentially dangerous, and students and athletes should avoid them completely.

- **Anabolic steroids:** The alleged benefit is an increase in muscle mass and strength. However, these substances are illegal and produce harmful side effects. Premature closure of growth plates in bones can occur if they are abused by a teenager, limiting growth. Other effects include bloody cysts in the liver, increased risk of cardiovascular disease, increased blood pressure, and dysfunction of the reproductive system.

- **Alcohol:** This is a legal substance for adults, but is very commonly abused. Moderate to excessive consumption can lead to an increased risk of cardiovascular disease, nutritional deficiencies, and dehydration. Alcohol also causes ill effects on various aspects of performance such as reaction time, coordination, accuracy, balance, and strength. Heavy alcohol use during teenage years has long-lasting effects on brain function and development.

- **Nicotine:** Another legal but often abused substance that can increase the risk of cardiovascular disease, pulmonary disease, and cancers of the mouth and lungs. Nicotine consumption through smoking severely hinders athletic performance by compromising lung function. Smoking especially affects performance in endurance activities.

Substance abuse can lead to adverse behaviors and increased risk of injury and disease.

- **Marijuana:** This is the most commonly abused illegal substance. Adverse effects include a loss of focus and motivation, decreased coordination, and lack of concentration.

- **Cocaine:** Another illegal and somewhat commonly abused substance. Effects include increased alertness and excitability. This drug can give the user a sense of overconfidence and invincibility, leading to a false sense of one's ability to perform certain activities. A high heart rate is associated with the use of cocaine, leading to an increased risk of heart attack, stroke, potentially deadly arrhythmias, and seizures.

> *It is important to note that the Federal Food and Drug Administration (FDA) does NOT have any legal right to review herbal supplements, including stimulants and herbal "steroids" at this time. Herbal supplements can be toxic, especially to children.*

Street drugs and misused over-the-counter or prescription drugs are a problem that changes constantly in the school environment. Because trends change, noticing changes in behavior (and particularly in sudden changes in physique) and keeping detailed reports and records of changes—as well as quick communication with administration, school nurses, and parents—is very important. There are many rules and regulations regarding student use of certain steroids and other performance-enhancing drugs. These rules and laws change as the trends and markets change, so it is up to the educator to keep an eye on his or her students' behaviors and perform drug tests when required or recommended.

COMPETENCY 2
STUDENT GROWTH AND DEVELOPMENT

SKILL 2.1 **Sequential and developmentally appropriate learning and practice opportunities based on growth and motor development stages, individual characteristics and individual needs of students, learning environment, and task**

In early childhood, the muscles follow a pattern of development that relates directly to a child's development. As the child develops through school age, development of certain skills is not necessarily predictable, but a child who is having noticeable difficulty with a motor skill might be having problems with a physical or mental development.

A positive and creative learning environment will positively impact the development of each child's skills in both independent work and in team sports. An environment of anger and ridicule will send negative messages about sports and fitness. The hippocampus section of the brain detects safety. It is the same part of the brain that lets in new information. If the child feels threatened or unsafe, the child will not learn. A negative experience in a fitness environment or with a teacher or coach could cause a child to become withdrawn or outspoken, but it will not improve his or her fitness level.

Relationship between Human Growth and Development and Appropriate Physical Activity

See Skill 1.4

> Many children are not exposed to any physical activity at home. This can cause a delay in what would be considered basic (walking, running, jumping, leaping, skipping) movement. For this reason, individual assessments are encouraged.

SKILL 2.2 Monitoring of individual performance and group performance in order to design safe instruction that meets students' developmental needs in the psychomotor, cognitive, and affective domains

---

Effective physical education supports psychomotor, cognitive, and affective development.

Psychomotor, Cognitive, and Affective Domains

Physical education through the psychomotor domain contributes to movement skills as a participant and spectator in sports and other physical activities; contributes skills to utilize leisure hours in mental and cultural pursuits; and contributes skills necessary to the preservation of the natural environment.

Physical education in the cognitive domain contributes to academic achievement; is related to higher thought processes via motor activity; contributes to knowledge of exercise, health, and disease; contributes to an understanding of the human body; contributes to an understanding of the role of physical activity and sport in American culture; and contributes to the knowledgeable consumption of goods and services.

Physical education in the affective domain contributes to self-actualization, self-esteem, and a healthy response to physical activity; contributes to an appreciation of beauty; contributes to directing one's life toward worthy goals; emphasizes humanism; affords individuals the chance to enjoy rich social experiences through play; assists cooperative play with others; teaches courtesy, fair play, and good sportsmanship; and contributes to humanitarianism.

Teaching methods and techniques

Teaching methods to facilitate psychomotor learning include:

- **Task/reciprocal:** The instructor integrates task learning into the learning setup by utilizing stations.
- **Command/direct:** Task instruction is teacher-centered. The teacher clearly explains the goals, explains and demonstrates the skills, allocates time for practice, and frequently monitors student progress.
- **Contingency/contract:** This is a style of task instruction that rewards the completion of tasks.

Techniques that facilitate psychomotor learning include:

- **Reflex movements:** Activities that create an automatic response to some stimuli; responses include flexing, extending, stretching, and postural adjustment
- **Basic fundamental locomotor movements:** Activities that utilize instinctive patterns of movement established by combining reflex movements
- **Perceptual abilities:** Activities that involve interpreting auditory, visual, and tactile stimuli in order to coordinate adjustments
- **Physical abilities:** Activities to develop physical characteristics of fitness, providing students with the stamina necessary for highly advanced, skilled movement
- **Skilled movements:** Activities that involve instinctive, effective performance of complex movement including vertical and horizontal components
- **Nondiscursive communication:** Activities necessitating expression as part of the movement

Teaching methods that facilitate cognitive learning include:

- **Problem solving:** The instructor presents the initial task and students come to an acceptable solution in unique and divergent ways
- **Conceptual theory:** The instructor's focus is on acquisition of knowledge
- **Guided inquiry:** Stages of instructions strategically guide students through a sequence of experiences

Techniques that facilitate cognitive learning include:

- Transfer of learning—that is, identifying similar movements of a previously learned skill in a new skill
- Planning for slightly longer instructions and demonstrations as students memorize cues and skills

- Using appropriate language according to the level of each student

- Conceptual learning—that is, giving students who are more capable more responsibility for their learning

Aids to facilitate cognitive learning include:

- Frequent assessments of student performance

- Movement activities incorporating principles of biomechanics

- Computers, software, and gaming programs

- Video recordings of student performance, NOT to be used outside of the classroom assessment process

Initially, performance of skills will be variable, inconsistent, error-prone, "off-time," and awkward. Students' focus will be on remembering what to do. Instructors should emphasize clear information regarding the skill's biomechanics. They should correct errors in gross movement that effect significant parts of the skill. To prevent students from being overburdened with too much information, they should only perform one or two elements at a time.

> *Motivation results from supportive and encouraging comments. Peer-to-peer encouragement is also very useful and helpful.*

SKILL 2.3 **Developmental readiness to learn and refine motor skills and movement patterns** *(e.g., biological, psychological, sociological, experimental, environmental)*

- **Biological readiness:** Is the child performing the preceding skills aptly enough to apply a new skill? Would his or her body be able to adapt to the new skill and be successful in some form?

- **Psychological readiness:** Is the child withdrawn or overly concerned about the previous skill? Would a new skill cause the child to react positively or negatively? An immediate negative response would indicate psychological limitations at the child's current state.

- **Sociological readiness:** Would the child relate to the new skill? Is it an acceptable skill in his or her environment? Would learning the new skill cause positive or negative feedback from the child and his or her family?

- **Experimental readiness:** Is the child ready to experiment to find out how his or her body responds to the new skill? Is he or she ready to try something in different ways to see what would work?

- **Environmental readiness:** Does the child's environment lend itself to a new skill? The Jamaican bobsled team comes to mind: Training for an ice sport would be difficult in an area that does not get any ice or snow. Also consider the direct environment for accessibility to the activity. Would their neighborhoods or homes have the equipment required to practice? Would they have access to the school or a parks and recreation center to practice?

SKILL 2.4 Perception in motor development

How a child perceives him or herself in motor development is important. The readiness factors outlined in Skill 2.3 are good indicators as to whether a child will feel like the new skill is appropriate.

Family and community standards are also important for learning new skills and sports. Sometimes these are stereotypes, which will not immediately disappear. Instead, if a teacher wants an individual or class to learn a skill that is new and different to the environment, the teacher must approach it through a skill that is already in the children's or community's idea of acceptability. For example, teaching dance movement to a boys' football team might be something new and awkward to the boys and their families. A slow introduction with a relationship to something they already know would make the skill more acceptable.

SKILL 2.5 Appropriate and effective instruction related to students' cultures and ethnicities, personal values, family structures, home environments, and community values

Communities and societies dictate much of what a child believes. Culture dictates what sports are considered to be of value. For example, ice hockey is a top sport in northern states, but goes mostly unstudied in southern states. This also has to do with environment. Our vast country has both states that are cold for months at a time, and states that rarely have any ice or snow.

Personal values and family values can also dictate what a child will respond to. For example, a girl's family might have trouble seeing their child as the kicker for the football team, or this choice may cause the community to be uncomfortable and critical of the teachers and student. These decisions by teachers and coaches are important to discuss openly and honestly with the child and his or her parents, understanding that the answer might be "no."

Our country is known as a melting pot because we embrace and accept people from all over the world as members of our communities. These cultures may have specific beliefs about what is acceptable for their children, for certain genders, or at certain times or on certain days. Open communication is important so that the teacher is informed of cultural or religious limitations. A teacher or any responsible adult should know that using slang that is disrespectful to any culture in front of or toward children is absolutely unacceptable.

A child that cites a religious reason for not doing something should be respected.

Children's families are also changing. With at least half of all marriages ending in divorce and 40 percent of all children being born out of wedlock, a teacher should not assume that the child has a mother and father at home. Teachers can assume nothing about a child's home life. In any situation, regardless of the type of family a child has, traumatic events can happen in a child's life, and sometimes the coach or physical education teacher is the first to see signs of a problem. Such signs could be a sudden change in personality or behavior, marks and bruises, discussions inappropriate for the school environment, or a lack of motivation or response in a child. Should the teacher or coach suspect a problem at home, she has certain laws to follow. Review the school and district policy. Contact the guidance counselor and/or principal immediately if abuse or neglect is suspected.

Many children are raised by grandparents and other guardians, many parents are not married, and many parents are gay couples or simply friends. None of these possibilities should make anyone assume less than a positive upbringing, and no judgments about the child's guardians and their life choices are necessary.

SKILL 2.6 Use of appropriate professional support services and resources to meet students' needs

In today's school and community, there are many support services and resources for both the student and the teacher. For example, it would be a good choice for the teacher to be a member of The National Association for Sports and Physical Education (NASPE). A certification through a reputable, ACSM-accredited association is a good idea as well. The newest initiative for student health and nutrition is First Lady Michelle Obama's "Let's Move" plan for movement and motivation in youth. Many other companies and celebrities have plans and endorsements to try to motivate a positive change in children so that they will want to exercise and will see the positive effects of fitness and sports.

Cooper Institute in Dallas, Texas has a powerful and informative youth initiative that is constantly researching and improving. They offer the Fitnessgram and the Nutriongram for students' data. Students and teachers can track progress and create goals.

Other sites for teachers include:

www.peuniverse.com

www.pecentral.com

DOMAIN II
MANAGEMENT, MOTIVATION, AND COMMUNICATION

PERSONALIZED STUDY PLAN

KNOWN MATERIAL/ SKIP IT

PAGE	COMPETENCY AND SKILL	
67	**3: Management and motivation**	☐
	3.1: Principles of classroom management practices that create effective learning experiences in physical educational settings	☐
	3.2: Psychological and social factors that affect individual learning and group learning, participation, cooperation, and performance in physical education settings	☐
	3.3: Organization, allocation, and management of resources to provide active and equitable learning experiences	☐
	3.4: Motivation of students to participate in physical activity both in school and outside of school	☐
	3.5: Promotion of positive relationships, encouragement of responsible personal and social behaviors among students, and establishment of a productive learning environment	☐
	3.6: Development and use of an effective behavior management plan	☐
74	**4: Communication**	☐
	4.1: Effective verbal and nonverbal communication skills in a variety of physical activity settings	☐
	4.2: Specific appropriate instructional feedback in skill acquisition, student learning, and motivation	☐
	4.3: Communication of classroom management and instructional information in a variety of ways	☐
	4.4: Communication in ways that show respect and consideration for students, colleagues, and parents	☐
	4.5: Communication in ways that show respect and consideration for students, colleagues, and parents	☐

COMPETENCY 3
MANAGEMENT AND MOTIVATION

SKILL 3.1 **Principles of classroom management practices that create effective learning experiences in physical educational settings**

Classroom management requires consistency and fairness. First, know your school's procedures for classroom management. Relate their rules to your own classroom. Post them and make the beginning of the school year about procedures and rules. Continue reminding children of these procedures and rules throughout the school year. Have effective and quick consequences for choices, and use them consistently with all students. Keep communication lines with the students' parents open. Know the students' names so that they can be addressed for positive behaviors first and negative behaviors second. Students want to feel like they matter and learning their names is the first step.

Also understand that each child is an individual, so while being fair and consistent, also understand that some children react differently to different stimuli in the classroom, and sometimes a child needs a second chance to get something right. Slight lapses in judgment or difficulty in decision-making happens to all children at some point. In these cases, a little understanding and tenderness goes a long way.

Many physical education classes have large numbers of students. Find out your school district's policy and the state laws on student–teacher ratio, and make your administrators aware if they are not following the law. Use the staff available to monitor all student activity in your classroom in terms of safety and legality.

Many schools have character curriculum and bullying standards to address both building a child's character and helping them with self-esteem. Most bullying occurs when children are unsupervised. Close proximity to an adult helps. Acts of bullying should be addressed immediately. A bully and his or her target should not be forced to work or play together. Separation of the two does help, but will not help the target once he or she has left your classroom. Other staff and personnel should be notified in instances where the teacher fears the child is being bullied. The bully will need some intervention to help with his or her behavior. An administrator or counselor can help with that.[8]

> *Classroom management requires consistency and fairness.*

> *Find out your school district's policy and the state laws on student–teacher ratio, and make your administrators aware if they are not following the law.*

> **SKILL 3.2** **Psychological and social factors that affect individual learning and group learning, participation, cooperation, and performance in physical education settings**

Personality Factors

Certain psychological factors might hinder participation in certain physical activities. These factors can depend on the individual, the group with which the individual will participate, and the activity itself.

An individual's personality type and interests can determine his or her level of participation. Outgoing, energetic, and aggressive personality types usually exhibit increased levels of participation. Reserved personality types are sometimes difficult to work with and motivate. Shy individuals are usually compliant, but might not feel completely comfortable in participation, especially in activities involving larger groups.

Physical education instructors often overlook the importance of activity groups for the psychological wellbeing of students. Instructors must construct groups with certain factors in mind. Children might feel intimidated by participating in activities with older individuals. In addition, girls might not feel comfortable participating with boys, and vice versa. Grouping students by age, gender, and skill level helps maintain self-confidence.

The type of activity can also affect participation. Everyone has different interests, and instructors should not necessarily force students to participate in activities they do not enjoy. Such action can lead to a diminished physical activity level throughout life. Instructors should introduce alternate activities to increase levels of participation for all individuals.

Everyone has different interests, and instructors should not necessarily force students to participate in activities they do not enjoy. Such action can lead to a diminished physical activity level throughout life.

Positive and Negative Influences of Participation in Physical Activity on Psycho-Social Factors

Physical activity can influence psycho-social development both positively and negatively. Thus, physical education instructors must create an environment that maximizes the benefits of physical activity and minimizes the potential negative aspects.

Positive Individual Influences	Positive Group Influences	Negative Influences
• Reduces tension and depression • Provides means of affiliation with others • Provides exhilarating experiences • Provides aesthetic experiences • Creates positive body image • Controls aggression • Provides relaxation and a change of pace from long hours of work, study, or other stresses • Provides challenge and sense of accomplishment • Provides a way to be healthy and fit • Improves self-esteem through skill mastery • Provides creative experiences • Creates positive addiction to exercise in contrast to negative addiction to substances	• Development of cooperation skills • Acceptance of and respect for all persons regardless of race, creed or origin • Assimilation of the group attitude • Opportunity to develop group relationships • Development of a spirit of fairness • Development of traits of good citizenship • Development of leadership and following skills • Development of self-discipline • Additional avenues for social acquaintances • Development of social poise and self-understanding • Development of a social consciousness with an accompanying sense of values • Individual and social development	• Ego-centered athletes • Winning at all costs • False values • Harmful pressures • Loss of identity • Role conflict • Aggression and violence • Compulsiveness • Over-competitiveness • Addiction to exercise, where commitment to exercise has a higher priority than commitments to family, interpersonal relationships, work, and medical advice • Escape or avoidance of problems • Exacerbation of anorexia nervosa • Exercise deprivation effects • Fatigue • Overexertion • Poor eating habits • Self-centeredness • Preoccupation with fitness, diet, and body image

Sometimes the coach or fitness instructor is the first to see signs of a serious psychological disorder called anorexia nervosa. If the coach sees signs that a student is not eating, has dropped a lot of weight quickly, or is lethargic, she might want to have a personal discussion with the student, and then take her concerns to the parents if necessary. The teacher cannot diagnose anything, but can tell the parents what she sees first-hand and let the parent handle the rest. The guidance counselor is also a good resource for these students.

The teacher or coach may or may not be privy to the signs of bulimia. This is also a serious psychological disorder with high physical stakes if not treated. Signs of bulimia are vomiting after eating (consistently), diarrhea (from taking laxatives), or exercising for hours. If bulimia is suspected, get all observations down on paper and share this with the student first, and, if necessary, with the guidance counselor and parents. Hold back all judgment and stick to direct observations.

> ### SKILL 3.3 Organization, allocation, and management of resources to provide active and equitable learning experiences (e.g., time, space, equipment, activities, teacher attention, students)

Management of resources

Time
Engage students from the beginning of class. Immediate activity gets children's attention and makes classroom management easier. Knowing what is realistic to accomplish in your time frame might take a little practice. Always over-plan so that there are plenty of activities to fill the time space. Never leave the children unattended while doing any activities. If children change their clothing for PE, allocate a certain amount of time to change and stick to it.

Space
Gymnasiums come in many sizes, and some schools do not even have a gymnasium and hold physical education in a classroom. Depending on the situation, classes might need to be broken up into groups that do different activities and then rotate, or an outside venue must be used. The teacher must know the policies on what space can be used and then use a system of student placement to make sure all students can perform the exercises or functions of the day.

Equipment
When equipment is part of the planned activities, make sure all children get a turn or have time sign-up lists to use a certain piece of equipment, such as in an independent study class where students have to share cardiovascular equipment.

Activities

Within the framework of the day, make sure the activities are age appropriate, time appropriate, and accessible to all the students of the class. In other words, a day that focuses on a difficult skill may be frustrating for students who are not athletes. A tiered plan may work better on these days, where practice at different levels of difficulty is in place before the most challenging moves are addressed. ALL children should be encouraged to try different levels of activity, without worry that their grade will be determined by their natural ability in that certain sport, or worry that their peers will judge them based on their performance of that sport.

Teacher Attention

Teachers should be able to see and address positive and negative behaviors. They should also be able to correct form and give advice quickly and efficiently so that children of all abilities are addressed. There should be enough staffing to have an adult present for each small group. If the group needs to be split between two rooms or locations, staffing must be split also.

SKILL 3.4 **Motivation of students to participate in physical activity both in school and outside of school**

Accessibility leads to compliance. Simple activities that can be done anywhere make simple lesson plans that work. The child can take that lesson home or to the park and perform well. A dance to a popular song, or an independent sport such as running or jumping rope, are easy activities that a child can do on his or her own and feel successful doing them. A positive classroom where students leave feeling good about their own performance can filter in to the rest of their day and make them want to continue moving.

Exercise releases endorphins (feel-good chemicals) in the brain. If a child feels those endorphins after exercising in school, he or she is going to want to feel that outside of school. Teachers can also take part in community teams and activities with their students and parents that can be done through local businesses or the parks and recreation department of the locality.

> *When a person of any age feels successful at something, he or she wants to continue doing it.*

Promotion of positive relationships, encouragement of responsible personal and social behaviors among students, and establishment of a productive learning environment

Relationships in the Physical Education Classroom

There are many relationships that are developed in the physical education classroom. First, there is the teacher–student relationship. If the student likes to be around the teacher and does not feel judged by him or her, the student will look forward to the class more and will perform better because he or she will not feel threatened.

Many schools use the Character Counts curriculum. If yours does, use the pillars at different times of the school year and keep revisiting them. Seven students must practice how to give each other feedback that shares their feelings in a positive way.

The second relationship is that of the students to each other. Negative feedback and negative feelings are more likely in these relationships. The teacher can turn negative situations into learning moments, where short character lessons are peppered into the curriculum. School guidance counselors can help with ideas for quick character lessons. Allow students to practice their feedback to each other with class demonstrations and scenarios. Do not ignore hurtful comments or bullying.

A third type of relationship is that between the teacher and parent or teacher and community. Parents should feel they can communicate with the teacher easily through phone calls, emails, or conferences. The community may be looking to the physical education teacher—especially if he or she is also a sport-specific coach—for quality sport education, character development, and athletic achievement in their youth. If the teacher is a coach, writing sports releases for the newspaper or putting information on the school district Website or television station is important. Even physical education classes that do not include a specific sport can reach out to the community through technology to show what children are learning and doing to promote self-esteem.

Please note that school districts have strict policies on sharing children's names on television or websites. Do not share student information online, and do not post anything without specific written permission per the school policy.

A productive learning environment will be filled with positive energy. When a child is having fun, that child is learning and remembering. The opposite is also true. A tormented child will learn that he or she is not capable, or that he or she is not accepted in the teacher's classroom. An effective teacher creates a productive learning environment for every child.

Development and use of an effective behavior management plan

An effective behavior management plan uses clear and simple rules, procedures, and positive and negative consequences.

Procedures

This is what we do in this class. For example:

1. Wear clothes and shoes for physical education

2. Start the class in assigned squad lines

3. Participate in the activities

4. Respect all others in the classroom

5. Use equipment responsibly

The procedures should be simple and concise. If a child is not following one, the teacher can simply remind that child of that procedure.

Positive Reinforcement

The best positive rewards are intrinsic. This is how a child feels about himself- or herself. Positive feelings promote positive self-esteem. Extrinsic consequences are effective as well, and can include appropriate rewards for following procedures. Follow the school's policy on this as well as negative consequences, making any adjustments to fit the physical education classroom.

A positive extrinsic reward could be getting to do something the children really like to do on a certain day. It could also be individual awards or rewards, depending on what the school and administrators choose to do.

Negative Consequences

A negative consequence is a punishment for a broken rule or procedure. It should be appropriate to the issue at hand, and it should be handled immediately. The teacher should try to handle any negative consequence in his or her own class-room by moving the individual away from the problem or changing that indi-vidual's activity for the day.

More severe cases or repetitive cases should include communication with parents and administrators. In a case where the teacher fears for the safety of children and adults present, additional administration must sometimes be called. Have a system in place for an emergency, such as an emergency phone number, a red card in the window, or an emergency sound. In a case of immediate physical danger to other children, make sure to move children away from the problem.

COMPETENCY 4
COMMUNICATION

> **SKILL 4.1** Effective verbal and nonverbal communication skills in a variety of physical activity settings

Verbal Communication to a Student

Students feel less cornered when addressed in a one-on-one situation, especially when addressing poor performance, a failure in an assessment, or behavioral concerns. When a student is addressed in front of a group, the result can be immediate defensiveness or withdrawal. The lasting impact of embarrassment can cause continuous problems in the current class and even across the curriculum. Verbal communication should be used in an attempt help the child make good choices or to help him or her reflect on his or her own choices effectively. Verbal communication could also be used to let a child know that his or her grade is slipping, or that he or she is not mastering a concept required by the class or sport. The conversation should then move to what can be done to improve his or her grade or skill level.

> *When a student is addressed in front of a group, the result can be immediate defensiveness or withdrawal. The lasting impact of embarrassment can cause continuous problems in the current class and even across the curriculum.*

Nonverbal Communication

Students can be quickly addressed with nonverbal communication, even from across the room. A simple point or motion can indicate what the children should be doing (perhaps instead of what they have chosen to do). A system should be in place that allows a teacher to get the group's attention when necessary. The system could be a clapped rhythm, a whistle or sound, or a raised hand (known as "give me five") instead of screaming over noise for attention. Part of the initial procedure practice at the beginning of school should be about knowing the signal and the response.

Proximity is another nonverbal communication. When a teacher needs to get a student back on task, sometimes just standing near the student helps the student realize that she needs to make a better choice. By moving closer, the teacher can also hear or see what the situation really is, such as student bullying, socialization problems, or problems adhering to general rules.

SKILL 4.2 Specific appropriate instructional feedback in skill acquisition, student learning, and motivation

Instructional feedback is important so that a child can continue on his or her path or choose to make a change. Quick classroom feedback that encourages skills or behaviors can sometimes be a quick "good job on that _____," or it can be detailed, describing what the student is doing right and what he or she can improve.

It is important to find something positive to use on each child in assessments and to be specific. For example, if the skill is general push-ups, the teacher's assessment of Susie can be, "You are doing great, Susie. I like that you are using the full range of motion. Just remember to treat your back like a board and try to hold it straight and still from the top to the bottom and back up." Do not leave it at that. Say, "Can I see another one, Susie?" Here, the teacher would see that it is better and say, "Yeah, like that! Did you feel how your back was straighter that time?" or would see that the advice was not quite enough and say, "Ok, let's try this on your knees like this, and let's move your hands out a little. Let's see if that makes your form a little better." Again, a short demonstration of the exercise should show the teacher whether to modify the exercise again, ask for practice, or teach the child how to develop that level and then move to the next.

This has a many-tiered effect on the child:

1. The child realizes she is capable of doing something

2. The child learns how to modify when necessary

3. The child feels a level of success and is motivated to gain more success

> We all must feel a level of success, or a comfort level with what we are doing. Otherwise, we would never try anything.

SKILL 4.3 Communication of classroom management and instructional information in a variety of ways (e.g., verbally and nonverbally and via bulletin boards, music, task cards, posters, technology)

To communicate behavioral expectations:

1. Post procedures in a place visible to all students in the classroom

2. Remind students verbally about their responsibility to the procedures and to the students around them

3. Show praise for following rules and procedures

4. Be consistent in consequences for positive and negative behaviors

5. Use Character Counts (*www.charactercounts.org*) curriculum or anti-bullying (*www.stopbullyingnow.hrsa.gov*) standards and lessons to adhere to campus, district, and state regulations

To communicate instructional information:

1. Present skills and lessons with movement and music to reach students who learn audially and kinesthetically. Model skills and lessons for visual learners.

2. Use digital cameras or other systems to show children their form and movement, NOT to be posted online, or for any other reason.

3. When correcting student form, point or verbalize. Do not touch students to show them muscles or areas.

4. Use Fitnessgram (*www.fitnessgram.net*) by the Cooper Institute (*www. cooperinstitute.org*) to track and monitor students' growth and development in their skills and strength, which is accessible to students and their parents.

SKILL 4.4 Communication in ways that show respect and consideration for students, colleagues, and parents

> To show respect and consideration for another human being, always turn the table and ask, "How would I feel if someone said this about me?"

Name calling, insults, threats, and ill treatment are never acceptable in education or in the workplace. Never attack a student's character or generalize his or her behavior. Making statements assuming a child's inability to achieve are also unacceptable. Do not generalize that a student or class of students is "all bad" or assume that an entire class is at fault when a student is acting out.

Instead, treat all children like they have potential and ability. They do because they are, after all, children. They all come from different walks of life, but it is our responsibility as educators to give them a safe place to learn. No child should feel belittled, humiliated, estranged, or frightened anywhere in school.

When communicating with colleagues, remember that they are also professionals. Quick communicating devices that are often used today, such as email and text messaging, should be used in an effective manner. Email should have proper grammar, and text messages sent to a colleague should always be concise.

A procedure at a school may be a "911" text to a certain number in an emergency. If this is the case, do not elaborate with additional information that could insult the students or staff involved. In professional emails, the teacher should treat the colleague as if he is composing a letter, including articles, complete sentences, paragraphs if necessary, and a signature or line for the teacher's name. In a phone call, address the person with their professional name and address the point right away. The phone should also be answered professionally.

In the case of a discipline referral, stick to the facts of the occurrence. Remember that administration and parents will have access to this form. In assessments, remember to quantify data specifically, not generally. A statement like "Jerry is not reaching goals" is not specific enough to help the student, teachers, or parents address the situation. "Jerry is performing 2 out of 9 assessment qualifications, and has completed none of the president's physical fitness test" helps the parents understand why he has his current grade and helps them see where their child needs to apply himself.

When addressing the public, make sure any letter home or press release has been edited by a trusted individual and that only the facts are stated. Any statements about feelings should be minimal, positive, and concise, such as, "We are proud of the varsity soccer team…" and then go on with the facts. In television or telephone interviews, come prepared with notes about the addressed event, dress profession- ally, and stick to the subject matter.

In parent conferences or parent discussions, make sure to follow the school's pro- cedures. For example, a certain number of staff might sometimes be required to be present. In some cases, the teacher might request the presence of an administrator, and this is perfectly acceptable. Stick to the matter at hand and the facts involved in any incident discussed in the meeting. Do not attack the child's character or generalize his or her behavior. Instead, cite specifics and bring documentation (write-up slips or a behavioral chart) of the behaviors or assessments. Never attack a child's or parent's character to the child, other children, staff members, parents, or the community.

It is advised that teachers keep folders or gradebooks updated with assessments, checklists, and any other notes that may need to be addressed.

DOMAIN III
PLANNING, INSTRUCTION, AND STUDENT ASSESSMENT

PERSONALIZED STUDY PLAN

✗ KNOWN MATERIAL/ SKIP IT

PAGE	COMPETENCY AND SKILL		KNOWN MATERIAL/ SKIP IT
81	**5:**	**Planning and instruction**	☐
	5.1:	Teaching of movement, physical activity, and fitness via numerous methods	☐
	5.2:	Sequencing of motor skill activities and use of strategies to improve learning in physical education activities and skill development	☐
	5.3:	Provision of feedback to enhance skill development	☐
	5.4:	Activities designed to improve health-related and skill-related fitness	☐
	5.5:	Current issues, trends, and laws affecting the choice of appropriate program and instructional goals and objectives	☐
	5.6:	Identification, development, and implementation of appropriate program and instructional goals and objectives	☐
	5.7:	Development of unit and lesson plans based on standards, goals, and students' needs	☐
	5.8:	Appropriate instructional strategies to facilitate learning in the physical activity setting	☐
	5.9:	Use of teaching resources and curriculum materials to design learning experiences	☐
	5.10:	Explanations, demonstrations, and appropriate instructional cues to link physical activity concepts to learning experiences	☐
	5.11:	General and specific safety and injury prevention guidelines for planning of movement and fitness activities	☐
102	**6:**	**Student assessment**	☐
	6.1:	Assessment of student skill performance and fitness via a variety of tools	☐
	6.2:	Gathering of data and assessment of student learning in the cognitive and affective domains by a variety of techniques	☐
	6.3:	Understanding of fitness assessments such as President's Challenge and Fitness program	☐
	6.4:	Types of assessments and assessment methods	☐
	6.5:	Validity, reliability, bias, and ways of interpreting assessment results	☐
	6.6:	Appropriate assessment techniques to assess and improve students' understanding and performance, provide feedback, communicate progress, guide personal goal setting, and guide curricular and instructional decisions	☐
	6.7:	Involvement of students in self-assessment and peer assessment	☐
	6.8:	Appropriate assessment of individuals with disabilities	☐
	6.9:	Referral procedures under the Individuals with Disabilities Education Act and Section 504 of the Vocational Rehabilitation Act	☐

COMPETENCY 5
PLANNING AND INSTRUCTION

> **SKILL 5.1** Teaching of skillful movement, physical activity, and fitness via pedagogy, sociology, psychology, anatomy and physiology, biomechanics and kinesiology, motor development and motor learning

Locomotor Skills

LOCOMOTOR SKILLS move an individual from one point to another.

Examples of locomotor skills include:

- **Walking:** This form of locomotion has one foot contacting the surface at all times. Walking shifts one's weight from one foot to the other while legs swing alternately in front of the body.

- **Running:** This is an extension of walking that has a phase where the body is propelled with no base of support (speed is faster, stride is longer, and arms add power).

- **Jumping:** This involves projectile movements that momentarily suspend the body in midair.

- **Vaulting:** Vaulting is coordinated movements that allow one to spring over an obstacle.

- **Leaping:** This is similar to running, but leaping has greater height, flight, and distance.

- **Hopping:** Hopping uses the same foot to take off from a surface and to land.

- **Galloping:** This is a forward or backward advanced elongation of walking combined and coordinated with a leap.

- **Sliding:** This is sideward stepping pattern that is uneven, long, or short.

- **Body rolling:** This involves moving across a surface by rocking back and forth, by turning over and over, or by shaping the body into a revolving mass.

- **Climbing:** This involves ascending or descending using the hands and feet with the upper body exerting the most control.

LOCOMOTOR SKILLS: move an individual from one point to another

Nonlocomotor Skills

NONLOCOMOTOR SKILLS are stability skills. These require little or no movement of one's base of support and do not result in a change of position.

Some examples of nonlocomotor skills include:

- Bending: Movement around a joint where two body parts meet
- Dodging: Sharp change of direction from original line of movement, such as away from a person or object
- Stretching: Extending or hyper-extending joints to make body parts as straight or as long as possible
- Twisting: Rotating the body or body parts around an axis with a stationary base
- Turning: Circular movement of the body through space releasing the base of support
- Swinging: Circular or pendular movements of the body or body parts below an axis
- Swaying: Same as swinging, but movement is above an axis
- Pushing: An act of applying force against an object or person to move it away from one's body or to move one's body away from the object or person
- Pulling: Executing force to cause objects/people to move towards one's body

> **NONLOCOMOTOR SKILLS:** stability skills that require little or no movement of one's base of support and do not result in a change of position

Manipulative Skills

MANIPULATIVE SKILLS use body parts to propel or receive an object, controlling objects primarily with the hands and feet. Two types of manipulative skills are receptive (catch and trap) and propulsive (throw, strike, and kick).

Examples of manipulative skills include:

- Bouncing/dribbling: Projecting a ball downwards
- Catching: Stopping momentum of an object (for control) using the hands
- Kicking: Striking an object with the foot
- Rolling: Initiating force on an object to instill contact with a surface
- Striking: Giving impetus to an object with the use of the hands or another object

> **MANIPULATIVE SKILLS:** use body parts to propel or receive an object, controlling objects primarily with the hands and feet

- **Throwing:** Using one or both arms to project an object into midair away from the body
- **Trapping:** Receiving and controlling a ball without the use of the hands,

Effects of Movement

Human growth and development

Movement activities promote personal growth and development physically by way of stimulating muscular development. They promote growth emotionally by raising personal confidence levels among children and by allowing them to explore concepts of inter-group equity that may at first seem threatening. To the insecure child, the concept that another group may be equal to his own may seem to "demote" his group, and, by extension, the child.

Psychology

Observation and interaction with children from diverse backgrounds in a training environment (where the training activities tend to focus more on "doing," which feels more genuine to children than the classroom setting of raising hands and answering questions) allows the child to see in others the same sorts of behavioral reasoning processes that he sees in himself. This humanizes others from diverse backgrounds, and promotes the concept of equity among diverse groups.

Aesthetics

Human movement activities create an opportunity for individual participation in activities with intrinsic aesthetic qualities. A gymnastic technique or a perfectly executed swing of a baseball bat relies on both physical training and a level of intuitive action. This is an artistic form of expression that is readily accessible to children. Recognizing beauty in the activities and performances of others (in some cases in groups different from that of the viewing student) is a humanizing experience.

Sociology

Student-centered activities that include social interaction are an important part of physical education and education in general, because team-building is a large part of higher education and careers. The student's involvement in a team means that he feels he fits a role on the team. He feels supported by the team and coaches. The ability he feels in this role will have a direct relationship with how he approaches his role and how he will show his ability. A child with high ability and low self-esteem will still not be able to achieve in his role. A child with high self-esteem that has not been trained in his role adequately will feel a sense of loss of self-worth when he is not able to perform the role as well as he expected.

Student-centered activities that include social interaction are an important part of physical education and education in general, because team-building is a large part of higher education and careers.

> ### SKILL 5.2 Sequencing of motor skill activities and use of movement concepts and effective strategies to improve learning in physical education activities and to improve skill development

A child must sit before crawling, crawl before walking, and walk before running. Very early in life we see a sequence of gross motor skills. As muscles and cognition develop, the skills can develop and progress to new skills.

Knowledge of Activities for Body Management Skill Development

Sequential development and activities for locomotor skills acquisition

Sequential development = crawl, creep, walk, run, jump, hop, gallop, slide, leap, skip, step-hop.

Sequential development = crawl, creep, walk, run, jump, hop, gallop, slide, leap, skip, step-hop.

- Activities to develop walking skills include walking more slowly and more quickly in place; walking forward, backward, and sideways with slower and faster paces in straight, curving, and zigzag pathways with various lengths of steps; pausing between steps; and changing the height of the body.

- Activities to develop running skills include having students pretend they are playing basketball, trying to score a touchdown, trying to catch a bus, finishing a lengthy race, or running on a hot surface.

- Activities to develop jumping skills include alternating jumping with feet together and feet apart, taking off and landing on the balls of the feet, clicking the heels together while airborne, and landing with one foot forward and one foot backward.

- Activities to develop galloping skills include having students play a game of Fox and Hound, with the lead foot representing the fox and the back foot the hound trying to catch the fox (alternate the lead foot).

- Activities to develop sliding skills include having students hold hands in a circle and sliding in one direction, then sliding in the other direction.

- Activities to develop hopping skills include having students hop all the way around a hoop and hopping in and out of a hoop, reversing direction. Students can also place ropes in straight lines and hop side-to-side over the rope from one end to the other and change (reverse) the direction.

- Activities to develop skipping skills include having students combine walking and hopping activities leading up to skipping.

- Activities to develop step-hopping skills include having students practice stepping and hopping activities while clapping hands to an uneven beat.

When a child gets stuck on one step, he or she may need to back up one step or more, may need help with a preceding skill, or may just need more practice. A little simple intervention with the teacher can lead that child down his or her path and end up in the same place as the other students, though perhaps not at the same time. This is because all people start from different places. It would be unrealistic to expect everyone to end at the same time. That would be like starting a runner's race with the same ending spot, but placing the runners at different starting points.

Flexibility in scheduling conceptual teaching helps the non-athletic or struggling students succeed at a higher rate. Flexibility in activities for students who are naturally ahead of other students keeps the class as a whole occupied and still working toward their goals.

SKILL 5.3 Provision of feedback to enhance skill development

Feedback can be something simple, like a quick statement to let a child know if he or she is performing a skill correctly. If the child needs help in correcting the skill, the teacher can lead the feedback into a short skill session, in which he takes the child through a series of actions that might improve his performance. The teacher can request a longer skill session for a student having a particularly hard time. The teacher might also need to modify lesson plans to help some students with certain skills, and she can then give feedback in smaller increments over a longer period of time. This promotes self-efficacy in the student because he feels more successful in smaller steps.

Feedback is also given in the form of Fitnessgrams, discussed in Skill 4.3, or in other written or verbal performance reviews.

SKILL
5.4 **Activities designed to improve health-related and skill-related fitness**

Invasion Games

Invasion games are a class of games that involve a player or team penetrating the territory of the opponent or opposing team in an attempt to score points by shooting, throwing, kicking, or striking an object or ball into the opponent's goal. Common invasion games in the physical education setting include basketball, soccer, flag football, lacrosse, and hockey.

Cooperative and Competitive Games

Cooperative games are a class of games that promote teamwork and social interaction. The emphasis is on activity, fitness, skill development, and cooperation rather than competition. There are many cooperative games available to the physical education instructor that helps develop various coordination skills and teamwork. Examples of cooperative games include throwing and catching, freeze tag, water tag, and parachute.

Water fitness activities and games should place emphasis on generating a lot of movement in the pool (gross motor activities). They also may incorporate activities that require more coordinated manipulations, like catching a ball (fine motor activities). Sample games include:

- Water tag: Children can attempt to catch each other in the pool. When someone is caught, he becomes "it". Variations include freeze tag (where a caught student isn't allowed to move until someone swims between their legs to free them) and base tag (where some sections of the pool, for example the ladders or the walls, are a safe "base"; rules must be in place limiting the time that a student can spend on the base). Water tag emphasizes gross motor activities. Safety issue: Students may not hold other students or grab other students in the water.

- Water dodgeball: Students divide into two teams, one on either side of the pool. They play dodgeball, throwing a ball from one side to the other. A student who is hit by the ball is captured by the opposing team, but if the ball is caught, the thrower is captured instead. Safety issue: Students may not throw the ball at another student's head at close range.

- Relay races: Students divide into teams and perform relay races (i.e., one student swims the length of the pool and back. When he returns, the next student in the team does the same. This is repeated until the whole team has completed the task). This can incorporate various swimming strokes; either all team members use the same stroke or each team member uses a different stroke.

Competitive games are a class of games that emphasize score, winning, and beating an opponent. Physical education instructors should integrate competitive games into the curriculum to generate student interest and teach concepts of fair play and sportsmanship. Competitive games are most suitable for students that are more mature and possess more developed skills. All traditional sporting events are competitive games.

Sequential Development and Activities for Nonlocomotor Skill Acquisition

Sequential development = stretch, bend, sit, shake, turn, rock and sway, swing, twist, dodge, and fall.

- Activities to develop stretching include lying on the back and stomach and stretching as far as possible; stretching as though one is reaching for a star, picking fruit off a tree, climbing a ladder, shooting a basketball, or placing an item on a high self; waking; and yawning. Yoga sequencing also develops stretching and lengthening.

- Activities to develop bending include touching knees and toes, then straightening the entire body and straightening the body halfway; bending as though picking up a coin, tying shoes, picking flowers or vegetables, and petting animals of different sizes.

- Activities to develop sitting include practicing sitting from standing, kneeling, and lying positions without the use of hands.

- Activities to develop falling skills include first collapsing in one's own space and then pretending to fall like bowling pins, raindrops, snowflakes, a rag doll, or Humpty Dumpty.

Sequential development = stretch, bend, sit, shake, turn, rock and sway, swing, twist, dodge, and fall.

Sequential Development and Activities for Manipulative Skill Development

Sequential development = striking, throwing, kicking, ball rolling, volleying, bouncing, catching, and trapping.

- Activities to develop striking begin with the striking of stationary objects by a participant in a stationary position. Next, the person remains still while trying to strike a moving object. Then, both the object and the participant are in motion as the participant attempts to strike the moving object.

- Activities to develop throwing include throwing yarn or foam balls against a wall, then at a big target, and finally at targets decreasing in size.

- Activities to develop kicking include alternating feet to kick balloons or beach balls, then kicking them under and over ropes. Change the type of ball as proficiency develops.

- Activities to develop ball rolling include rolling differently sized balls to a wall, then to targets decreasing in size.

- Activities to develop volleying include using a large balloon and first hitting it with both hands, then one hand (alternating hands), and then using different parts of the body. Change the object as students progress (from balloon, to beach ball, to foam ball, etc.).

- Activities to develop bouncing include starting with large balls and first using both hands to bounce and then using one hand (alternate hands).

- Activities to develop catching include using various objects (balloons, beanbags, balls, etc.) to catch. First, catch the object the participant has thrown himself or herself, then catch objects someone else has thrown, and finally increase the distance between the catcher and the thrower.

- Activities to develop trapping include trapping slow and fast rolling balls; trapping balls (or other objects such as beanbags) that are lightly thrown at waist, chest, and stomach levels; and trapping different size balls.

Skills

Overhand throw

The overhand throw consists of a sequence of four movements: a stride, hip rotation, trunk rotation, and forward arm movement. The thrower should align his body sideways to the target (with opposite shoulder pointing towards the target). The overhand throw begins with a step or stride with the opposite foot (e.g., left foot for a right-handed thrower). As the stride foot contacts the ground, the pivot foot braces against the ground and provides stability for the subsequent movements.

Hip rotation is the natural turning of the hips toward the target. Trunk rotation follows hip rotation. The hips should rotate before the trunk because the stretching of the torso muscles allows for stronger muscle contraction during trunk rotation. Following trunk rotation, the arm moves forward in two phases. In the first phase, the elbow is bent. In the second phase, the elbow joint straightens and the thrower releases the ball.

Development of the overhand throwing motion in children occurs in three stages: elementary, mature, and advanced. In the elementary stage, the child throws mainly with the arm and does not incorporate other body movements. The signature characteristic of this stage is striding with the foot on the same side of the body as the throwing arm (e.g., placing the right foot in front when throwing with the right hand). In the mature stage, the thrower brings the arm backward in preparation for the throw. Use of body rotation is still limited. Children in the advanced stage incorporate all the elements of the overhand throw. The thrower displays an obvious stride and body rotation.

Underhand throw

The thrower places the object in the dominant hand. When drawing the arm back, the triceps straighten the elbow and, depending on the amount of power behind the throw, the shoulder extends or hyperextends using the posterior deltoid, latissimus dorsi, and the teres major. At the time of drawback, a step forward is taken with the leg opposite to the throwing arm. When coming back down, the thrower moves the shoulder muscles (primarily the anterior deltoid) into flexion. When the object in hand moves in front of the body, the thrower releases the ball. The wrist may be firm or slightly flexed. The thrower releases the object shortly after planting the foot, and the biceps muscle contracts, moving the elbow into flexion during follow through.

Kick

In executing a kick, the object needs to be in front of the body and in front of the dominant leg. The kicker steps and plants with the opposite leg while drawing the kicking leg back. During drawback, the hamstring muscle group flexes the knee. When the kicker plants the opposite foot, the hips swing forward for power and the knee moves into extension using the quadriceps muscle group. The contact point is approximately even with the plant foot and a comfortable follow through completes the action.

SKILL 5.5 **Current issues, trends, and laws affecting the choice of appropriate program and instructional goals and objectives**

State Legislation

See Skill 1.8

Impact of Education Reforms

See Skill 1.8

Because of the steady increase in childhood obesity and childhood diseases such as Type II Diabetes, lawmakers are getting involved in improving standards of physical education. The constant updating of mandates and requirements means that physical education teachers must stay on top of current events in their field and respond appropriately. New teaching tools are created constantly, and there is pressure to keep a physically fit student classroom for all students, not just the athletes.

Liability Concerns in Physical Education

See Skill 1.8

SKILL 5.6 **Identification, development, and implementation of appropriate program and instructional goals and objectives**

Goal-Setting and Assessment

> *Keep in mind that maintaining a current fitness level is an adequate goal, provided that the individual is in a healthy state.*

Goal-setting is an effective way of achieving progress. In order to preserve and increase self-confidence, you and your students must set goals that are consistently reachable. One way of achieving this is to set several small, short-term goals to attain one long-term goal. Be realistic in goal-setting to increase fitness levels gradually. As students reach their goals, set more in order to continue performance improvement. Reward your students when they reach goals. Rewards serve as motivation to reach the next goal. Also, be sure to prepare for lapses. Try to get back on track as soon as possible.

In assessment of a program, look at previous data. This could be previous physical fitness tests, or data from journals and workbooks of the students. For a specific sport, the statistics of the previous season are a good indicator of success. From the data, identify needs and goals of the students. Design future units based on both the state requirements and the students' needs. For example, if a teacher notices that in the previous year, the students were only 50 percent to their running goal, he or she can base new objectives on the old data.

- Was the old goal an appropriate one?

- Do the goals need adjustment?

- Why did the students fail?

- Is there a skill missing in their lesson plans that would help their running scores? After looking at this data, these adjustments can be made for a new marking period.

When reviewing an entire semester course, set goals as a timeline. Start with the end, such as "students will complete a 5k run in less than 30 minutes." Assuming that the students are starting at zero, the teacher should set appropriate time-related goals. Then, as the semester moves on, goals should be reassessed. The teacher should set multiple goals for a fitness class, based on their state's standards. A sporting coach should set goals not only based on wins, but on development of student skills. For example, if the sport is soccer and the past year shows high-scoring games from the opponent, the teacher should focus on defensive attributes of the game and create appropriate goals for being a more defensive team.

SKILL 5.7 Development of unit and lesson plans based on local, state, and national standards; program goals; instructional goals; and students' needs

National Standards

The National Standards for Physical Education indicate that a physically educated student:

1. Demonstrates competency in many movement forms and proficiency in a few movement forms

2. Applies involvement concepts and principles to the learning and development of motor skills

3. Exhibits a physically active lifestyle

4. Achieves and maintains a health-enhancing level of physical fitness

5. Demonstrates responsible personal and social behavior in physical activity settings

6. Demonstrates understanding and respect for differences among people in physical activity settings

7. Understands that physical activity provides opportunities for enjoyment, challenge, self-expression, and social interaction

The first and most general set of standards used to set program and instructional goals is the basic national standards for a physically fit student.

State Standards

The second way to structure curriculum units and goals is to refer to the state requirements and standards. For example, the state of Texas has the Texas Essential Knowledge and Skills documents for every subject area in every grade level. Using this document, a teacher can build large units and then individual lessons teaching the skills defined by the TEKS 9. To implement these skills, the teacher must assess the classroom, materials, and class sizes available. Program goals and instructional goals are to be made based on requirements, and also on student needs. Comparing the required goals and objectives of the state with student data shows the teacher which aspects are missing from the program and which need some adjustments.

District Standards

Writing down ideas and then creating one large overall goal and assessment sheet that can be modified will help continue to mold the new curriculum for the current students.

Finally, look locally for further goals and instructional planning. Does the district have certain criteria and expectations? Does the school principal? What happened last year or last semester that would cause the teacher to reassess the current direction?

> **SKILL 5.8** Appropriate instructional strategies to facilitate learning in the physical activity setting based on selected content, students' needs, safety concerns, facilities and equipment, and instructional models

---

See Skills 2.2, 2.3, 2.6, 3.2, 3.3, and 3.4

Strategies must address appropriate content for the age group and fitness level of the students and available resources. Space size may impact what specific activities are appropriate. Program materials may also impact what sport or skill is taught. If an instructor does not yet understand the skill himself, or if the skill is too new to him, this skill may have to wait until the teacher is properly trained. If the instructor feels underqualified in an area that is mandated or necessary to teach, the teacher must seek out assistance from others and workshops for skill development. If the teacher is concerned that the skill is inappropriate or unsafe and wants to take it out of the curriculum, assistance from administration may be necessary. Modification of the space and time allotted may also be the solution.

SKILL 5.9 Use of teaching resources and curriculum materials to design learning experiences

There are too many physical education resources to list here, and not all of them would work for every classroom. Some materials include visual resources, such as posters for safety or reminders of body mechanics; audio resources, such as music designed for physical fitness; and kinesthetic resources, such as training materials that challenge the students differently to impact their speed and stamina.

Programs with online and visual aids can also be found through the main site for NASPE. The American Heart Association, American Lung Association, and American Red Cross are also very forthcoming with visual aids and other free help for public schools.

Audio resources would be fitness podcasts that use certain music at certain speeds (beats per minute) to help a class or an individual move to a beat. The teacher must listen in advance to podcasts and other music used in the classroom to ensure appropriate lyrics.

Kinesthetic resources can challenge students in new ways. Equipment such as weighted vests and parachutes create drag when a student runs. Agility equipment such as floor ladders and cones can be used to set up courses for lateral movement. Stability balls can be used to help with balance exercises and stability training. Such equipment can be found through Power Systems or a similar company (*http://www.power-systems.com/*).

Using popular dance or movement can be a big motivator to get students moving and learning. More classes are also teaching their students mind–body exercise such as yoga and Pilates, which can impact their state of mind as well as their balance and strength.

For visual aids, see:
www.aahperd.org/naspe/

Check out these audio resources online:
itunes.com
motiontraxx.com
fitmusic.com

When teaching kids' yoga or Pilates, additional certifications are required and can count toward the teacher's inservice credit hours.

Check out these nationally recognized certification companies:
www.yogafit.com
www.physicalmind.com

SKILL 5.10 Explanations, demonstrations, and appropriate instructional cues and prompts to link physical activity concepts to learning experiences and to facilitate motor skill performance

See Skills 5.1, 5.2, and 5.4

Form is always important. When teaching any skill, make sure the students learn the form correctly before adding additional weight, rotation, or supplemental movement. For example, if the skill is a plyometric squat, the squat must be done correctly first. Check the students' backs for straightness, and then check that the knees stay over the feet and do not extend past the toes. Give verbal and visual cues to help the children find where that spot is on their feet and knees. When loading for the jump, make sure their form does not slip. Jump and land softly on the balls of the feet, not on the heels.

If the skill of the day is more complex, break it into small parts. Use physical demonstration and time to practice, and verbal or audial cues for help on what is and is not working for each individual. Different students need to practice for different lengths of time and with different cues. Some children may be ready to move on, while others struggle with the first part of the lesson. This is why lesson design must allow for flexibility in time and space. Students who learn visually will need a demonstration to watch before performing the activity. Audial learners will need to hear about it before trying or completing an activity. Kinesthetic learners will have to physically practice before they will feel ready to perform, and they may jump up and start practicing during instructional time because that is their way of understanding instructions. In a case where kinesthetic learners become a distraction, remind them that they will have help in practice after instructions are given.

> SKILL 5.11 **General and specific safety and injury prevention guidelines for planning of movement and fitness activities** (e.g., first aid, cardiopulmonary resuscitation)

Actions That Promote Safety and Injury Prevention

1. Having an instructor who is properly trained and qualified

2. Organizing the class by size, activity, and conditions of the class

3. Inspecting buildings and other facilities regularly and immediately giving notice of any hazards

4. Avoiding overcrowding

5. Using adequate lighting

6. Ensuring that students dress in appropriate clothing and shoes

7. Presenting organized activities

8. Inspecting all equipment regularly

9. Adhering to building codes and fire regulations

10. Using protective equipment

11. Using spotters

12. Eliminating hazards

13. Teaching students correct ways to perform skills and activities

14. Teaching students how to use the equipment properly and safely

Emergency Action Plans

The first step in establishing a safe physical education environment is creating an emergency action plan (EAP). The formation of a well-planned EAP can make a significant difference in the outcome of an injury situation.

Components of an emergency action plan

To ensure the safety of students during physical activity, an EAP should be easily comprehensible yet detailed enough to facilitate prompt, thorough action.

> Each district requires a school-wide consistent emergency action plan that is to be followed. Physical education teachers need to know this plan and review it often.

Implementing the emergency plan

The main thing to keep in mind when implementing an EAP is to remain calm. Maintaining a sufficient level of control and activating appropriate medical assistance will facilitate the process and will leave less room for error.

Communication

Instructors should communicate rules and expectations clearly to students. This information should include pre-participation guidelines, emergency procedures, and proper game etiquette. Instructors should collect emergency information sheets from students at the start of each school year. First-aid kits, facility maps, and incident report forms should also be readily available. Open communication between students and teachers is essential. Creating a positive environment within the classroom allows students to feel comfortable enough to approach an adult or teacher if she feels she has sustained a potential injury.

> Instructors should collect emergency information sheets from students at the start of each school year.

Teacher education

Teachers must have a certain number of continuing education hours to stay certified. A physical education teacher should use this time to improve skills or stay updated on mandates and changes in physical educational systems. These hours can also be for first aid and CPR certifications, as well as crisis prevention and Intervention (CPI) training. These three certifications can help the teacher keep a safe classroom.

Facilities and equipment

It is the responsibility of the teacher and school district to provide a safe environment, playing area, and equipment for students. Instructors and maintenance staff should regularly inspect school facilities to confirm that the equipment and location is adequate and safe for student use.

First aid equipment

It is essential to have a properly stocked first aid kit in an easily reachable location. Instructors might need to include asthma inhalers and special care items to meet the specific needs of certain students. Instructors should clearly mark these special care items to avoid a potentially harmful mix-up.

An Automatic External Defibrilator Device (AED) should be in every school, and several should be posted in obvious places in a larger school. The physical education teacher and nurse, as well as other personnel, should be trained in AED usage along with their CPR training. Most CPR trainings also teach AED usage. It is very effective in the first few minutes of cardiac arrest and has been shown to save lives. A person not trained in AED can still use one because after pressing the "On" button, the system will tell the user what to do. It is highly recommended that staff in contact with children and parents who may go into cardiac arrest are trained in AED and know where it is on campus.

Strategies for Injury Prevention
See Skill 1.8

Prevention of Common Athletic Injuries
See Skill 1.8

Care for Common Athletic Injuries

The most common injuries that physical education instructors will encounter include muscle sprains and strains, soft tissue injuries, and cuts and bruises. Instructors should apply the RICE principle when caring for muscle sprains, strains, and soft tissue injuries. The RICE principle stands for: rest, ice, compression, and elevation.

> *The most common injuries that physical education instructors will encounter include muscle sprains and strains, soft tissue injuries, and cuts and bruises.*

- Rest: Injured students should stop using the injured body part immediately
- Ice: The instructor should apply ice to the injured area to help reduce swelling

- Compression: The instructor should wrap the injured area to help reduce swelling

- Elevation: The student should raise the injured area above heart level

In addition, physical education instructors should have a well-stocked first aid kit that allows the treatment of routine cuts and bruises. Finally, instructors must recognize more serious injuries that require immediate medical attention. For example, injuries to the head or neck require medical attention and extreme caution.

Treating Specific Illnesses

Diabetes

Type I DIABETES limits the pancreas's ability to produce insulin, a hormone vital to life. Without insulin, the body cannot use the sugar found in blood. In order to stay alive, an individual suffering from Type I diabetes must take one or more injections of insulin daily.

Diabetics control their disease by keeping the level of blood sugar (glucose) as close to normal as possible. The means to achieve diabetes control include proper nutrition, exercise, and insulin. Most children with diabetes self-monitor blood glucose levels to track their condition and respond to changes.

Some rules of thumb to keep in mind when dealing with a diabetic child are:

- Food makes the glucose level rise

- Exercise and insulin make the glucose level fall

- Hypoglycemia occurs when the blood sugar level is low

- Hyperglycemia occurs when the blood sugar level is high

Type II diabetes is more and more common in children, and it is increasingly unlikely that the child will be aware of it before showing symptoms. The physical education coach should be made aware of any child with Type II diabetes. The school nurse should have the child's insulin or medication. Any emergency for that child should be directed immediately to the nurse. A child who shows signs of diabetes, such as blurry vision, constant thirst, or a sore that will not heal should be referred to the school nurse, who may in turn refer the child to a doctor for treatment.

> **DIABETES:** a condition that limits the pancreas's ability to produce insulin, a hormone vital to life

Low blood sugar (Hypoglycemia)

This is the diabetic emergency most likely to occur. Low blood sugar may result from eating too little, engaging in too much physical activity without eating, or by injecting too much insulin.

Symptoms	• Headache • Sweating • Shakiness • Pale, moist skin • Fatigue/weakness • Loss of coordination
Treatment	Provide sugar immediately. You may give the student ½ cup of fruit juice, non-diet soda, or two to four glucose tablets. The child should feel better within the next 10 minutes. If so, the child should eat some additional food (e.g. half a peanut butter sandwich, or a meat or cheese sandwich). If the child's status does not improve, treat the reaction again.

High blood sugar (Hyperglycemia)

Hyperglycemia can result from eating too much, engaging in too little physical activity, not injecting enough insulin, or illness. You can confirm high blood sugar levels by testing with a glucose meter.

Symptoms	• Increased thirst • Weakness/fatigue • Blurred vision • Frequent urination • Loss of appetite
Treatment	If hyperglycemia occurs, the instructor should contact the student's parent or guardian immediately.

Dehydration

DEHYDRATION occurs when a person loses more fluids than he or she takes in. The amount of water present in the body subsequently drops below the level needed for normal body functions. The two main causes of dehydration are

DEHYDRATION: person loses more fluids than he or she takes in

gastrointestinal illness (vomiting, diarrhea) and sports. It is essential to replace fluids lost by sweating to prevent dehydration, especially on a hot day.

Symptoms	• Thirst
	• Dizziness
	• Dry mouth
	• Producing less/darker urine
Prevention/ Treatment	• Drink lots of fluids. Water is usually the best choice.
	• Dress appropriately (i.e., loose-fitting clothes and a hat).
	• If you begin to feel thirsty or dizzy, take a break and sit in the shade.
	• Drink fluids prior to physical activity and then at 20-minute intervals after activity commences.
	• Refer the student to a doctor or hospital if necessary.
	• Play sports or train in the early morning or late afternoon to avoid the hottest part of the day.

CPR BASICS

CARDIOPULMONARY RESUSCITATION (CPR) is a first-aid technique used to keep cardiac arrest victims alive. It also prevents brain damage while the individual is unconscious and more advanced medical help is on the way. CPR keeps blood flowing through the body and in and out of the lungs.

> **CARDIOPULMONARY RESUSCITATION (CPR):** a first-aid technique used to keep cardiac arrest victims alive; it also prevents brain damage while the individual is unconscious and more advanced medical help is on the way

CPR steps

As of October 18, 2010, the method of CPR has changed through recommendation by the American Heart Association. They changed their methods to allow quicker action on a person's heart and so that untrained people can help if there is not a trained person available. If a person is unconscious:

1. Always have someone call 911 first.

2. Make sure the victim is in a safe place to start compressions. If a back injury is feared, do not move the victim. Otherwise, the victim must be flat on his or her back to start compressions.

3. Next, start compressions. Compressions are the act of pushing down the victim's chest by two inches. Younger children (under 12) will need

compressions to be less deep. Put the heel of one hand directly over the sternum, between the nipples. Put the other hand over the first and lace the fingers. Press straight down with straight elbows. The American Heart Association now says to continue compressions if the caregiver does not have training in proper CPR until the victim regains consciousness or until help arrives.

4. A person trained in CPR should give 30 compressions at the rate of 100 BPM (the tempo for the song "Stayin' Alive" by the Beegees) and then open the airway by tilting the head back.

5. Check the airway for breathing. If there is no visible sign of breathing (chest not rising) or the caregiver does not feel any breath, give two rescue breaths and go back to 30 chest compressions.

6. If the victim is breathing, check for a pulse. If there is a pulse and breathing, monitor the situation until help arrives.

General and Specific Safety Considerations for All Movement Activities

Water safety basics

> *Most school districts require that physical education instructors are trained in CPR and first aid. Companies with accredited CPR training are the American Heart Association and the American Red Cross.*

- Get a partner. Even experienced swimmers get tired or get muscle cramps. When swimming with a partner you can help each other or go for help in case of an emergency.

- Learn some life-saving techniques (e.g., CPR).

- Know your limits. If you're a novice swimmer, don't go into water that is so deep that you're unable to touch the bottom. Also, don't try to keep up with advanced swimmers.

- Swim only in places with lifeguard supervision.

- When swimming in an open body of water, don't fight the current, swim with it, gradually trying to make your way to shore.

- Dive only in areas that are safe for diving.

- Watch the sun and reapply sunscreen often.

- Drink plenty of fluids to prevent dehydration.

- Don't stay in cool water for too long. This can lower your body temperature. Get out of the water if you feel your muscles cramp or you begin to shiver.

Aquatics

To promote water safety, physical education instructors should make students familiar with appropriate medical responses to life-threatening situations (e.g., recognizing signs that someone needs medical attention—not moving, not breathing, etc.; knowledge of the proper response—who to contact and where to find them). With older children, instructors can introduce rudimentary first-aid training. Finally, instructors must ensure that students are aware and observant of safety rules (e.g., no running near the water, no chewing gum while swimming, no swimming without a lifeguard, no roughhousing near or in the water, etc.).

Outdoor education

Related safety education should emphasize the importance of planning and research. Instructors should ask students to consider in advance what the potential dangers of an activity might be and to prepare and plan accordingly. Of course, educator supervision is required. Outdoor education activities require first-aid equipment and properly trained educators. Students should use appropriate safety gear (e.g., helmets, harnesses, etc.). Instructors should generally obtain parental consent for outdoor education activities.

Combative activities

The potential harm that these activities can cause (stressing specific damage potential to musculoskeletal systems) should be stressed, emphasizing students' responsibility for the well-being of their training partners. Discipline must be maintained throughout the class (ensuring that students remain focused on their training activities and alert to the instructor's instructions), and students must be aware and observant of the limits of force that they may apply (e.g., no-striking zones, like above the neck and below the belt; limits on striking force, like semi-contact or no-contact sparring; and familiarity with the concept of a tap-out indicating submission). Students should perform warm-up, cool-down, and stretching as with any physical training program.

COMPETENCY 6
STUDENT ASSESSMENT

SKILL 6.1 **Assessment of student skill performance and fitness via a variety of tools** *(e.g., observations, data, charts, graphs, rating scales)*

- Observations: Students can be assessed through simple observations, planned or unplanned.

- Data: Keep data records from start to finish for the semester class or sport season.

- Charts and graphs: Assess the data and then plug it into appropriate charts or graphs. When assessing each child singularly, look at a chart or line graph to show the change in the child's skills from the beginning to the current point. When assessing the structure of the class, compare students' data by making a class chart or graph. With this assessment, the teacher can see whether the students are getting the information and understanding the skill or not.

- Rating scales: A rating scale can be created using a number line, such as 1–10, and then placing the student where he or she would fall at the current time. In something as developmental as physical education, a rating scale might not show the teacher the rate of improvement for the child.

> A flat line on a graph, showing no improvement, would mean that the teacher needs to reassess how the course is taught and the methods for teaching each individual skill.

SKILL 6.2 **Gathering of data and assessment of student learning in the cognitive and affective domains by a variety of techniques** *(e.g., written assessments, rating scales, observations)*

Fitness Appraisals

The trend in physical education assessment is to move increasingly away from norm- and criterion-referenced evaluations (i.e., measuring a student's achievements against the achievements of a normative group or against criteria that are arbitrarily set by either the educator or the governing educational body) and toward performance-based, or "authentic," evaluations. This creates difficulty for physical educators because it eliminates preset reference points.

> The advantage of performance-based evaluations is that they are equally fair to individuals with diverse backgrounds, special needs, and disabilities. The instructor evaluates students based on their personal performance.

Portfolio construction is one way of assessing the performance of a student. The student chooses the achievements to add to the portfolio. This creates a tool that assesses current abilities and serves as a benchmark against which the instructor can measure future performance (thus evaluating progress over time, and evaluating more than a localized achievement).

VALID PHYSICAL FITNESS TEST ITEMS TO MEASURE HEALTH-RELATED FITNESS COMPONENTS	
Cardiorespiratory Fitness Tests	Maximal stress test, sub-maximal stress test, Bruce Protocol, Balke Protocol, Astrand and Rhyming Test, PWC Test, Bench Step Test, Rockport Walking Fitness Test, and Cooper 1.5 Mile Run/Walk Fitness Test
Muscle Strength Tests	Dynamometers (hand, back, and leg), cable tensiometer, the 1-RM Test (repetition maximum: bench press, standing press, arm curl, and leg press), bench-squat, sit-ups (one sit-up holding a weight plate behind the neck), and lateral pull-down
Muscle Endurance Tests	Squat-thrust, pull-ups, sit-ups, lateral pull-down, bench press, arm curl, push-ups, and dips
Flexibility Tests	Sit and reach, Kraus-Webber Floor Touch Test, trunk extension, forward bend of trunk, Leighton Flexometer, shoulder rotation/flexion, and goniometer
Body Composition Determination	Hydrostatic weighing, skin fold measurements, limb/girth circumference, and body mass index

SKILL 6.3 Understanding of fitness assessments such as President's Challenge and Fitness program

To help realize fitness goals, several organizations exist to educate and encourage physical fitness. Three such programs include Physical Best, President's Challenge, and Fitnessgram.

Physical Best is a comprehensive health-related fitness education program developed by physical educators for physical educators. The purpose of Physical Best is to educate, challenge, and encourage all children to develop the knowledge, skills, and attitudes for a healthy and fit life. The goal of the program is to move students from dependence to independence for their own fitness and health by promoting regular, enjoyable physical activity. The focus of Physical Best is to educate ALL children regardless of athletic talent, physical, and mental abilities or disabilities.

The President's Challenge is a program that encourages all Americans to make regular physical activity a part of their everyday lives. No matter what your activity and fitness level, the President's Challenge can help motivate you to improve.

Physical Best:

www.aahperd.org/NASPE
/physicalbest/

The President's Challenge:

www.presidentschallenge
.org/

The Cooper Institute:

www.cooperinst.org
/ftginfo.asp#Overview

The Cooper Institute in Dallas, Texas, introduced Fitnessgram in 1982. The objective was to increase parental awareness of children's fitness levels. This was done by developing an easy way for physical education teachers to report the results of physical fitness assessments.

SKILL 6.4 **Types of assessments and assessment methods** *(e.g., formative, summative, authentic, portfolio, standardized, rubric, criterion, referenced, norm-referenced)*

- **Baseline assessments:** These are assessments that determine where the student is starting. They are assessments of skills the child already knows when starting the class. It is good to have a baseline for children to monitor growth.

- **Formative assessments:** These are assessments that are made along the way in education to keep track of development in small steps. Some ways to keep formative assessments wo uld be through checklists that the teacher keeps on skill mastery and portfolios that the students keep tracking what skills they are accomplishing, what the students' times or levels were on each skill, and checklists of understanding skills or physical comfort in certain skills.

- **Summative assessments:** Summatives are assessments that look at a student's progress over a marking period or unit to create a general picture of how a student has progressed. This requires application of skills learned. For example, if the unit has been based on skills necessary to play basketball, then the summative would be a game.

- **Authentic assessments:** Authentic assessments are summative assessments for what the child has learned, using analytical thinking: The student takes skills mastered and uses them in a self-directed project. In physical education, this could be a child-centered organized game or sport using skills already learned.

- **Standardized testing:** This is the testing used by a school district or state to assess whether the students are mastering necessary objectives. Many states have mandated physical fitness tests. Each child must be tested on each skill individually and scored. Data is then used to assess the efficacy of the teachers and schools, according to district or state administration.

- **Rubric:** A rubric is a chart to keep track of a student's level of ability in a given unit. The left hand column lists the skills for the unit. The columns at the top are levels of understanding (usually 1 being the lowest level, 4 being the highest). As the teacher goes through each skill, he or she assesses where the student would be if he or she were at level 1, 2, 3, or 4 and notates in the appropriate box what they would be doing to show their level at that given time. Then, the teacher keeps track of where each student is at the given assessment time.

- Criterion-referenced assessments: These are tests based on what the student shows. They are straight skill-related tests without regard to growth and development. They list only the criteria of the test and what criteria the student has mastered. Most standardized tests are criterion-referenced.
- Norm-referenced assessments: These are assessments that interpret the skill based on comparison. Within a group of students, the teacher or test administrator would decide what is average, above average, and below average, and then place students figuratively on the curve of comparison with peers.

SKILL 6.5 Validity, reliability, bias, and ways of interpreting assessment results

Assessments themselves must be assessed. A test is valid if the teacher or administrator can assess a child's skill based on the test. A reliable test is consistent. In class after class, the test is accurate in assessing students' skill level.

BIAS is teacher or administrator opinion. In terms of grades, if the grade does not match the assessment, then the teacher has used some bias to change the grade. The teacher might think the child is capable of doing better, but changes the grade without reassessment, or the teacher might think the child does not deserve the grade, based on willingness to participate, even with a high mark on the test. Biases cannot be upheld in a court of law. A teacher must have concrete evidence to support changing a grade or mark.

BIAS: teacher or administrator opinion

SKILL 6.6 Appropriate assessment techniques to assess and improve students' understanding and performance, provide feedback, communicate students' progress, guide students' personal goal setting, and guide curricular and instructional decisions

See Skills 6.1, 6.2, 6.3 and 6.4

Technology is a wonderful thing when referring to a student's form or a team's performance. Digital photography with a good, simple photography and video program can run plays, stop plays, view mistakes close up, and show off assets! The day after a game or activity, the teacher can review what he remembers before showing the students, and then they can see it for themselves. This is a great way to assess and make new goals. Keeping it positive is important, especially because students will be self-conscious at first about seeing their own mistakes. Remember to show not only the problems, but also the positives, such as "Remember the onside kick play we worked on last week? Let's watch it in action!" Students can then celebrate the small victories.

Technology is not the only way to review and assess. Simple notes with simple verbal reviews are effective, too. Practice is great for kinesthetic memory, so repetition may be the key that day at practice, with quick reminders of the key elements of the skill.

SKILL 6.7 Involvement of students in self-assessment and peer assessment

Student self-assessment is often an important part of portfolios. The instructor should encourage children to ask themselves questions like, "Where am I now? Where am I trying to go? What am I trying to achieve? How can I get from here to there?" This type of questioning involves the child more deeply in the learning process. Students can keep a journal of progress in sports or fitness goals on paper or online.

Students can peer assess as well, under certain guidelines. Students should be well-trained in pillars of character so that they know how to speak positively to each other. They should not assign grades to each other, but give feedback with guidelines, such as:

- What was good about the student's performance?

- What is one thing the student can improve on?

A lot of student feedback is overwhelming to the child, so limit the feedback to a few students at a time.

Student feedback often happens on the playing field, when a student yells at another for getting something right or wrong. Students taught good sportsmanship will focus on the positive, but all kids get frustrated at some point and can say something negative to another player on the team. Keeping the game or activity upbeat and reminding students of how to assess each other is important.

SKILL 6.8 Appropriate assessment of individuals with disabilities

Human Development, Motor Behavior, and Prescribed Exercises

Standards for measures of success and evaluation include parameters that set the benchmarks for change in motor-related skills and stock knowledge. A special criterion is set for students with disabilities and special needs in consonance with the Individuals with Disabilities Education Act (IDEA). The criteria for coverage under IDEA include people with symptoms of:

- Mental retardation

- Deafness or profound hearing loss

- Blindness or profound sight loss

- Autism

- Emotional disturbance

- Traumatic brain injury

- Developmental delay

IDEA covers a free education appropriate to these students and protects their rights to a fair education by qualified professionals. Some qualified professionals may include behavioral therapists, music therapists, and occupational therapists. Students may come to the classroom with one of these professionals or with an aide assigned to them.

> *Instructors must consider student disabilities and specific needs when setting personal fitness goals. Instructors should evaluate proposed activities and set standards for desired motor behavioral change, taking into account the diverse student population.*

SKILL 6.9 Referral procedures under the Individuals with Disabilities Education Act and Section 504 of the Vocational Rehabilitation Act

Under Section 504, all children have the right to a public education access, regardless of disabilities.

> *Under Section 504, all children have the right to a public education access, regardless of disabilities.*

An important part of 504 is that students with disabilities must be included in educational activities with other students. In most cases, their inclusion must be in physical education.

MODIFICATIONS: learning tools that are used to educate students with different needs

A student is described as disabled under Section 504 if:

1. He cannot participate in the normal activities of others of the same age

2. He has been diagnosed with a disability

3. His actions warrant concern of a disability

Students protected under Section 504 have the right to an appropriate education for their abilities and disabilities. One way to ensure this education is through an Individual Educational Plan (IEP). An IEP, however, is NOT required, only recommended. A teacher should recommend an IEP if there are concerns over what exactly a child needs. A committee close to the student and the specialists who work with the student can make a plan about the child's physical education requirements and any modifications for that child. MODIFICATIONS are learning tools that are used to educate students with different needs. Modifications could include when and where the child is assessed, what fine and gross motor skills can be assessed, and where the child is to be placed in the classroom.

DOMAIN IV
COLLABORATION, REFLECTION, AND TECHNOLOGY

PERSONALIZED STUDY PLAN

KNOWN MATERIAL/ SKIP IT

PAGE	COMPETENCY AND SKILL	
111	**7: Collaboration**	☐
	7.1: Current educational issues that cross subject matter boundaries	☐
	7.2: Integration of knowledge and skills from multiple subject areas in physical education	☐
	7.3: Establishment of productive relationships to support student growth and well-being with school colleagues and administrators, parents and guardians, community members, and organizations	☐
	7.4: Promotion of a variety of opportunities for physical activity in the school and the community	☐
113	**8: Reflection**	☐
	8.1: Use of the reflective cycle to facilitate change in teacher performance, student learning, and instructional goals and decisions	☐
	8.2: Use of available resources to develop and grow as a reflective professional	☐
115	**9: Technology**	☐
	9.1: Design, development, and implementation of student learning activities that integrate information technology	☐
	9.2: Use of technologies to communicate, instruct, assess, keep records, network, locate resources, present information, and enhance professional development	☐

COMPETENCY 7
COLLABORATION

Health

Science and fitness work together to teach students to make healthy choices about their nutrition and their movement outside of school. Current science has elements focused on how the body processes and burns calories. This is a good segue for fitness and health education. Teachers can coordinate lessons in health science to enhance student learning that will last a lifetime.

Character

Many teachers have themes and units based on character. Think of sportsmanship and teamwork when coordinating with these teachers. Social studies may touch on citizenship and cultural diversity, which relate to character in interpersonal fitness or team sports.

Biomechanics

The science of how the body works bridges the subjects of health and science as well. The way the cells react to movement, the way the body moves, and the way nerves and brain waves work are all related to physical exercise.

The fundamental concepts of science, math, and social studies can be integrated into physical education instruction. Each content area has multiple topics that relate to health and fitness and are good starting points for building cross-curricular lesson plans.

- Science: Anatomy, study of forces, biology, and nutrition are all health and fitness related subjects
- Mathematics: Statistics, graphs, charts, formulas, ratios
- Social Studies: History of a sport or activity, such as the Olympics

When teaching students about any of these topics, coordinate with other teachers, and check sources. Study and cross-curricular workshops can also help.

SKILL 7.3 **Establishment of productive relationships to support student growth and well-being with school colleagues and administrators, parents and guardians, community members, and organizations**

It's overstated but true that it takes a village to raise a child. Through the family, school, and community, the same themes are true: character counts, be responsible, and keep learning.

A good rapport with parents and colleagues is very important for any teacher, but the physical education teacher works directly with everyone in the school. Keeping a professional atmosphere, taking care of the classroom, reaching students and parents, and coordinating lessons are all ways to integrate all of these people for the good of the child. Being a leader and keeping a positive attitude are professional attributes that help colleagues and parents associate the teacher with positivity. Print and online newsletters let the school staff and community see what goes on in the classroom. Other teachers that support students may come to a game if they see a pupil listed on the team.

Community members like to be involved in the social wellbeing of students. Invite respected guests to observe or lead a presentation for the class. The Parent–Teacher Organization could have funds for a special presentation about health and fitness, so it does not hurt to ask. Many times the parents will go out of their way to get funding for something they see as worthwhile. A written letter of request helps with this.

Other organizations that may help with activities and presentations are the local YMCA, American Red Cross, American Heart Association, and American Lung Association. They have resources for programs and presentations about various subjects, such as physical activity awareness and Red Ribbon Week (an anti-drug program offered at most schools nationally).

SKILL 7.4 Promotion of a variety of opportunities for physical activity in the school and the community

Most communities have a parks and recreation department as well as small businesses that are in the business of helping kids stay healthy. The physical education teacher can sometimes be parents' main resource for what is going on in the community. The parent may not always seek out a brochure from parks and recreation, but if the PE teacher sends it home, or even sends home a link to a Web site about fitness clubs or sports, the parent may be inclined to look the information over.

If the teacher sees an opportunity for cooperation with the parks and recreation department, she may plan an activity outside of school for the students to see first-hand what is available to them. Parks and recreation departments can facilitate community clean-ups, walks, races, and other volunteer activities that promote socialization within the community. If the PE teacher shares this opportunity with the students and meets them at an event, it may encourage the students to try an activity offered by parks and recreation or another local club for sports and activities.

COMPETENCY 8
REFLECTION

SKILL 8.1 Use of the reflective cycle to facilitate change in teacher performance, student learning, and instructional goals and decisions *(e.g., planning, teaching, assessment, reflection)*

In the reflective cycle (Graham Gibbs), a professional or teacher goes through a constant cycle of learning:

1. Description: What is going on, or what occurred during the incident (or class period)?

2. Feelings: What thoughts and feelings occurred?

3. Evaluation: What pros and cons did you see in the occurrence?

4. Analysis: How would you see this problem as an outsider?

5. Conclusion: What could be done with this problem?

6. Action plan: What will you do if something similar happens again?

The new action plan would then lead to a new description. The point of this cycle is that we as teachers must constantly reevaluate our own teaching. What works and what doesn't? How can the lesson be tweaked to get the same message across? How can we reach all of the students? How can we avoid pitfalls and hiccoughs in our plans?

Every teacher has a plan that does not work in the classroom every once in a while or has an incident that alerts the teacher to something that needs to be changed. For instance, a teacher may have a great lesson plan incorporating cooperation and team-building, only to find that students spend the lesson socializing instead of participating. The Graham Gibbs cycle helps that teacher see the positive and negative in the socializing activity, and then make a new action plan to use the positive side of the occurrence in a different way for a different outcome. This cycle can continue until the teacher has gotten the kinks out of the lesson.

SKILL 8.2 Use of available resources to develop and grow as a reflective professional (e.g., students, colleagues, literature, professional organization memberships, professional development opportunities)

Students teach us every day. If they are not feeling stronger, if they are not excelling where they did before, and if they are not enjoying what they are doing, then we must refocus, rebuild, and redeliver our message. If colleagues are with us in our plans, then things will go smoothly all day long. If they see problems or shortcomings, the lesson may not work and the PE teacher may feel he or she is losing clout.

Many companies and nonprofits are accredited and led by research and development, and they all offer conferences and workshops for professionals. Gaining additional continuing education credit may be possible through online workshops or correspondence courses from any of these organizations.

The American Council on Exercise (ACE) performs research into modern exercise science and provides information for teachers on overall fitness and youth fitness.

The National Association for Sport and Physical Education (NASPE) is the certifying agency for professional physical education teachers. The American College of Sports Medicine (ACSM) defines many of the accreditation standards for fitness organizations and companies. The Cooper's Institute is a leader in health and fitness education and has redefined health education for youth.

To learn more about this profession, check out these sites:

aahperd.org/naspe
www.acefitness.org
www.ideafit.com
www.issaonline.com
www.acsm.org
www.nasm.org

COMPETENCY 9
TECHNOLOGY

| SKILL 9.1 | Design, development, and implementation of student learning activities that integrate information technology |

Many technological game systems are movement-driven instead of joystick-driven. The Sony Wii is the first marketed system that reads the player's body movements rather than signals from buttons. Many others are following suit. By using a remote signal, the game player can move like the joystick controller, making movement important to the outcome of the game. This is not to say that the Wii can replace sports and games, but it is an alternative to sitting and playing.

There are also games online or using computer technology that use dance mats to test the player on foot accuracy. This timing game is great for athletes who are trying to improve their timing. This game requires quick pace, timing, and coordination, all of which are important in general fitness.

In an independent fitness class, students can journal about their nutrition and movement. One site that is dedicated to voluntary and independent journaling is *www.peertrainer.com*. A person can join a group or team with similar goals or create one with similar goals and make notes. A teacher could have a peer trainer team for each class and motivate students through a social network by reviewing exercise and nutritional trends for the students.

For sites that have lesson plans or interactive applications for the students, look here:

- *www.bam.gov /sub_physicalactivity /index.html (CDC kids site)*
- *www.cooperinstitute.org /ourkidshealth/index.cfm (Cooper's Institute site for teachers, parents, and kids)*
- *www.aahperd.org /naspe/advocacy /letsmoveinschool/cspap .cfm (Michelle Obama's initiative for action in students and schools)*

SKILL 9.2 Use of technologies to communicate, instruct, assess, keep records, network, locate resources, present information, and enhance professional development

Using technology to communicate: The modern technological world is one of social networking. A chance for students to network positively could be created with something like peer trainer (*see Skill 9.1*).

Teachers can maintain a website about physical fitness and keep general information as well as sports-related achievements online. Keep in mind that student confidentiality is also important when dealing with an online community or a Web site showing students.

Using technology to instruct: Wikis, blogs, websites, and applications can all instruct when used in a positive and not overwhelming way. A balance of modern technology with physical training basics could even out an otherwise sedentary technological world.

Using technology to network: Many social spaces are opening to teachers. Spaces such as *www.linkedin.com* group together people of certain interests and occupations so that they can compare notes and share. *www.wellsphere.com* is a networking site for professionals in the field of health and fitness, as well as a network for people interested in getting fit or in a certain sport or activity.

Using technology to assess: Many assessments are now online, including the president's plan and the Cooper's Institute Fitnessgram. This is fine as long as true assessments can be taken and applied through the technology. Most districts now have an online gradebook.

Using technology to present and teach: Most schools now have a setup allowing teachers to use technology to present material. Document cameras with computer access can display documents, presentations, or online content on a large screen for the class, or even an auditorium full of people, to see. With this comes the responsibility for reviewing all online data first and only using data for student learning and learning enhancement.

Technology in professional development allows teachers to attend webinars and conferences online. This is a privilege allowed these last few years that has widened teachers' horizons. They can now attend more workshops than ever before, without spending money on travel or losing precious time with students.

Many online gradebooks have parent/student applications so that parents and students can see their grades before report cards or other printed material is sent home.

DOMAIN V
SUPPLEMENTAL CONTENT

Exercises that Benefit the Major Muscle Groups of the Body

Some of the major muscle groups of the body important to physical fitness are the traps, delts, pecs, lats, obliques, abs, biceps, quadriceps, hamstrings, adductors, triceps, biceps, and gluts.

Dumbbell Shoulder Shrug
(Trapezius)

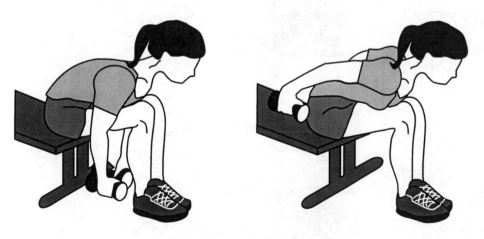

Seated Bent-Over Rear Deltoid Raise
(Rear Deltoids)

Seated Side Lateral Raise
(Front and Outer Deltoids)

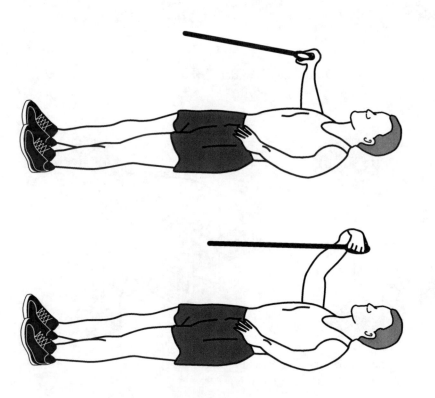

Lying Low-Pulley One-Arm Chest
(Lateral Pectorals)

Flat Dumbbell Press
(Pectorals)

Medium-Grip Front-to-Rear Lat Pull Down
(Lats)

Straight-Arm Close-Grip Lat Pull Down
(Lats)

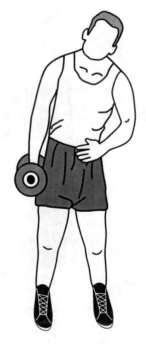

Dumbbell Side Bend
(Obliques)

Seated Barbell Twist
(Obliques)

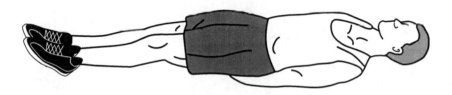

Leg Pull-In
(Lower Abdominals)

Jackknife Sit-Up
(Upper and Lower Abdominals)

Standing Alternated Dumbbell Curl
(Biceps)

Standing Medium-Grip Barbell Curl
(Biceps)

Standing Close-Grip Easy-Curl-Bar Triceps Curl
(Triceps)

Standing Bent-Over One-Arm-Dumbbell Triceps Extension
(Triceps)

Flat-Footed Medium-Stance Barbell Half-Squat
(Thighs)

Freehand Front Lunge
(Thighs and Hamstrings)

Thigh Curl on Leg Extension Machine
(Hamstrings)

One-at-a-Time Thigh Curl on Leg Extension Machine
(Hamstings)

Hip Abduction
(Hips)

Hip Adduction
(Inner Thigh)

Standing Toe Raise on Wall Calf Machine
(Main Calf Muscles)

Standing Barbell Toe Raise
(Main Calf Muscles)

Hip Extension
(Hips and Thighs)

Hip Flexion
(Hip Flexors)

Knowledge of Mechanical Principles of Body Management

Concepts of equilibrium and center of gravity applied to movement

Body mass redistributes when body segments move independently. This changes the location of the body's center of gravity. Segments also move to change the body's base of support from one moment to the next to cope with imminent loss of balance.

The entire center of gravity of the body shifts in the same direction of movement of the body's segments. As long as the center of gravity remains over the base of support, the body will remain in a state of equilibrium. The more the center of gravity is situated over the base, the greater the stability. A wider base of support and/or a lower center of gravity enhances stability. To be effective, the base of support must widen in the direction of the force produced or opposed by the body. Shifting weight in the direction of the force in conjunction with widening the base of support further enhances stability.

Constant interaction of forces that move the body in the elected direction results in dynamic balance. The smooth transition of the center of gravity changing from one base of support to the next produces speed.

Concept of force applied to movement

Force is any influence that can change the state of motion of an object; we must consider the objective of movement.

Magnitude of force means that force must overcome the inertia of the object and any other resisting forces for movement to occur.

For linear movement, force applied close to the center of gravity requires a smaller magnitude of force to move the object than does force applied farther from the center of gravity.

For rotational movement, force applied farther from the center of gravity requires a smaller magnitude of force to rotate the object than does force applied closer to the center of gravity.

For objects with a fixed point, force applied anywhere other than through the point of fixation results in object rotation.

Energy is the capacity to do work—the more energy a body has, the greater the force with which it can move something (or change its shape) and/or the farther it can move it.

Movement (mechanical energy) occurs in two forms:

1. Potential energy, or energy possessed by virtue of position, absolute location in space, or change in shape

   A. Gravitational potential energy: Potential energy of an object that is in a position where gravity can act on it

   B. Elastic (strain) potential energy: Energy potential of an object to do work while recoiling (or reforming) after stretching, compressing, or twisting

2. Kinetic energy, or energy possessed by virtue of motion that increases with speed

Force absorption refers to maintaining equilibrium while receiving a moving object's kinetic energy without sustaining injury and without losing balance while rebounding. The force of impact is dependent on an object's weight and speed. The more abruptly kinetic energy is lost, the more likely injury or rebound will occur. Thus, absorbing force requires gradually decelerating a moving mass by utilization of smaller forces over a longer period of time. Stability is greater when the force is received closer to the center of gravity.

Striking resistive surfaces means that the force of impact per unit area decreases when the moving object's area of surface making contact increases and the surface area that the object strikes increases.

Striking non-resistive surfaces means that the force of impact decreases if the moving object's area of surface making contact decreases because it is more likely to penetrate.

The more time and distance that it takes to stop a moving object when striking any surface, the more gradually the surface absorbs the force of impact; also the reaction forces acting upon the moving object decrease.

Equilibrium returns easily when the moving body (striking a resistive surface) aligns the center of gravity more vertically over the base of support.

Angular force against a body decreases when the distance between a contacting object and the body decreases and the contact occurs closer to the center of gravity. Also, widening the base of support in the direction of the moving object will increase stability.

Concept of Leverage Applied to Movement
A first-class lever is where the axis is between the points of application of the force and the resistance.

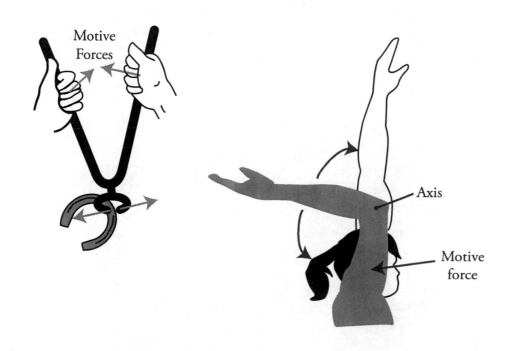

A second-class lever is where the force arm is longer than the resistance arm (operator applies resistance between the axis and the point of application of force).

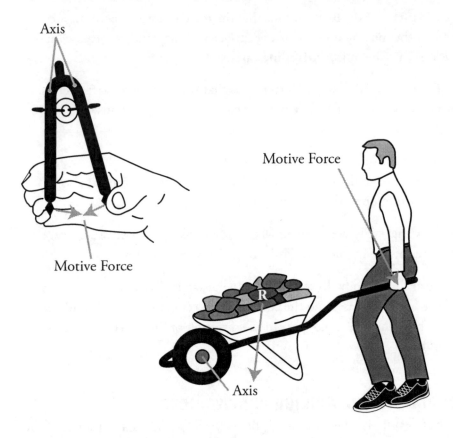

Axis

Motive Force

Motive Force

R

Axis

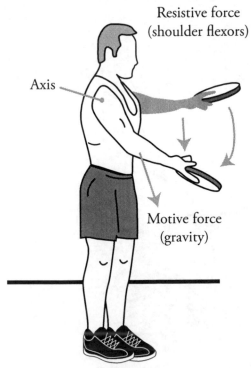

Resistive force
(shoulder flexors)

Axis

Motive force
(gravity)

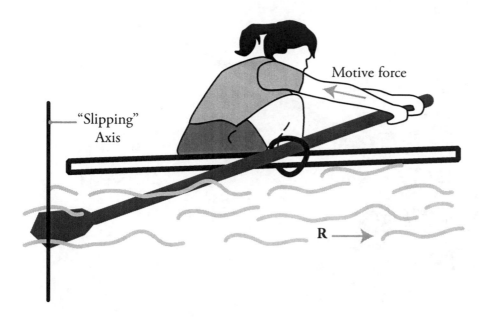

"Slipping" Axis

Motive force

R →

A third-class lever is where the force works at a point between the axis and the resistance (resistance arm is always longer than the force arm).

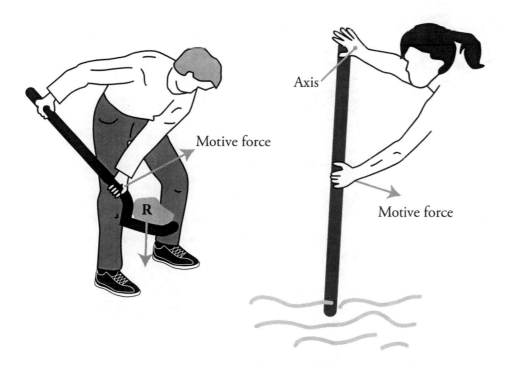

Motive force

R

Axis

Motive force

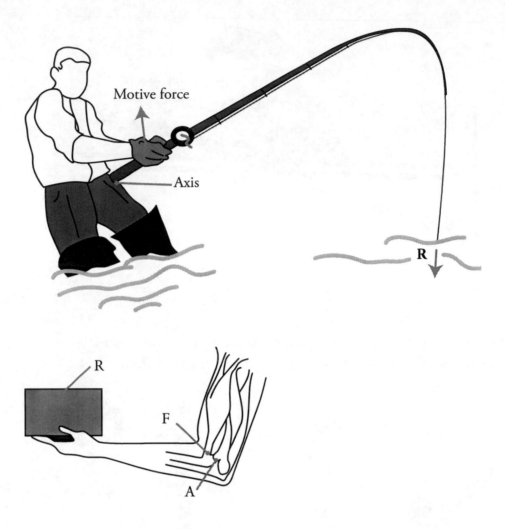

Muscle force is applied where muscles insert on bones.

With a few exceptions, the body consists primarily of third-class levers, with bones functioning as the levers and contracting innervated muscles acting as the fulcrums or by gravity acting on various body masses. As a result, the human body favors speed and range of motion over force.

Because most human body levers are long, their distal ends can move rapidly. Thus, the body is capable of swift, wide movements at the expense of abundant muscle force.

The human body easily performs tasks involving rapid movement with light objects. Very heavy tasks require a device for the body to secure an advantage of force.

Sports instruments increase body levers, thereby increasing the speed of an object's imparting force. However, the use of sports instruments requires more muscle force.

The body's leverage rarely includes one part of the body (a simple, singular lever). Movement of the body is an outcome of a system of levers operating together. However, levers do function in sequence when the force produced by the system of levers is dependent on the speed at the extremity. Many levers function simultaneously for a heavy task (e.g., pushing).

SAMPLE TEST

SAMPLE TEST

Content Knowledge and Student Growth and Development

(Average) (Skill 1.1)

1. **Which is the correct formula for determining the BMI (body mass index)?**

    A. BMI = (weight in pounds) × 880/ height in inches

    B. BMI = (weight in pounds) × 110/ height in inches

    C. BMI = (weight in pounds) × 703/ height in inches

    D. BMI = (weight in pounds) × 910/ height in inches

(Rigorous) (Skill 1.1)

2. **Which of the following is functional exercise?**

    A. Bending to lift an object

    B. Smith machine squat

    C. Bench press

    D. Warrior pose

(Rigorous) (Skill 1.2)

3. **When watching the beginning of a play in football, which sequence defines summation of forces?**

    A. The quarterback's ability to rotate his arm with the deltoid muscles

    B. The defense begins the motion with pressure into the feet, which pushes upward into the core of the body, lifting the player upward, and then steps forward to block his opponent

    C. The running back's ability to shift his body center as he changes direction

    D. The team working together to achieve a goal

(Rigorous) (Skill 1.3)

4. **Which is an example of body awareness?**

    A. BMI testing

    B. Exercise bulimia

    C. Playing a game that requires finding body parts or using specific body parts when asked to

    D. Comparing muscle sizes with a peer

(Easy) (Skill 1.4)

5. **When would overload training be appropriate?**

    A. For an advanced athlete, to increase muscle size and strength

    B. For a small child, to learn to skip

    C. For a pubescent-aged child, to start developing stronger muscles

    D. In a case of injury and recovery

(Easy) (Skill 1.4)

6. **You find a student gasping for air as he is performing a long distance run. He is in the:**

   A. Aerobic state

   B. Anaerobic state

   C. Psychomotor state

   D. Analytic state

(Rigorous) (Skill 1.4)

7. **The student gasping for air while performing a long distance run should do which of the following?**

   A. Stop immediately

   B. Push through the pain

   C. Slow down

   D. Change activities

(Rigorous) (Skill 1.4)

8. **What is the difference between the results of muscle strength training and the results of muscle endurance training?**

   A. There is no difference in the results of muscle strength training and muscle endurance training

   B. Muscle strength training increases flexibility and agility, whereas muscle endurance training increases power and balance

   C. Muscle strength training increases slow-twitch muscle tissue, and muscle endurance training increases fast-twitch muscle tissue

   D. Muscle strength training increases fast-twitch muscle tissue, and muscle endurance training increases slow-twitch muscle tissue

(Easy) (Skill 1.4)

9. **220 – age is:**

   A. Target heart rate

   B. Optimum resting heart rate

   C. Maximum heart rate, according to the Karvonean scale

   D. Minimum heart rate, according to Cooper's Fitnessgram

(Easy) (Skill 1.5)

10. **Digestion begins in the:**

    A. Mouth

    B. Gastrointestinal tract

    C. Stomach

    D. Large intestine

(Easy) (Skill 1.5)

11. **Gross motor skills include:**

    A. Writing

    B. Jumping

    C. Reading

    D. Pinching

(Easy) (Skill 1.5)

12. **The thyroid is part of the:**

    A. Endocrine system

    B. Respiratory system

    C. Skeletal system

    D. Muscular system

(Easy) (Skill 1.5)

13. **Antigens are sometimes known as:**

    A. Rusty nails

    B. Germs

    C. Hair

    D. Mucous

(Easy) (Skill 1.5)

14. **Pulmonary arteries carry blood from the heart to the:**

    A. Legs

    B. Arms

    C. Brain

    D. Lungs

(Easy) (Skill 1.5)

15. **Which type of muscle do we train in weight-bearing exercise?**

    A. Smooth muscle

    B. Skeletal muscle

    C. Cardiac muscle

    D. The weak ones

(Average) (Skill 1.6)

16. **Title IX Law mandates that:**

    A. Special education students receive the same physical education as non-special education students

    B. Nine hours of physical activity per week are required in and out of school

    C. Women's sports will receive the same funding and educational rights as men's sports

    D. Girls are not required to attend a coed PE class

(Easy) (Skill 1.6)

17. **A high-quality physical education class in a public school (as reported by NASPE) includes:**

    A. Snack time

    B. 60 minutes of daily exercise

    C. Visual charts of daily improvements

    D. Meaningful content

(Rigorous) (Skill 1.6)

18. **Accountability for a physical education teacher would include:**

    A. Having classes of 22 students or fewer

    B. Administering a physical standardized test to every student

    C. Knowing the standards of the local and state government

    D. Giving grades

(Easy) (Skill 1.7)

19. **In a softball game, the base runner is out if:**

    A. The opposition tags the player before the player reaches a base

    B. The player runs outside of the base path to avoid a tag

    C. The ball reaches the base before the player does

    D. All of the above

(Average) (Skill 1.7)

20. **In a tennis match, if the server's foot crosses the back line for the first time, then:**

    A. The opponent gets to serve

    B. The opponent gets a point

    C. The server gets a point

    D. The server gets a "fault"

(Average) (Skill 1.7)

21. **In track and field, if a runner goes into another runner's lane, then:**

    A. He must quickly return to his lane

    B. He is disqualified

    C. He gets a 5-second penalty

    D. He must stop immediately

(Easy) (Skill 1.7)

22. **In volleyball, the server is:**

    A. In the front

    B. In the middle

    C. In the back right

    D. In the back left

(Average) (Skill 1.7)

23. **In basketball, what would qualify as a technical foul?**

    A. Not starting on time

    B. Catching the ball, dribbling, stopping, and dribbling again

    C. Playing zone defense

    D. Knocking a player over

(Rigorous) (Skill 1.8)

24. **What is the most appropriate way to prevent injuries in the classroom?**

    A. Have the students run only on mats

    B. Have the students dress appropriately for the activity at hand

    C. Have an AED available

    D. Have the school nurse's phone number by the phone

(Rigorous) (Skill 1.8)

25. **What would be an example of an attractive nuisance?**

    A. A poster of a model with a milk moustache

    B. A flashing light for a fire drill

    C. Markings on the floor for drills

    D. A pile of toys in the corner of the gym floor

(Rigorous) (Skill 1.8)

26. **An exercise that would reduce the frequency of shin splints would be:**

    A. Running

    B. Calf raises

    C. Hurtles

    D. Pointe

(Average) (Skill 1.8)

27. **Before purchasing a new piece of equipment for the weight room, the teacher can check the website of _____ for safety specifications.**

    A. astm.org

    B. nasm.org

    C. Acefitness.org

    D. acsm.org

(Rigorous) (Skill 1.8)

28. **Two trustworthy students want to use the weight room on Saturday. You should:**

    A. Be there at the beginning and end of the workout to secure all items and lock up

    B. Know they are trained properly in form and in spotting before leaving them

    C. Let the custodian know they are there and come back to check on them later

    D. Never leave students unattended in workout or exercise situations at school

(Average) (Skill 1.9)

29. **What is a warning sign that a student might be using illegal drugs or harmful supplements?**

    A. A sudden change in physique

    B. Excitability

    C. A gradual growth in musculature

    D. A sudden interest in diet and exercise

(Rigorous) (Skill 1.9)

30. **Which of the following are some of the potential risks of nicotine use?**

    A. Premature closure of growth plates in bones and bloody cysts in the liver

    B. Nutritional deficiencies and dehydration

    C. Increased risk of cardiovascular disease and pulmonary disease

    D. A loss of focus and motivation

(Average) (Skill 2.1)

31. **In motor development, a normal sequence is:**

    A. Walk, step, crawl, run

    B. Hop, step, run, walk

    C. Jump, leap, run, 5k

    D. Crawl, stand, walk, run

(Rigorous) (Skill 2.2)

32. **What is an example of a physical reflex?**

    A. Seeing a hallway and running down it as fast as possible

    B. Jumping when excited

    C. Blocking a punch

    D. Tiptoeing to be quiet

(Rigorous) (Skill 2.2)

33. **Allowing students to design and run their own plays in team sports would be an example of:**

    A. Conceptual learning

    B. Transfer of learning

    C. Appropriate language

    D. Timed learning

(Rigorous) (Skill 2.2)

34. **How can a teacher use cognitive learning in the PE environment?**

    A. By asking the students how they can improve their performance

    B. By repetitive practicing

    C. By posting pie graphs of statistics

    D. By testing more often

(Rigorous) (Skill 2.3)

35. **When learning a new skill, experimental readiness compares to environmental readiness in which of the following ways?**

    A. Experimental readiness depends on the student performing the preceding skills well enough to apply a new skill and environmental readiness depends on the student's ability to relate to the new skill emotionally

    B. Experimental readiness depends on the resources available to the student, and environmental readiness depends on the problem solving ability of the student

    C. Experimental readiness is a student's readiness to experiment with what will work for him or her and how to make it work; environmental readiness depends on the student's home environment and/or what he or she already recognizes

    D. None of the above

(Easy) (Skill 2.5)

36. **A child may not see himself as an athlete because:**

    A. Of a lack of opportunity in his past to perform in athletic functions

    B. Of a dismissal of athletics by his family

    C. He sees himself as "fat"

    D. All of the above

Management, Motivation, and Communication

(Easy) (Skill 3.1)

37. **Classroom procedures are:**

    A. Announcements

    B. Basic rules

    C. Schedules

    D. Character counts pillars

(Rigorous) (Skill 3.1)

38. **Classroom procedures should be:**

    A. Mentioned

    B. Reviewed occasionally

    C. Posted in the classroom and reviewed regularly

    D. Discussed in student evaluations

(Average) (Skill 3.2)

39. **A child who is hesitant to participate in an activity may be:**

    A. Lazy

    B. Shy

    C. Neglected or abused

    D. Not intelligent

(Rigorous) (Skill 3.2)

40. **Knowing that students will do better in a positive environment, something a teacher can do to help would be:**

    A. Play positive and upbeat music in class

    B. Have posters of sports stars up in the classroom

    C. Create an elite team of athletes and show them off as "the best"

    D. Compare students' athleticism publicly

(Rigorous) (Skill 3.3)

41. **The teacher has 30 minutes to assess 60 students. He or she can:**

    A. Have the whole group perform the test at once, hoping to catch the students who have not mastered the concept

    B. Break the students up into groups according to ability and grade them accordingly

    C. Break the students up into random pairs or very small groups and rotate the groups to be assessed

    D. Ask teachers to hold students late

(Rigorous) (Skill 3.3)

42. **In an independent fitness class, all of the students want to use the Fitness game, but only two students can use it at a time. A fair way to handle this is:**

    A. First come, first serve

    B. Use it only on certain days

    C. Let only the strongest kids use it

    D. Have a sign-up system with time limitations

(Rigorous) (Skill 3.3)

43. Today's activity is dribbling the basketball while pivoting. Which is the best framework for that activity?

   A. Set up centers with different dribbling activities and let all students rotate around the centers

   B. Have a competitive game of basketball and whistle every time someone double dribbles

   C. Set up an obstacle course and let all the students try to dribble around it

   D. Set up centers, but require mastery of each one before moving on

(Average) (Skill 3.4)

44. Any child who lives anywhere can:

   A. Run around outside

   B. Play baseball

   C. Skate

   D. Learn to dance

(Average) (Skill 3.4)

45. Physical education lasts a lifetime when someone:

   A. Finds something they like

   B. Is at the top of the class

   C. Learns perfect form

   D. Loses weight

(Easy) (Skill 3.5)

46. The girls' softball coach has noticed that her team does not have any local press for a winning season. She should:

   A. Create a press release highlighting their season

   B. Call the principal and ask why the football team gets all the attention

   C. Send out a mass email to the staff, comparing the girls' softball team to the football team

   D. Have a pizza party for the girls

(Rigorous) (Skill 3.6)

47. The teacher notices a group of children are calling another child "Fatty." The teacher should:

   A. Call it out in front of the group

   B. Plan a meeting with the bullying students and the guidance counselor or other trusted campus administrators

   C. Call the parents immediately

   D. Let it go

(Average) (Skill 3.6)

48. An example of an intrinsic reward is:

   A. A sticker

   B. A good grade

   C. Release of endorphins

   D. Pain

(Easy) (Skill 3.6)

49. A negative consequence could be:

   A. Sitting out a run

   B. Being benched for the next game

   C. Being sent to another classroom for a while

   D. No response from the teacher

(Average) (Skill 4.1)

50. **A disapproving look toward students who are not focused on the task at hand is an example of:**

    A. Positive nonverbal communication

    B. Negative nonverbal communication

    C. Positive verbal communication

    D. Negative verbal communication

(Average) (Skill 4.2)

51. **An example of positive verbal communication with specificity would be:**

    A. "Great job on that handstand. You placed your hands exactly right and are even pointing your toes!"

    B. "That was good, but let's try again."

    C. "No, I don't like that. This time try harder."

    D. "Great job!"

(Easy) (Skill 4.3)

52. **A procedure list for the classroom could include:**

    A. Rules for equipment usage

    B. Rules for dress

    C. Rules for character

    D. All of the above

(Average) (Skill 4.3)

53. **Telling students, "You did a terrible job in today's game," is an example of:**

    A. Positive nonverbal communication

    B. Negative nonverbal communication

    C. Positive verbal communication

    D. Negative verbal communication

(Average) (Skill 4.3)

54. **Telling a student, "What a great somersault!" is an example of:**

    A. Positive nonverbal communication

    B. Negative nonverbal communication

    C. Positive verbal communication

    D. Negative verbal communication

(Average) (Skill 4.3)

55. **When handling a negative situation with students, it is best to:**

    A. Confront every situation head-on, immediately, and with vigor

    B. Take a step back and decide if the situation requires immediate verbal communication or intervention

    C. Embarrass students behaving badly so they won't do it again

    D. Handle every situation behind closed doors

(Average) (Skill 4.3)

56. **To communicate behavior expectations visually, you can:**

    A. Demonstrate bad behaviors

    B. Tell the students what you expect

    C. Correct someone verbally

    D. Post procedures on the wall

(Average) (Skill 4.3)

57. **To communicate performance expectations kinesthetically, you can:**

    A. Have children practice the skill physically

    B. Have students sit down to watch a demonstration

    C. Tell students about someone who is doing a great job

    D. Give quick verbal assessments

(Average) (Skill 4.3)

58. **To communicate performance expectations verbally, you can:**

    A. Run with the students

    B. Demonstrate the skill for them

    C. Give quick verbal cues as they are performing the skill

    D. Use proximity

(Average) (Skill 4.3)

59. **Use technology to correct form by:**

    A. Using a digital camera to record or take still shots and showing the students what they are doing and how to correct it

    B. Having the children watch a professional sport and comment on the athletes' skills

    C. Using a laser pointer to point out flaws

    D. Using a document camera to show a list of proper alignment techniques on the board

(Rigorous) (Skill 4.3)

60. **On your Facebook page, you post a video of a student you consider to be a star performing a skill. This could lead to:**

    A. The student and parents being proud that you have highlighted their child

    B. Your termination

    C. Raising your popularity with students when they see you have a Facebook page

    D. Getting calls from college recruiters about the student

(Average) (Skill 4.4)

61. **Good email etiquette includes which of the following:**

    A. Abbreviating sentences by dropping articles (a, the) so that they are fast and easy to read

    B. Composing the email as one continuous paragraph in order to shorten the overall length

    C. Using the same conventional abbreviations for words and phrases that are used in text messaging (lol, btw, etc.)

    D. None of the above

(Rigorous) (Skill 4.4)

62. **A colleague has made negative comments about your students' performances at this season's games. You should:**

    A. Tell school authorities

    B. Write a letter to the papers

    C. Send out a mass email defending your character and that of your students

    D. Communicate professionally, one-on-one with the colleague

(Rigorous) (Skill 4.4)

63. You get a text message from a parent that she is pulling her child off your team because her child came home crying from last night's game. You should:

   A. Ignore it

   B. Immediately call the parent and ask about the situation

   C. Text her back and say "OK"

   D. Forward her text to the principal

(Rigorous) (Skill 4.4)

64. When sending an email to an administrator, you should:

   A. Be quick about the details, but use correct grammar and appropriate language

   B. Send it in shorthand because she doesn't have time for your details

   C. Make it as detailed as possible

   D. Use the *MLA Handbook*

(Average) (Skill 4.4)

65. You get a text message from a colleague that is inappropriate. You should:

   A. Text him back "LOL"

   B. Text him back "No thanks"

   C. Text him back "Take me off your text list"

   D. Call him or see him face to face to address it

(Rigorous) (Skill 4.4)

66. The teacher is writing a discipline referral for a child who pulled a chair out from under another child today. Which detail can the referral list?

   A. The student pulled a chair out from under another student, who was sitting down at the time

   B. The student bullied another student

   C. The student acted out of spite

   D. All of the above

(Average) (Skill 4.4)

67. For a parent–teacher conference, you should:

   A. Bring photographs

   B. Come with an open mind

   C. Bring data, such as assessments and discipline referrals

   D. Bring a list of websites the parent should see

Planning, Instruction, and Student Assessment

(Easy) (Skill 5.1)

68. Which of the following is a locomotor skill?

   A. Running

   B. A bridge

   C. Throwing a ball

   D. Writing

(Easy) (Skill 5.1)

69. **Which of the following is a non-locomotor skill?**

    A. Running

    B. A bridge

    C. Throwing a ball

    D. Writing

(Easy) (Skill 5.1)

70. **Which of the following is a manipulative skill?**

    A. Running

    B. A bridge

    C. Throwing a ball

    D. Writing

(Rigorous) (Skill 5.1)

71. **A student with high ability and low self-esteem can increase self-esteem through:**

    A. Psychological intervention

    B. Being in an aesthetically pleasing environment

    C. Being given a part on the team at which he can excel

    D. Being assessed

(Average) (Skill 5.2)

72. **A student having trouble with locomotor skills might need:**

    A. Practice in different ways, such as new directions or heights, using the same skill

    B. Repetition

    C. Remediation

    D. Intervention

(Rigorous) (Skill 5.2)

73. **In a boxing class, how would the teacher use sequencing in teaching a jab-punch combination?**

    A. Repetition

    B. Using flexibility

    C. Practicing similar combinations

    D. Practicing the sequence of events slowly

(Average) (Skill 5.3)

74. **Feedback for a student who is behind on a skill should be:**

    A. Rigorous

    B. Light-handed

    C. Constant

    D. Informative

(Rigorous) (Skill 5.4)

75. **Competitive games are useful in PE classes when:**

    A. Students are practicing a skill and are feeling successful

    B. You want to find the best athlete of the group

    C. You need to individually assess the students

    D. Students are bullying each other

(Average) (Skill 5.5)

76. **The national legislature has gotten involved in physical education through:**

   A. Equality legislation for genders and special education

   B. Nationally mandating physical education in every grade level at every public school

   C. Funding a national physical education program

   D. Raising the physical education requirements for advanced high school students

(Average) (Skill 5.5)

77. **State legislatures have passed mandates for physical education because of the sudden rise in:**

   A. Bullying

   B. Female population

   C. Special populations

   D. Overweight children and type II diabetes

(Average) (Skill 5.5)

78. **The new National Standards for Health and Fitness Education are based on the overall goal that all students:**

   A. Will be athletes

   B. Will lead healthy lifestyles

   C. Will change their neighborhoods

   D. Will love exercise

(Average) (Skill 5.6)

79. **Creating new goals requires taking an honest look at:**

   A. Last year's assessments

   B. Last year's goals

   C. This year's new requirements

   D. All of the above

(Rigorous) (Skill 5.6)

80. **A physical education teacher has the goal of teaching all her students to play volleyball. She has 60 students at a time and one volleyball court and net. The problem with her goal is:**

   A. She does not have the funding for another net

   B. She does not have the time in a 30-minute class period

   C. The ratio of kids per court will not allow productivity in practicing the game

   D. Her students are not tall enough

(Average) (Skill 5.9)

81. **A floor ladder is:**

   A. Kinesthetic equipment

   B. Audial equipment

   C. Visual equipment

   D. Special education equipment

(Rigorous) (Skill 5.10)

82. When teaching a 3-point jump, the teacher could start by:

    A. Reviewing how to run

    B. Reviewing how to leap

    C. Reviewing how to mark the final jump

    D. Attaching a kinesthetic piece of practice equipment to the student

(Average) (Skill 5.11)

83. The EAP for the school should be:

    A. Located by the front office

    B. Located in the coach's office

    C. Easily accessed

    D. In a file, hidden from students

(Rigorous) (Skill 5.11)

84. A student falls on the floor suddenly and is unconscious. An AED is nearby. The teacher is not AED or CPR certified. What should the teacher do?

    A. Call for help and wait

    B. Tell someone close by to call 911 and wait

    C. Tell someone to call 911, pull out the AED, and follow the directions

    D. Tell someone close by to call 911, have the AED ready for someone else to use, and begin CPR

(Easy) (Skill 5.11)

85. The RICE acronym for treating sports injuries stands for rest, ice, compression, and:

    A. Education

    B. Emulation

    C. Emanation

    D. Elevation

(Rigorous) (Skill 5.11)

86. A student did not eat lunch and is now shaking and behaving erratically. The teacher should assume the student has _____ and should contact the nurse.

    A. hypoglycemia

    B. hyperglycemia

    C. Type I Diabetes

    D. anorexia nervosa

(Rigorous) (Skill 5.11)

87. A student practicing outside takes off his helmet and staggers around. He is red in the face and soaked from sweat. He may be:

    A. Sick

    B. Tired

    C. Dehydrated

    D. Hungry

(Rigorous) (Skill 5.11)

88. The above student should be:

    A. Brought inside

    B. Given fluids

    C. Referred to a doctor or the hospital

    D. All of the above

(Average) (Skill 5.11)

89. **The new CPR:**

    A. Teaches rescue breathing first

    B. Teaches calling for help instead of immediate help

    C. Teaches compressions first

    D. Teaches that only CPR-certified people should act in an emergency

(Average) (Skill 5.11)

90. **In an open body of water, a teacher gets caught in the current. He or she should:**

    A. Swim parallel to the shore

    B. Call for help

    C. Swim toward the shore

    D. Swim out farther into the sea

(Average) (Skill 6.1)

91. **Comparing students in a perceived scale of competency is a:**

    A. Chart

    B. Rating scale

    C. Graph

    D. Journal

(Rigorous) (Skill 6.1)

92. **A teacher wants to show a comparison of each student's softball pitches. Each student has had 10 pitches. She could use a:**

    A. Pie graph

    B. Rating scale

    C. Line graph

    D. Chart

(Rigorous) (Skill 6.2)

93. **A portfolio can show more _____ than typical assessments.**

    A. skills

    B. data

    C. opinions

    D. development over time

(Average) (Skill 6.3)

94. **National student assessments, such as the President's Challenge and Cooper's Fitnessgram, are a positive way to:**

    A. Give students research-based information

    B. Motivate students

    C. Keep assessment data over time

    D. All of the above

(Average) (Skill 6.4)

95. **A tennis match would be which kind of assessment?**

    A. Baseline

    B. Formative

    C. Authentic

    D. Standardized

(Average) (Skill 6.4)

96. **A multiple choice test is a:**

    A. Non-criterion referenced test

    B. Rubic

    C. Criterion-referenced test

    D. Authentic assessment

(Rigorous) (Skill 6.9)

97. **A 504 plan gives a student the right to:**

    A. A fair education, regardless of disabilities

    B. An IEP

    C. The same education as everyone else

    D. Play on a sports team

Collaboration, Reflection, and Technology

(Rigorous) (Skill 7.1)

98. **Sports games can teach:**

    A. Science of summation of forces

    B. Sportsmanship

    C. Equations

    D. First aid and CPR

(Rigorous) (Skill 7.2)

99. **The next class unit is about immunity and the endocrine system. The teacher could consult which other teacher for cross-curricular study?**

    A. Math

    B. English

    C. Science

    D. Social studies

(Average) (Skill 7.2)

100. **Another unit intended for study is sports and games from different cultures. The teacher could also see the curriculum of which class for more information?**

    A. Math

    B. English

    C. Science

    D. Social studies

(Easy) (Skill 7.2)

101. **Which of the following subject areas can be integrated into physical education instruction?**

    A. Anatomy, study of forces, biology, and nutrition

    B. Statistics, graphs, charts, and ratios

    C. History of sports or activities, such as the Olympics

    D. All of the above

(Average) (Skill 7.4)

102. **Physical education teachers can send information home about community walks, races, or other volunteer community events in order to:**

    A. Raise parental awareness about fitness-related opportunities outside of the classroom

    B. Raise parental awareness about the importance of community involvement

    C. Raise parental awareness about the active role of the PE department

    D. None of the above

(Rigorous) (Skill 7.4)

103. The PE teacher has heard great things about a local dance studio. She should:

   A. Talk about the dance studio to classes

   B. Send home flyers from the one dance studio

   C. Contact many dance studios to request information for students

   D. Post the dance studio information on the school website

   Answer: C. Contact many dance studios

(Rigorous) (Skill 7.4)

104. To provide students with many choices for physical activities outside of school, the teacher can:

   A. Stay after school daily to let the kids play in the gym

   B. Advertise with a local business that targets children

   C. Take students on a field trip to a baseball game

   D. Present information from the city parks and recreation department

Directions: Questions 105–108. Use the following situation and apply it to the reflective cycle.

A teacher has a lesson plan to teach the skills of a great new dance that was popularized by a song on the radio. When the teacher started class, the kids refused to try the dance moves. The teacher tried to inspire them, only for the children to ignore the teacher and then go on to something else. The teacher was left to scramble for a second plan because he felt his plan was rejected by the class.

(Rigorous) (Skill 8.1)

105. The decision aspect is:

   A. The decision to scrap the dance and go on to something else

   B. The decision to teach the dance moves

   C. The decision to let the children choose to participate or not

   D. The decision to give the students a zero for the day

(Rigorous) (Skill 8.1)

106. If an administrator had walked in to observe, the evaluation would be:

   A. That the initial plan failed

   B. That the kids were having a good time

   C. That the original plan was disorganized

   D. That the teacher cannot teach well

(Rigorous) (Skill 8.1)

107. **Later, the teacher analyzes the lesson and concludes that:**

A. He is a failure as a teacher

B. He should never teach music again

C. He should start with something the students can already do, and then work from there

D. He should scrap a bad lesson plan and let the kids play if he fails to get his lesson across

(Average) (Skill 8.1)

108. **The new action plan leads to the:**

A. New feelings about the action plan

B. New description for a new lesson

C. New conclusion of the new lesson

D. Evaluation of the new lesson

(Easy) (Skill 8.2)

109. **NASPE is the certifying agency for:**

A. Professional physical education teachers

B. Personal trainers

C. Weight management trainers

D. Equipment advice

(Average) (Skill 8.2)

110. **ACE is:**

A. A hardware company

B. A research agency for fitness

C. Equipment safety regulations

D. National requirements for fitness

(Average) (Skill 8.2)

111. **ACSM is the:**

A. Accreditation for many other fitness companies and is the litmus test for professional fitness organizations

B. Scientific information for health class

C. Council for sports medications

D. Constitution for sports teachers

(Easy) (Skill 8.2)

112. **Cooper's Institute is known to be a:**

A. Leader in alternative medicine

B. Leader in assessment

C. Leader in health and fitness education

D. Leader in state standards for education

(Average) (Skill 9.1)

113. **When using technology in fitness education:**

A. The more the better

B. There are only a couple of resources

C. You shouldn't trust anything

D. There is a lot of information, but sources should be checked for credibility

(Average) (Skill 9.1)

114. **When using technology in the classroom:**

A. Use sources for demonstration only

B. Use sources that allow kinesthetic practice only

C. Use a variety of sources, but use time management and judgment in usage

D. Technology is not necessary in the PE environment.

(Rigorous) (Skill 9.1)

115. Many new gaming systems use gross motor skills instead of fine motor skills. What would be a good game to use for the best form of aerobic exercise?

    A. A dance game with foot placement requirements

    B. A racing game with a steering wheel

    C. A musical game with instruments

    D. A trivia game

(Average) (Skill 9.1)

116. A teacher wants to keep track of students' health habits. She could require:

    A. An upload on a mobile phone

    B. A daily email of students' activities outside of school

    C. Each student to join her team on *www.peertrainer.com*

    D. Each student to take daily measurements

(Average) (Skill 9.2)

117. A teacher wants to create an online interaction with students that is direct and immediate. She could create a:

    A. Blog

    B. Wiki

    C. .com site

    D. Poster

(Average) (Skill 9.2)

118. A teacher wants to share her exercise videos with others. She should use a:

    A. Blog

    B. Wiki

    C. .com site

    D. Vlog or podcast

(Average) (Skill 9.2)

119. A teacher wants to share her own story. She should use a:

    A. Blog

    B. Wiki

    C. .com site

    D. Podcast

(Average) (Skill 9.2)

120. A teacher blog or vlog should never include:

    A. Personal stories

    B. Student names or information

    C. Scientific research

    D. Opinions

Answer Key

ANSWER KEY							
1. C	16. C	31. D	46. A	61. D	76. A	91. B	106. A
2. A	17. D	32. C	47. B	62. D	77. D	92. C	107. C
3. B	18. B	33. A	48. C	63. B	78. B	93. D	108. B
4. C	19. D	34. A	49. B	64. A	79. D	94. D	109. A
5. A	20. D	35. C	50. B	65. D	80. C	95. C	110. B
6. B	21. B	36. D	51. A	66. A	81. A	96. C	111. A
7. C	22. C	37. B	52. D	67. C	82. B	97. A	112. C
8. D	23. D	38. C	53. D	68. A	83. C	98. B	113. D
9. C	24. B	39. B	54. C	69. B	84. C	99. C	114. C
10. A	25. D	40. A	55. B	70. C	85. D	100. D	115. A
11. B	26. B	41. C	56. D	71. C	86. A	101. D	116. C
12. A	27. A	42. D	57. A	72. A	87. C	102. A	117. B
13. B	28. D	43. A	58. C	73. D	88. D	103. C	118. D
14. D	29. A	44. D	59. A	74. B	89. C	104. D	119. A
15. B	30. C	45. A	60. B	75. A	90. A	105. B	120. B

Rigor Table

RIGOR TABLE	
Rigor level	**Questions**
Easy 20%	5, 6, 9, 10, 11, 12, 13, 14, 15, 17, 19, 22, 36, 37, 46, 49, 52, 68, 69, 70, 85, 101, 109, 112
Average 40%	1, 16, 20, 21, 23, 27, 29, 31, 39, 44, 45, 48, 50, 51, 53, 54, 55, 56, 57, 58, 59, 61, 65, 67, 72, 74, 76, 77, 78, 79, 81, 83, 89, 90, 91, 94, 95, 96, 100, 102, 108, 110, 111, 113, 114, 116, 117, 118, 119, 120
Rigorous 40%	2, 3, 4, 7, 8, 18, 24, 25, 26, 28, 30, 32, 33, 34, 35, 38, 40, 41, 42, 43, 47, 60, 62, 63, 64, 66, 71, 73, 75, 80, 82, 84, 86, 87, 88, 92, 93, 97, 98, 99, 103, 104, 105, 106, 107, 115

Sample Test with Rationales

Content Knowledge and Student Growth and Development

(Average) (Skill 1.1)

1. **Which is the correct formula for determining the BMI (body mass index)?**

   A. BMI = (weight in pounds) × 880/ height in inches

   B. BMI = (weight in pounds) × 110/ height in inches

   C. BMI = (weight in pounds) × 703/ height in inches

   D. BMI = (weight in pounds) × 910/ height in inches

   Answer: C. BMI = (weight in pounds) × 703/height in inches

   Body mass index (BMI) is used by doctors and insurance companies as an easy way to test for obesity. It is a flawed test because it only relies on height and weight. Someone who is not fat but extremely fit and muscular could be considered obese by this test. It is, however, a reality that employers and insurance companies—as well as some standards for excellence in fitness education awards and grants—use this formula, so the teacher should know what BMI is and how to check it.

(Rigorous) (Skill 1.1)

2. **Which of the following is functional exercise?**

   A. Bending to lift an object

   B. Smith machine squat

   C. Bench press

   D. Warrior pose

   Answer: A. Bending to lift an object

   Functional exercise is the kind of movement the body does on a regular basis in regular movements. By training this way, the body is training to use the muscles it would use in daily life.

(Rigorous) (Skill 1.2)

3. **When watching the beginning of a play in football, which sequence defines summation of forces?**

   A. The quarterback's ability to rotate his arm with the deltoid muscles

   B. The defense begins the motion with pressure into the feet, which pushes upward into the core of the body, lifting the player upward, and then steps forward to block his opponent

   C. The running back's ability to shift his body center as he changes direction

   D. The team working together to achieve a goal

Answer: B. The defense begins the motion with pressure into the feet, which pushes upward into the core of the body, lifting the player upward, and then steps forward to block his opponent

Summation of forces is defined as the muscle systems working together to create one fluid movement at the right time. The defense has to go through this sequence on every play so that their muscles will move them to the right place at the right time in the right way.

(Rigorous) (Skill 1.3)

4. **Which is an example of body awareness?**

   A. BMI testing

   B. Exercise bulimia

   C. Playing a game that requires finding body parts or using specific body parts when asked to

   D. Comparing muscle sizes with a peer

   Answer: C. Playing a game that requires finding body parts or using specific body parts when asked to

   Body awareness is knowing the body parts and being able to use them when directed to do so.

(Easy) (Skill 1.4)

5. **When would overload training be appropriate?**

   A. For an advanced athlete, to increase muscle size and strength

   B. For a small child, to learn to skip

   C. For a pubescent-aged child, to start developing stronger muscles

   D. In a case of injury and recovery

Answer: A. For an advanced athlete, to increase muscle size and strength

Overload training is a principle designed for advanced athletes to increase muscle size and strength.

(Easy) (Skill 1.4)

6. **You find a student gasping for air as he is performing a long distance run. He is in the:**

   A. Aerobic state

   B. Anaerobic state

   C. Psychomotor state

   D. Analytic state

Answer: B. Anaerobic state

The anaerobic state is the state past the aerobic threshold. The body is no longer functioning in a way that increases strength and burns calories.

(Rigorous) (Skill 1.4)

7. **The student gasping for air while performing a long distance run should do which of the following?**

   A. Stop immediately

   B. Push through the pain

   C. Slow down

   D. Change activities

Answer: C. Slow down

The student should slow down to re-enter the aerobic state. The anaerobic state is not safe for a long period of time.

(Rigorous) (Skill 1.4)

8. **What is the difference between the results of muscle strength training and the results of muscle endurance training?**

    A. There is no difference in the results of muscle strength training and muscle endurance training

    B. Muscle strength training increases flexibility and agility, whereas muscle endurance training increases power and balance

    C. Muscle strength training increases slow-twitch muscle tissue, and muscle endurance training increases fast-twitch muscle tissue

    D. Muscle strength training increases fast-twitch muscle tissue, and muscle endurance training increases slow-twitch muscle tissue

    Answer: D. Muscle strength training increases fast-twitch muscle tissue, and muscle endurance training increases slow-twitch muscle tissue

    Muscle strength is the ability of muscle groups to contract and support a given amount of weight. Muscle endurance is the ability of muscle groups to contract continually over a period of time and support a given amount of weight. Training for muscle strength increases the fast-twitch muscle tissue and training for muscle endurance increases the slow-twitch muscle tissue.

(Easy) (Skill 1.4)

9. **220 – age is:**

    A. Target heart rate

    B. Optimum resting heart rate

    C. Maximum heart rate, according to the Karvonean scale

    D. Minimum heart rate, according to Cooper's Fitnessgram

    Answer: C. Maximum heart rate, according to the Karvonean scale

    The general practice in Karvonean scale is to take 220 – age, and then multiply it by 0.65 to 0.9 to find an approximate safe and effective zone for cardiovascular exercise.

(Easy) (Skill 1.5)

10. **Digestion begins in the:**

    A. Mouth

    B. Gastrointestinal tract

    C. Stomach

    D. Large intestine

    Answer: A. Mouth

    Digestion begins in the mouth with the chewing of food and the mixing of food with saliva from the salivary glands.

(Easy) (Skill 1.5)

11. **Gross motor skills include:**

    A. Writing

    B. Jumping

    C. Reading

    D. Pinching

Answer: B. Jumping

Gross motor skills are skills using larger muscle groups.

(Easy) (Skill 1.5)

12. **The thyroid is part of the:**

    A. Endocrine system

    B. Respiratory system

    C. Skeletal system

    D. Muscular system

Answer: A. Endocrine system

The thyroid is part of the endocrine system, which regulates the release of hormones and controls many functions of the body.

(Easy) (Skill 1.5)

13. **Antigens are sometimes known as:**

    A. Rusty nails

    B. Germs

    C. Hair

    D. Mucous

Answer: B. Germs

Antigens are foreign germs carrying illness that enter the body.

(Easy) (Skill 1.5)

14. **Pulmonary arteries carry blood from the heart to the:**

    A. Legs

    B. Arms

    C. Brain

    D. Lungs

Answer: D. Lungs

Pulmonary means "related to the lungs."

(Easy) (Skill 1.5)

15. **Which type of muscle do we train in weight-bearing exercise?**

    A. Smooth muscle

    B. Skeletal muscle

    C. Cardiac muscle

    D. The weak ones

Answer: B. Skeletal muscle

Skeletal muscles are the muscles attached to bone, which give the body shape and strength. These are the muscles whose sizes and densities we can control to some extent through exercise.

(Average) (Skill 1.6)

16. **Title IX Law mandates that:**

    A. Special education students receive the same physical education as non-special education students

    B. Nine hours of physical activity per week are required in and out of school

    C. Women's sports will receive the same funding and educational rights as men's sports

    D. Girls are not required to attend a coed PE class

Answer: C. Women's sports will receive the same funding and educational rights as men's sports

Title IX refers to the equality of sports education and funding for boys and girls in public schools.

(Easy) (Skill 1.6)

17. **A high-quality physical education class in a public school (as reported by NASPE) includes:**

    A. Snack time

    B. 60 minutes of daily exercise

    C. Visual charts of daily improvements

    D. Meaningful content

    Answer: D. Meaningful content

    NASPE gives four criteria for a standard physical education class, one of which is meaningful content. While the 60 minutes of daily exercise is recommended, it is to be achieved over the course of a day, not over the course of a class.

(Rigorous) (Skill 1.6)

18. **Accountability for a physical education teacher would include:**

    A. Having classes of 22 students or fewer

    B. Administering a physical standardized test to every student

    C. Knowing the standards of the local and state government

    D. Giving grades

    Answer: B. Administering a physical standardized test to every student

    Standardized testing helps teachers and administrators compare data to requirements and make goals for upcoming classes.

(Easy) (Skill 1.7)

19. **In a softball game, the base runner is out if:**

    A. The opposition tags the player before the player reaches a base

    B. The player runs outside of the base path to avoid a tag

    C. The ball reaches the base before the player does

    D. All of the above

    Answer: D. All of the above

    The rules of softball dictate that the player is out if any of the above circumstances occur. Additionally, the player is out if a batted ball strikes the player in fair territory.

(Average) (Skill 1.7)

20. **In a tennis match, if the server's foot crosses the back line for the first time, then:**

    A. The opponent gets to serve

    B. The opponent gets a point

    C. The server gets a point

    D. The server gets a "fault"

    Answer: D. The server gets a "fault"

    A foot fault is a warning. The second time, the server loses the ball to the opponent.

(Average) (Skill 1.7)

21. **In track and field, if a runner goes into another runner's lane, then:**

    A. He must quickly return to his lane

    B. He is disqualified

    C. He gets a 5-second penalty

    D. He must stop immediately

    Answer: B. He is disqualified

    A change of lanes is illegal and makes the runner's score null and void.

(Easy) (Skill 1.7)

22. **In volleyball, the server is:**

    A. In the front

    B. In the middle

    C. In the back right

    D. In the back left

    Answer: C. In the back right

    The server is always in the back on the team's right side.

(Average) (Skill 1.7)

23. **In basketball, what would qualify as a technical foul?**

    A. Not starting on time

    B. Catching the ball, dribbling, stopping, and dribbling again

    C. Playing zone defense

    D. Knocking a player over

    Answer: D. Knocking a player over

    A technical foul is for misconduct or disrespectful behavior.

(Rigorous) (Skill 1.8)

24. **What is the most appropriate way to prevent injuries in the classroom?**

    A. Have the students run only on mats

    B. Have the students dress appropriately for the activity at hand

    C. Have an AED available

    D. Have the school nurse's phone number by the phone

    Answer: B. Have the students dress appropriately for the activity at hand

    Students must wear appropriate clothing and footwear for the sport or event at hand. Doing so is a measure of prevention because it reduces the chance of injury.

(Rigorous) (Skill 1.8)

25. **What would be an example of an attractive nuisance?**

    A. A poster of a model with a milk moustache

    B. A flashing light for a fire drill

    C. Markings on the floor for drills

    D. A pile of toys in the corner of the gym floor

    Answer: D. A pile of toys in the corner of the gym floor

    A pile of randomly placed toys would be an attractive nuisance that would disrupt class and possibly be harmful if the students dug through it and possibly threw objects around.

(Rigorous) (Skill 1.8)

26. **An exercise that would reduce the frequency of shin splints would be:**

    A. Running

    B. Calf raises

    C. Hurtles

    D. Pointe

    Answer: B. Calf raises

    Calf raises strengthen the gastrocnemius, the tibealis anterior, and the smaller muscles around the ankle. Stability here reduces injury to the shin.

(Average) (Skill 1.8)

27. **Before purchasing a new piece of equipment for the weight room, the teacher can check the website of _____ for safety specifications.**

    A. astm.org

    B. nasm.org

    C. Acefitness.org

    D. acsm.org

    Answer: A. astm.org

    ASTM is federally regulated to test fitness equipment.

(Rigorous) (Skill 1.8)

28. **Two trustworthy students want to use the weight room on Saturday. You should:**

    A. Be there at the beginning and end of the workout to secure all items and lock up

    B. Know they are trained properly in form and in spotting before leaving them

    C. Let the custodian know they are there and come back to check on them later

    D. Never leave students unattended in workout or exercise situations at school

    Answer: D. Never leave students unattended in workout or exercise situations at school

    Unless you or another professional teacher or trainer employed by the school district is present the entire time the students are there, they should not be allowed to go.

(Average) (Skill 1.9)

29. **What is a warning sign that a student might be using illegal drugs or harmful supplements?**

    A. A sudden change in physique

    B. Excitability

    C. A gradual growth in musculature

    D. A sudden interest in diet and exercise

    Answer: A. A sudden change in physique

    Drugs can cause a sudden change in physique, such as sudden muscle changes, weight gain or loss, and sudden voice changes.

(Rigorous) (Skill 1.9)

30. **Which of the following are some of the potential risks of nicotine use?**

    A. Premature closure of growth plates in bones and bloody cysts in the liver

    B. Nutritional deficiencies and dehydration

    C. Increased risk of cardiovascular disease and pulmonary disease

    D. A loss of focus and motivation

    Answer: C. Increased risk of cardiovascular disease and pulmonary disease

    Nicotine is a legal substance for adults but can increase the risk of cardiovascular disease, pulmonary disease, and cancers of the mouth and lungs. Nicotine consumption through smoking severely hinders athletic performance by compromising lung function. Smoking especially affects performance in endurance activities.

(Average) (Skill 2.1)

31. **In motor development, a normal sequence is:**

    A. Walk, step, crawl, run

    B. Hop, step, run, walk

    C. Jump, leap, run, 5k

    D. Crawl, stand, walk, run

    Answer: D. Crawl, stand, walk, run

    Motor development is the sequence of muscle changes leading to new body movements.

(Rigorous) (Skill 2.2)

32. **What is an example of a physical reflex?**

    A. Seeing a hallway and running down it as fast as possible

    B. Jumping when excited

    C. Blocking a punch

    D. Tiptoeing to be quiet

    Answer: C. Blocking a punch

    Keeping the body from getting hurt is an automatic response, or reflex.

(Rigorous) (Skill 2.2)

33. **Allowing students to design and run their own plays in team sports would be an example of:**

    A. Conceptual learning

    B. Transfer of learning

    C. Appropriate language

    D. Timed learning

    Answer: A. Conceptual learning

    Conceptual learning is analysis of learned material to create new ideas.

(Rigorous) (Skill 2.2)

34. **How can a teacher use cognitive learning in the PE environment?**

    A. By asking the students how they can improve their performance

    B. By repetitive practicing

    C. By posting pie graphs of statistics

    D. By testing more often

Answer: A. By asking the students how they can improve their performance

Cognitive learning is about analysis. Having students analyze their own performance data teaches them to use their cognition skills. It will also make them personally invested in learning and improving their data or scores on assessments.

(Rigorous) (Skill 2.3)

35. **When learning a new skill, experimental readiness compares to environmental readiness in which of the following ways?**

    A. Experimental readiness depends on the student performing the preceding skills well enough to apply a new skill and environmental readiness depends on the student's ability to relate to the new skill emotionally

    B. Experimental readiness depends on the resources available to the student, and environmental readiness depends on the problem solving ability of the student

    C. Experimental readiness is a student's readiness to experiment with what will work for him or her and how to make it work; environmental readiness depends on the student's home environment and/or what he or she already recognizes

    D. None of the above

Answer: C. Experimental readiness is a student's readiness to experiment with what will work for him or her and how to make it work; environmental readiness depends on the student's home environment and/or what he or she already recognizes

Experimental readiness is a student's readiness to experiment with what will work for him or her and how to make it work. Is the child ready to experiment to find out his or her body responds to the new skill? Is he or she ready to try something in different ways to see what would work? Environmental readiness depends on the student's home environment and/or what he or she already recognizes. Does the child's environment lend itself to a new skill? Would their neighborhoods or homes have the equipment required to practice?

(Easy) (Skill 2.5)

36. **A child may not see himself as an athlete because:**

    A. Of a lack of opportunity in his past to perform in athletic functions

    B. Of a dismissal of athletics by his family

    C. He sees himself as "fat"

    D. All of the above

Answer: D. All of the above

All of these factors affect how a child sees himself with respect to athletics.

Management, Motivation, and Communication

(Easy) (Skill 3.1)

37. **Classroom procedures are:**

    A. Announcements

    B. Basic rules

    C. Schedules

    D. Character counts pillars

    Answer: B. Basic rules

    Basic rules, or the ways things are done in this classroom, are called *procedures*.

(Rigorous) (Skill 3.1)

38. **Classroom procedures should be:**

    A. Mentioned

    B. Reviewed occasionally

    C. Posted in the classroom and reviewed regularly

    D. Discussed in student evaluations

    Answer: C. Posted in the classroom and reviewed regularly

    Procedures keep a class moving smoothly. Post them and review them as often as they need to be revisited, which could be many times per class.

(Average) (Skill 3.2)

39. **A child who is hesitant to participate in an activity may be:**

    A. Lazy

    B. Shy

    C. Neglected or abused

    D. Not intelligent

Answer: B. Shy

A hesitant student may have a shy personality and may need some time to warm up to the class and the other participants.

(Rigorous) (Skill 3.2)

40. **Knowing that students will do better in a positive environment, something a teacher can do to help would be:**

    A. Play positive and upbeat music in class

    B. Have posters of sports stars up in the classroom

    C. Create an elite team of athletes and show them off as "the best"

    D. Compare students' athleticism publicly

    Answer: A. Play positive and upbeat music in class

    A positive learning environment for all would include something positive for all. Elitist activities and groups may not be inspiring, whereas positive and inspiring music can help everyone in the class.

(Rigorous) (Skill 3.3)

41. **The teacher has 30 minutes to assess 60 students. He or she can:**

    A. Have the whole group perform the test at once, hoping to catch the students who have not mastered the concept

    B. Break the students up into groups according to ability and grade them accordingly

    C. Break the students up into random pairs or very small groups and rotate the groups to be assessed

    D. Ask teachers to hold students late

Answer: C. Break the students up into random pairs or very small groups and rotate the groups to be assessed

All students should be seen and assessed fairly with no assumptions made about their abilities.

(Rigorous) (Skill 3.3)

42. In an independent fitness class, all of the students want to use the Fitness game, but only two students can use it at a time. A fair way to handle this is:

   A. First come, first serve

   B. Use it only on certain days

   C. Let only the strongest kids use it

   D. Have a sign-up system with time limitations

   Answer: D. Have a sign-up system with time limitations

   All students should have access to equipment, which may mean a sign-up system and schedule should be used for more popular pieces of equipment.

(Rigorous) (Skill 3.3)

43. Today's activity is dribbling the basketball while pivoting. Which is the best framework for that activity?

   A. Set up centers with different dribbling activities and let all students rotate around the centers

   B. Have a competitive game of basketball and whistle every time someone double dribbles

   C. Set up an obstacle course and let all the students try to dribble around it

   D. Set up centers, but require mastery of each one before moving on

Answer: A. Set up centers with different dribbling activities and let students rotate around the centers

All students should be able to try the centers on a day of introduction to a skill and new learning.

(Average) (Skill 3.4)

44. Any child who lives anywhere can:

   A. Run around outside

   B. Play baseball

   C. Skate

   D. Learn to dance

   Answer: D. Learn to dance

   Children do not need special equipment, a big yard, or a safe neighborhood to learn to dance.

(Average) (Skill 3.4)

45. Physical education lasts a lifetime when someone:

   A. Finds something they like

   B. Is at the top of the class

   C. Learns perfect form

   D. Loses weight

   Answer: A. Finds something they like

   Fun is the priority when creating a lifestyle of fitness and health.

(Easy) (Skill 3.5)

46. The girls' softball coach has noticed that her team does not have any local press for a winning season. She should:

   A. Create a press release highlighting their season

   B. Call the principal and ask why the football team gets all the attention

   C. Send out a mass email to the staff, comparing the girls' softball team to the football team

   D. Have a pizza party for the girls

Answer: A. Create a press release highlighting their season

Students should be recognized for what they do, and many times that requires the teacher to release the information. Please note that school districts have strict policies on sharing children's names on television or websites. Do not share student information online, and do not post anything without specific written permission per the school policy.

(Rigorous) (Skill 3.6)

47. The teacher notices a group of children are calling another child "Fatty." The teacher should:

   A. Call it out in front of the group

   B. Plan a meeting with the bullying students and the guidance counselor or other trusted campus administrators

   C. Call the parents immediately

   D. Let it go

Answer: B. Plan a meeting with the bullying students and the guidance counselor or other trusted campus administrators

Teachers have a responsibility to address bullying when it comes to their attention. Bullying must be addressed with sensitivity toward the bullied child.

(Average) (Skill 3.6)

48. An example of an intrinsic reward is:

   A. A sticker

   B. A good grade

   C. Release of endorphins

   D. Pain

Answer: C. Release of endorphins

Intrinsic means "from the inside." The release of endorphins (the "feel good" hormones) experienced during exercise can be considered an intrinsic reward because they come from within as a result of our own activities.

(Easy) (Skill 3.6)

49. A negative consequence could be:

   A. Sitting out a run

   B. Being benched for the next game

   C. Being sent to another classroom for a while

   D. No response from the teacher

Answer: B. Being benched for the next game

A negative consequence is a punishment for breaking a rule or procedure.

(Average) (Skill 4.1)

50. **A disapproving look toward students who are not focused on the task at hand is an example of:**

    A. Positive nonverbal communication

    B. Negative nonverbal communication

    C. Positive verbal communication

    D. Negative verbal communication

    Answer: B. Negative nonverbal communication

    Sometimes saying nothing gets the point across.

(Average) (Skill 4.2)

51. **An example of positive verbal communication with specificity would be:**

    A. "Great job on that handstand. You placed your hands exactly right and are even pointing your toes!"

    B. "That was good, but let's try again."

    C. "No, I don't like that. This time try harder."

    D. "Great job!"

    Answer: A. "Great job on that handstand. You placed your hands exactly right and are even your pointing toes!"

    Verbal communication is spoken, and specificity refers to sharing details. Sharing details helps students understand what it is they are doing right so that they can do it right again.

(Easy) (Skill 4.3)

52. **A procedure list for the classroom could include:**

    A. Rules for equipment usage

    B. Rules for dress

    C. Rules for character

    D. All of the above

    Answer: D. All of the above

    Procedures are a positive way to list rules and could include anything important to classroom management.

(Average) (Skill 4.3)

53. **Telling students, "You did a terrible job in today's game," is an example of:**

    A. Positive nonverbal communication

    B. Negative nonverbal communication

    C. Positive verbal communication

    D. Negative verbal communication

    Answer: D. Negative verbal communication

    Saying something negative is negative verbal communication.

(Average) (Skill 4.3)

54. **Telling a student, "What a great somersault!" is an example of:**

    A. Positive nonverbal communication

    B. Negative nonverbal communication

    C. Positive verbal communication

    D. Negative verbal communication

Answer: C. Positive verbal communication

Saying something nice is positive verbal communication.

(Average) (Skill 4.3)

55. **When handling a negative situation with students, it is best to:**

   A. Confront every situation head-on, immediately, and with vigor

   B. Take a step back and decide if the situation requires immediate verbal communication or intervention

   C. Embarrass students behaving badly so they won't do it again

   D. Handle every situation behind closed doors

Answer: B. Take a step back and decide if the situation requires immediate verbal communication or intervention

Every situation is different. Assess the situation before acting.

(Average) (Skill 4.3)

56. **To communicate behavior expectations visually, you can:**

   A. Demonstrate bad behaviors

   B. Tell the students what you expect

   C. Correct someone verbally

   D. Post procedures on the wall

Answer: D. Post procedures on the wall

Posting procedures helps remind visual learners of behavioral expectations.

(Average) (Skill 4.3)

57. **To communicate performance expectations kinesthetically, you can:**

   A. Have children practice the skill physically

   B. Have students sit down to watch a demonstration

   C. Tell students about someone who is doing a great job

   D. Give quick verbal assessments

Answer: A. Have children practice the skill physically

Sometimes physical practice is what students need to succeed, especially kinesthetic learners.

(Average) (Skill 4.3)

58. **To communicate performance expectations verbally, you can:**

   A. Run with the students

   B. Demonstrate the skill for them

   C. Give quick verbal cues as they are performing the skill

   D. Use proximity

Answer: C. Give quick verbal cues as they are performing the skill

Speak quickly and clearly to reinforce or correct performance of a skill.

(Average) (Skill 4.3)

59. **Use technology to correct form by:**

   A. Using a digital camera to record or take still shots and showing the students what they are doing and how to correct it

   B. Having the children watch a professional sport and comment on the athletes' skills

   C. Using a laser pointer to point out flaws

   D. Using a document camera to show a list of proper alignment techniques on the board

   Answer: A. Using a digital camera to record or take still shots and showing the students what they are doing and how to correct it

   Seeing one's own performance is a good way to self-correct a skill.

(Rigorous) (Skill 4.3)

60. **On your Facebook page, you post a video of a student you consider to be a star performing a skill. This could lead to:**

   A. The student and parents being proud that you have highlighted their child

   B. Your termination

   C. Raising your popularity with students when they see you have a Facebook page

   D. Getting calls from college recruiters about the student

Answer: B. Your termination

Any posting online of a student could get you fired. Online permission is necessary to post any pictures or videos of students. Even then, students' full names cannot be posted. Your personal pages are off-limits for student pictures and video.

(Average) (Skill 4.4)

61. **Good email etiquette includes which of the following:**

   A. Abbreviating sentences by dropping articles (a, the) so that they are fast and easy to read

   B. Composing the email as one continuous paragraph in order to shorten the overall length

   C. Using the same conventional abbreviations for words and phrases that are used in text messaging (lol, btw, etc.)

   D. None of the above

Answer: D. None of the above

In drafting professional emails, the teacher should write in the same manner as if they were composing a letter. This includes using complete sentences, paragraphs, proper grammar, and a signature line.

(Rigorous) (Skill 4.4)

62. **A colleague has made negative comments about your students' performances at this season's games. You should:**

   A. Tell school authorities

   B. Write a letter to the papers

   C. Send out a mass email defending your character and that of your students

   D. Communicate professionally, one-on-one with the colleague

Answer: D. Communicate professionally, one-on-one with the colleague

Professional communication includes communicating directly and discreetly with colleagues.

(Rigorous) (Skill 4.4)

63. You get a text message from a parent that she is pulling her child off your team because her child came home crying from last night's game. You should:

A. Ignore it

B. Immediately call the parent and ask about the situation

C. Text her back and say "OK"

D. Forward her text to the principal

Answer: B. Immediately call the parent and ask about the situation

Sometimes technology does not facilitate communication as fully as a direct conversation would.

(Rigorous) (Skill 4.4)

64. When sending an email to an administrator, you should:

A. Be quick about the details, but use correct grammar and appropriate language

B. Send it in shorthand because she doesn't have time for your details

C. Make it as detailed as possible

D. Use the *MLA Handbook*

Answer: A. Be quick about the details, but use correct grammar and appropriate language

Consider not only what details need to be shared, but the way it is presented. Shorthand and poor grammar are not appropriate in the professional workplace.

(Average) (Skill 4.4)

65. You get a text message from a colleague that is inappropriate. You should:

A. Text him back "LOL"

B. Text him back "No thanks"

C. Text him back "Take me off your text list"

D. Call him or see him face to face to address it

Answer: D. Call him or see him face to face to address it

Do not encourage poor behavior using technology, and do not text him back. Address the issue to the person directly so that he knows not to send you negative or inappropriate texts.

(Rigorous) (Skill 4.4)

66. The teacher is writing a discipline referral for a child who pulled a chair out from under another child today. Which detail can the referral list?

A. The student pulled a chair out from under another student, who was sitting down at the time

B. The student bullied another student

C. The student acted out of spite

D. All of the above

Answer: A. The student pulled a chair out from another student, who was sitting down at the time

A discipline referral should include facts only.

(Average) (Skill 4.4)

67. For a parent–teacher conference, you should:

   A. Bring photographs

   B. Come with an open mind

   C. Bring data, such as assessments and discipline referrals

   D. Bring a list of websites the parent should see

   Answer: C. Bring data, such as assessments and discipline referrals

   Bring any assessments or other written material that can help the student and parent see grades or behavioral problems.

Planning, Instruction, and Student Assessment

(Easy) (Skill 5.1)

68. Which of the following is a locomotor skill?

   A. Running

   B. A bridge

   C. Throwing a ball

   D. Writing

   Answer: A. Running

   Locomotor skills are skills that involve movement from one place to another.

(Easy) (Skill 5.1)

69. Which of the following is a non-locomotor skill?

   A. Running

   B. A bridge

   C. Throwing a ball

   D. Writing

   Answer: B. A bridge

   A movement that does not require propulsion forward or backward is non-locomotor, such as many movements in Pilates and yoga.

(Easy) (Skill 5.1)

70. Which of the following is a manipulative skill?

   A. Running

   B. A bridge

   C. Throwing a ball

   D. Writing

   Answer: C. Throwing a ball

   Manipulative skills include movement of a piece of equipment.

(Rigorous) (Skill 5.1)

71. A student with high ability and low self-esteem can increase self-esteem through:

   A. Psychological intervention

   B. Being in an aesthetically pleasing environment

   C. Being given a part on the team at which he can excel

   D. Being assessed

Answer: C. Being given a part on the team at which he can excel

A student can see his or her own success through the sociology of sports and games.

(Average) (Skill 5.2)
72. **A student having trouble with locomotor skills might need:**

A. Practice in different ways, such as new directions or heights, using the same skill

B. Repetition

C. Remediation

D. Intervention

Answer: A. Practice in different ways, such as new directions or heights, using the same skill

Students may need to feel the skill through other directions or avenues. A new view of the same problem may create a new solution for a challenged child.

(Rigorous) (Skill 5.2)
73. **In a boxing class, how would the teacher use sequencing in teaching a jab-punch combination?**

A. Repetition

B. Using flexibility

C. Practicing similar combinations

D. Practicing the sequence of events slowly

Answer: D. Practicing the sequence of events slowly

When using a sequence, breaking it down into individual movements helps teach correct form.

(Average) (Skill 5.3)
74. **Feedback for a student who is behind on a skill should be:**

A. Rigorous

B. Light-handed

C. Constant

D. Informative

Answer: B. Light-handed

Feedback should be quick, direct, and helpful, not lengthy and discouraging.

(Rigorous) (Skill 5.4)
75. **Competitive games are useful in PE classes when:**

A. Students are practicing a skill and are feeling successful

B. You want to find the best athlete of the group

C. You need to individually assess the students

D. Students are bullying each other

Answer: A. Students are practicing a skill and are feeling successful

Healthy competition applies skill to something real. The analysis of a learned behavior comes from using the behavior in a real circumstance, such as a competitive game.

(Average) (Skill 5.5)

76. The national legislature has gotten involved in physical education through:

A. Equality legislation for genders and special education

B. Nationally mandating physical education in every grade level at every public school

C. Funding a national physical education program

D. Raising the physical education requirements for advanced high school students

Answer: A. Equality legislation for genders and special education

The only mandates by federal law are regulation of standards for genders and special education students.

(Average) (Skill 5.5)

77. State legislatures have passed mandates for physical education because of the sudden rise in:

A. Bullying

B. Female population

C. Special populations

D. Overweight children and type II diabetes

Answer: D. Overweight children and type II diabetes

The increase of overweight and obese students, as well as a rapidly growing number of kids with type II diabetes, has caused state legislatures to mandate new laws in hopes of decreasing mortality and disease.

(Average) (Skill 5.5)

78. The new National Standards for Health and Fitness Education are based on the overall goal that all students:

A. Will be athletes

B. Will lead healthy lifestyles

C. Will change their neighborhoods

D. Will love exercise

Answer: B. Will lead healthy lifestyles

The goal of modern fitness education is to help students make choices that lead to healthier lives.

(Average) (Skill 5.6)

79. Creating new goals requires taking an honest look at:

A. Last year's assessments

B. Last year's goals

C. This year's new requirements

D. All of the above

Answer: D. All of the above

It takes assessment of old assessments and goals, as well as of new requirements, in order to start making new goals.

(Rigorous) (Skill 5.6)

80. **A physical education teacher has the goal of teaching all her students to play volleyball. She has 60 students at a time and one volleyball court and net. The problem with her goal is:**

   A. She does not have the funding for another net

   B. She does not have the time in a 30-minute class period

   C. The ratio of kids per court will not allow productivity in practicing the game

   D. Her students are not tall enough

   Answer: C. The ratio of kids per court will not allow productivity in practicing the game

   She cannot have all 60 kids practice, so it will not be practical to keep all 60 kids actively involved in learning the game.

(Average) (Skill 5.9)

81. **A floor ladder is:**

   A. Kinesthetic equipment

   B. Audial equipment

   C. Visual equipment

   D. Special education equipment

   Answer: A. Kinesthetic equipment

   Kinesthetic equipment is equipment used to challenge someone physically when practicing a skill.

(Rigorous) (Skill 5.10)

82. **When teaching a 3-point jump, the teacher could start by:**

   A. Reviewing how to run

   B. Reviewing how to leap

   C. Reviewing how to mark the final jump

   D. Attaching a kinesthetic piece of practice equipment to the student

   Answer: B. Reviewing how to leap

   Link the new skill to an old one, like a movement in the final skill that links back to a locomotor skill learned previously.

(Average) (Skill 5.11)

83. **The EAP for the school should be:**

   A. Located by the front office

   B. Located in the coach's office

   C. Easily accessed

   D. In a file, hidden from students

   Answer: C. Easily accessed

   The emergency action plan must be easily accessible in case of emergency.

(Rigorous) (Skill 5.11)

84. A student falls on the floor suddenly and is unconscious. An AED is nearby. The teacher is not AED or CPR certified. What should the teacher do?

   A. Call for help and wait

   B. Tell someone close by to call 911 and wait

   C. Tell someone to call 911, pull out the AED, and follow the directions

   D. Tell someone close by to call 911, have the AED ready for someone else to use, and begin CPR

Answer: C. Tell someone to call 911, pull out the AED, and follow the directions

If an AED is nearby, someone should use it. If that person is not trained, the AED instructions will instruct the user exactly what to do, and the machine will only administer a shock if one is necessary.

(Easy) (Skill 5.11)

85. The RICE acronym for treating sports injuries stands for rest, ice, compression, and:

   A. Education

   B. Emulation

   C. Emanation

   D. Elevation

Answer: D. Elevation

Elevation of the injured body part above the level of the heart reduces swelling around it.

(Rigorous) (Skill 5.11)

86. A student did not eat lunch and is now shaking and behaving erratically. The teacher should assume the student has _____ and should contact the nurse.

   A. hypoglycemia

   B. hyperglycemia

   C. Type I Diabetes

   D. anorexia nervosa

Answer: A. Hypoglycemia

A person with hypoglycemia can have erratic behavior when the body needs sugar.

(Rigorous) (Skill 5.11)

87. A student practicing outside takes off his helmet and staggers around. He is red in the face and soaked from sweat. He may be:

   A. Sick

   B. Tired

   C. Dehydrated

   D. Hungry

Answer: C. Dehydrated

The child may need water or may be overheated.

(Rigorous) (Skill 5.11)

88. The above student should be:

   A. Brought inside

   B. Given fluids

   C. Referred to a doctor or the hospital

   D. All of the above

Answer: D. All of the above

Signs of dehydration and overheating should not be ignored. Both conditions can lead to organ damage and death.

(Average) (Skill 5.11)

89. **The new CPR:**

    A. Teaches rescue breathing first

    B. Teaches calling for help instead of immediate help

    C. Teaches compressions first

    D. Teaches that only CPR-certified people should act in an emergency

Answer: C. Teaches compressions first

The American Heart Association believes that compressions administered as soon as possible will save more lives, so the new CPR calls for quick intervention with compressions, even by uncertified individuals.

(Average) (Skill 5.11)

90. **In an open body of water, a teacher gets caught in the current. He or she should:**

    A. Swim parallel to the shore

    B. Call for help

    C. Swim toward the shore

    D. Swim out farther into the sea

Answer: A. Swim parallel to the shore

Currents will pull any person out to sea if that person stays in the current, so the person should swim parallel to the shore. Students should also be trained to do this in case they encounter a current.

(Average) (Skill 6.1)

91. **Comparing students in a perceived scale of competency is a:**

    A. Chart

    B. Rating scale

    C. Graph

    D. Journal

Answer: B. Rating scale

A rating scale is usually not the best assessment, because it is highly subjective.

(Rigorous) (Skill 6.1)

92. **A teacher wants to show a comparison of each student's softball pitches. Each student has had 10 pitches. She could use a:**

    A. Pie graph

    B. Rating scale

    C. Line graph

    D. Chart

Answer: C. Line graph

A line graph can show many different stages of development for several players at once.

(Rigorous) (Skill 6.2)

93. **A portfolio can show more _____ than typical assessments.**

    A. skills

    B. data

    C. opinions

    D. development over time

Answer: D. development over time

Portfolios are designed to follow a student over time. They will show data for the student over the course of the class, semester, year, or several years.

(Average) (Skill 6.3)

94. **National student assessments, such as the President's Challenge and Cooper's Fitnessgram, are a positive way to:**

    A. Give students research-based information

    B. Motivate students

    C. Keep assessment data over time

    D. All of the above

    Answer: D. All of the above

    All of these assessments educate the students and families, motivate the students, and keep data for comparison.

(Average) (Skill 6.4)

95. **A tennis match would be which kind of assessment?**

    A. Baseline

    B. Formative

    C. Authentic

    D. Standardized

    Answer: C. Authentic

    A real game or match is an assessment that includes using all of the previous lessons and analyzing them for performance in competition.

(Average) (Skill 6.4)

96. **A multiple choice test is a:**

    A. Non-criterion referenced test

    B. Rubic

    C. Criterion-referenced test

    D. Authentic assessment

    Answer: C. Criterion-referenced test

    Criterion-referenced tests assess the student based on a list of criteria or standards to be learned.

(Rigorous) (Skill 6.9)

97. **A 504 plan gives a student the right to:**

    A. A fair education, regardless of disabilities

    B. An IEP

    C. The same education as everyone else

    D. Play on a sports team

    Answer: A. A fair education, regardless of disabilities

    A 504 plan gives a student the right to a fair education, which may be different for each child with a 504.

Collaboration, Reflection, and Technology

(Rigorous) (Skill 7.1)

98. **Sports games can teach:**

    A. Science of summation of forces

    B. Sportsmanship

    C. Equations

    D. First aid and CPR

Answer: B. Sportsmanship

Though games can, in theory, teach many mathematical equations and scientific theories, students will most likely get the lesson of sportsmanship or character.

(Rigorous) (Skill 7.2)

99. The next class unit is about immunity and the endocrine system. The teacher could consult which other teacher for cross-curricular study?

A. Math

B. English

C. Science

D. Social studies

Answer: C. Science

The endocrine system, or hormonal balance, is a study of body systems, or human biology.

(Average) (Skill 7.2)

100. Another unit intended for study is sports and games from different cultures. The teacher could also see the curriculum of which class for more information?

A. Math

B. English

C. Science

D. Social studies

Answer: D. Social studies

Anthropology or culture would be included in the social studies curriculum.

(Easy) (Skill 7.2)

101. Which of the following subject areas can be integrated into physical education instruction?

A. Anatomy, study of forces, biology, and nutrition

B. Statistics, graphs, charts, and ratios

C. History of sports or activities, such as the Olympics

D. All of the above

Answer: D. All of the above

Knowledge and skills from science, mathematics, and social studies can be effectively integrated into physical education instruction. Coordinate with fellow teachers when building cross-curricular instructional programs.

(Average) (Skill 7.4)

102. Physical education teachers can send information home about community walks, races, or other volunteer community events in order to:

A. Raise parental awareness about fitness-related opportunities outside of the classroom

B. Raise parental awareness about the importance of community involvement

C. Raise parental awareness about the active role of the PE department

D. None of the above

Answer: A. Raise parental awareness about fitness-related opportunities outside of the classroom

Physical education teachers can be important parental resources for information about community opportunities related to fitness. In addition to facilitating community events, the PE teacher can send information home about local resources such as parks and recreation events and resources.

(Rigorous) (Skill 7.4)

103. The PE teacher has heard great things about a local dance studio. She should:

    A. Talk about the dance studio to classes

    B. Send home flyers from the one dance studio

    C. Contact many dance studios to request information for students

    D. Post the dance studio information on the school website

Answer: C. Contact many dance studios to request information for students

To be fair to local businesses and to avoid a lawsuit, teachers should request information from several local businesses and distribute information from studios interested in the school promotion.

(Rigorous) (Skill 7.4)

104. To provide students with many choices for physical activities outside of school, the teacher can:

    A. Stay after school daily to let the kids play in the gym

    B. Advertise with a local business that targets children

    C. Take students on a field trip to a baseball game

    D. Present information from the city parks and recreation department

Answer: D. Present information from the city parks and recreation department

City and local parks and recreation departments are in the business of affordable recreation for kids, and this is an appropriate business to discuss with students.

Directions: Questions 105–108. Use the following situation and apply it to the reflective cycle.

A teacher has a lesson plan to teach the skills of a great new dance that was popularized by a song on the radio. When the teacher started class, the kids refused to try the dance moves. The teacher tried to inspire them, only for the children to ignore the teacher and then go on to something else. The teacher was left to scramble for a second plan because he felt his plan was rejected by the class.

(Rigorous) (Skill 8.1)

105. The decision aspect is:

A. The decision to scrap the dance and go on to something else

B. The decision to teach the dance moves

C. The decision to let the children choose to participate or not

D. The decision to give the students a zero for the day

Answer: B. The decision to teach the dance moves

The decision phase is the initial phase of the lesson: the idea.

(Rigorous) (Skill 8.1)

106. If an administrator had walked in to observe, the evaluation would be:

A. That the initial plan failed

B. That the kids were having a good time

C. That the original plan was disorganized

D. That the teacher cannot teach well

Answer: A. That the initial plan failed

The failure of the initial plan is the teacher's failure, so the next evaluation would depend on how the teacher turns the lesson around to something that works.

(Rigorous) (Skill 8.1)

107. Later, the teacher analyzes the lesson and concludes that:

A. He is a failure as a teacher

B. He should never teach music again

C. He should start with something the students can already do, and then work from there

D. He should scrap a bad lesson plan and let the kids play if he fails to get his lesson across

Answer: C. He should start with something the students can already do, and then work from there

Starting with success yields a higher rate of confidence, thereby encouraging students to try to succeed in the next lesson.

(Average) (Skill 8.1)

108. The new action plan leads to the:

A. New feelings about the action plan

B. New description for a new lesson

C. New conclusion of the new lesson

D. Evaluation of the new lesson

Answer: B. New description for a new lesson

The action plan leads directly back to the description of the new plan.

(Easy) (Skill 8.2)

109. **NASPE is the certifying agency for:**

A. Professional physical education teachers

B. Personal trainers

C. Weight management trainers

D. Equipment advice

Answer: A. Professional physical education teachers

NASPE is an agency for professionals in the field of physical education.

(Average) (Skill 8.2)

110. **ACE is:**

A. A hardware company

B. A research agency for fitness

C. Equipment safety regulations

D. National requirements for fitness

Answer: B. A research agency for fitness

ACE is responsible for a lot of research in modern exercise science, and helps teachers with information on overall fitness and youth fitness.

(Average) (Skill 8.2)

111. **ACSM is the:**

A. Accreditation for many other fitness companies and is the litmus test for professional fitness organizations

B. Scientific information for health class

C. Council for sports medications

D. Constitution for sports teachers

Answer: A. Accreditation for many other fitness companies and is the litmus test for professional fitness organizations

ACSM defines many of the accreditation standards for other fitness organizations.

(Easy) (Skill 8.2)

112. **Cooper's Institute is known to be a:**

A. Leader in alternative medicine

B. Leader in assessment

C. Leader in health and fitness education

D. Leader in state standards for education

Answer: C. Leader in health and fitness education

Cooper's Institute sets the standards for health and fitness education and has redefined much of the health and fitness education for youth.

(Average) (Skill 9.1)

113. **When using technology in fitness education:**

A. The more the better

B. There are only a couple of resources

C. You shouldn't trust anything

D. There is a lot of information, but sources should be checked for credibility

Answer: D. There is a lot of information, but sources should be checked for credibility

There is a lot of true information and a lot of false information in the fitness and health industry. Teachers should quantify anything they use by researching it first.

(Average) (Skill 9.1)

114. When using technology in the classroom:

A. Use sources for demonstration only

B. Use sources that allow kinesthetic practice only

C. Use a variety of sources, but use time management and judgment in usage

D. Technology is not necessary in the PE environment.

Answer: C. Use a variety of sources, but use time management and judgment in usage

There is a lot of information available, but a balance of technology and real-feel movement is important.

(Rigorous) (Skill 9.1)

115. Many new gaming systems use gross motor skills instead of fine motor skills. What would be a good game to use for the best form of aerobic exercise?

A. A dance game with foot placement requirements

B. A racing game with a steering wheel

C. A musical game with instruments

D. A trivia game

Answer: A. A dance game with foot placement requirements

A dancing game would require foot placement and sometimes even arm placement, raising the heart rate and creating aerobic exercise.

(Average) (Skill 9.1)

116. A teacher wants to keep track of students' health habits. She could require:

A. An upload on a mobile phone

B. A daily email of students' activities outside of school

C. Each student to join her team on *www.peertrainer.com*

D. Each student to take daily measurements

Answer: C. Each student to join her team on *www.peertrainer.com*

Peertrainer or similar systems allow students to journal daily food, exercise, and feelings. The teacher and team members can check up on the students daily.

(Average) (Skill 9.2)

117. A teacher wants to create an online interaction with students that is direct and immediate. She could create a:

A. Blog

B. Wiki

C. .com site

D. Poster

Answer: B. Wiki

A wiki gives members control of the content and can allow students to upload information, ideas, questions, and their own research.

(Average) (Skill 9.2)

118. **A teacher wants to share her exercise videos with others. She should use a:**

    A. Blog

    B. Wiki

    C. .com site

    D. Vlog or podcast

    Answer: D. Vlog or podcast

    Vlogs and podcasts allows people to upload and send out videos and audial recordings.

(Average) (Skill 9.2)

119. **A teacher wants to share her own story. She should use a:**

    A. Blog

    B. Wiki

    C. .com site

    D. Podcast

    Answer: A. Blog

    A blog is an online journal of opinions and personal experiences.

(Average) (Skill 9.2)

120. **A teacher blog or vlog should never include:**

    A. Personal stories

    B. Student names or information

    C. Scientific research

    D. Opinions

    Answer: B. Student names or information

    Student information, names, or any implication of any student would be unacceptable in any practice on the Internet. Teachers should also refrain from giving away personal information, such as addresses and phone numbers, and should use a code of caution when discussing personal stories.

Endnotes

1. Dorgo, S., King, GA., Candelaria, NG., Bader, JO., Brickey, GD., and Adams, CE. Effects of manual resistance training on fitness in adolescents. *J Strength Cond Res* 23(8): 2287–2294, 2009.

2. 2008 Physical Activity Guidelines for Americans, Physical Activity Guidelines Advisory Committee, Michael O. Leavitt, September 2008. *http://www.health.gov/paguidelines/guidelines /chapter3.aspx*.

3. National Association for Sport and Physical Education, Moving into the Future: National Standards of Physical Education, Second Edition, 2008. *http://www.aahperd.org/naspe/standards /nationalStandards/PEstandards.cfm*.

4. The "QPE" as listed on the NASPE website, 2010. *http://www.aahperd.org/naspe/publications /teachingTools/QualityPE.cfm*.

5. *http://law.onecle.com/texas/education/28.002.00.html*, law last modified 2007, Texas State Legislature.

6. Pellman, E., et. al. "Concussion in Professional Football *Neurosurgery*. Vol 58: 2, 263–274.

7. *www.astm.org*

8. *www.stopbullying.now.hrsa.gov*

Sources

National Institute of Health
http://www.nlm.nih.gov/medlineplus/exerciseandphysicalfitness.html

Government Standards on Children's Health
www.kidshealth.org
www.mypyramid.gov

American Council on Exercise
http://www.acefitness.org/getfit/research.aspx

Mayo Clinic
www.mayoclinic.com

President's Council on Fitness
www.fitness.gov

Federal Government Resources on Physical Fitness and Special Education
http://www.fitness.gov/resources-and-grants/related-links/barriers_ncpadfinal.pdf

Federal Government Guidelines for Fitness
http://www.health.gov/paguidelines/

Physical Education National Standards
http://www.aahperd.org/naspe/standards/nationalStandards/PEstandards.cfm

National Guidelines: Components of Physical Education
http://www.aahperd.org/naspe/publications/teachingTools/QualityPE.cfm

CDC BAM
http://www.bam.gov/sub_physicalactivity/index.html

ACSM research database
http://www.acsm.org/AM/Template.cfm?Section=Home_Page&Template=/CM/HTMLDisplay.cfm&ContentID=6117

Physical Education State Guidelines
http://www.aahperd.org/naspe/standards/stateStandards/

Cooper Institute Youth Initiative
http://www.cooperinstitute.org/ourkidshealth/index.cfm

Stand Up and Eat
http://www.standupandeat.org/index.aspx?id=library

Let's Move First Lady initiative for movement in school
http://www.aahperd.org/naspe/advocacy/letsmoveinschool/cspap.cfm

Equipment Standards
http://www.astm.org/SNEWS/NOVEMBER_2004/voris_nov04.html

BONUS
SAMPLE TEST

**To provide you with even more value, we're including a
free BONUS sample test with this guide.**

 The extra Praxis Physical Education 091 test will help you practice
for the real exam with state-aligned questions.
XAMonline: dedicated to helping you succeed the first time.

BONUS Sample Test

Content Knowledge and Student Growth and Development

(Average) (Skill 1.1)

1. The ability for a muscle(s) to repeatedly contract over a period of time is:

    A. Cardiovascular endurance

    B. Muscle endurance

    C. Muscle strength

    D. Muscle force

(Rigorous) (Skill 1.1)

2. A 17-year-old male has a body fat composition of 20%. Which is the best interpretation of his obesity level?

    A. Obese

    B. Overweight

    C. Normal

    D. Underweight

(Rigorous) (Skill 1.1)

3. What is the name of the main chest muscle?

    A. Pectoralis major

    B. Latissimus Dorsi

    C. Deltoids

    D. Rectus Abdominis

(Easy) (Skill 1.1)

4. Which of the following are muscles of the leg?

    A. Hamstrings, gluteus maximus, triceps brachii, rectus abdominis

    B. Quadriceps, gastrocnemius, biceps brachii, hamstrings

    C. Quadriceps, hamstrings, gastrocnemius, gluteus maximus

    D. Pectoralis major, latissimus dorsi, triceps brachii

(Rigorous) (Skill 1.3)

5. There are two sequential phases to the development of spatial awareness. What is the order of these phases?

    A. Locating more than one object in relation to each other; locating objects in relation to one's own body in space

    B. Locating an object in relation to ones' own body in space; locating more than one object in relation to one's own body

    C. Locating more than one object independent of one's body; locating objects in relation to one's own body

    D. Locating objects in relation to one's own body in space; locating more than one object in relation to each other and independent of one's own body

(Rigorous) (Skill 1.3)

6. Students that paddle balls against a wall or jump over objects with various heights are demonstrating which quality of movement?

    A. Balance

    B. Time

    C. Force

    D. Inertia

(Rigorous) (Skill 1.3)

7. Which movement concept involves students making decisions about an object's positional changes in space?

    A. Spatial awareness

    B. Effort awareness

    C. Body awareness

    D. Motion awareness

(Rigorous) (Skill 1.3)

8. Applying the mechanical principles of balance, time, and force describes which movement concept?

    A. Spatial awareness

    B. Effort awareness

    C. Body awareness

    D. Motion awareness

(Average) (Skill 1.3)

9. Having students move on their hands and knees, move on lines, and/or hold shapes while moving develops which quality of movement?

    A. Balance

    B. Time

    C. Force

    D. Inertia

(Average) (Skill 1.3)

10. Playing "Simon Says" and having students touch different body parts applies which movement concept?

    A. Spatial awareness

    B. Effort awareness

    C. Body awareness

    D. Motion awareness

(Average) (Skill 1.3)

11. Having students move in a specific pattern while measuring how long they take to do so develops which quality of movement?

    A. Balance

    B. Time

    C. Force

    D. Inertia

(Rigorous) (Skill 1.4)

12. Aerobic dance develops or improves each of the following skills or health components except:

    A. Cardio-respiratory function

    B. Body composition

    C. Coordination

    D. Flexibility

(Rigorous) (Skill 1.4)

13. Rowing develops which health- or skill-related component of fitness?

    A. Muscle endurance

    B. Flexibility

    C. Balance

    D. Reaction time

(Average) (Skill 1.4)

14. Calisthenics develops all of the following health- and skill-related components of fitness except:

    A. Muscle strength

    B. Body composition

    C. Power

    D. Agility

(Average) (Skill 1.4)

15. **Which health- or skill-related component of fitness is developed by rope jumping?**

    A. Muscle force

    B. Coordination

    C. Flexibility

    D. Muscle strength

(Rigorous) (Skill 1.4)

16. **Working at a level that is above normal is which exercise training principle?**

    A. Intensity

    B. Progression

    C. Specificity

    D. Overload

(Rigorous) (Skill 1.4)

17. **Students on a running program to improve cardio-respiratory fitness apply which exercise principle?**

    A. Aerobic

    B. Progression

    C. Specificity

    D. Overload

(Average) (Skill 1.4)

18. **Adding more repetitions to a weightlifting set applies which exercise principle?**

    A. Anaerobic

    B. Progression

    C. Overload

    D. Specificity

(Rigorous) (Skill 1.4)

19. **Which of the following does not modify overload?**

    A. Frequency

    B. Perceived exertion

    C. Time

    D. Intensity

(Rigorous) (Skill 1.4)

20. **Overloading for muscle strength includes all of the following except:**

    A. Lifting heart rate to an intense level

    B. Lifting weights every other day

    C. Lifting with high resistance and low reps

    D. Lifting 60% to 90% of assessed muscle strength

(Rigorous) (Skill 1.4)

21. **Which of the following applies the concept of progression?**

    A. Beginning a stretching program every day

    B. Beginning a stretching program with 3 sets of reps

    C. Beginning a stretching program with ballistic stretching

    D. Beginning a stretching program holding stretches for 15 seconds and working up to holding stretches for 60 seconds

(Rigorous) (Skill 1.4)

22. Which of following overload principles does not apply to improving body composition?

    A. Aerobic exercise three times per week

    B. Aerobic exercise at a low intensity

    C. Aerobic exercise for about an hour

    D. Aerobic exercise with intervals of high intensity

(Average) (Skill 1.4)

23. The ability to change the direction of the body rapidly is:

    A. Coordination

    B. Reaction time

    C. Speed

    D. Agility

(Rigorous) (Skill 1.4)

24. Students are performing the vertical jump. What component of fitness does this activity assess?

    A. Muscle strength

    B. Balance

    C. Power

    D. Muscle endurance

(Rigorous) (Skill 1.4)

25. Using the Karvonean Formula, compute the 60% − 80% THR for a 16-year-old student with a RHR of 60.

    A. 122–163 beats per minute

    B. 130–168 beats per minute

    C. 142–170 beats per minute

    D. 146–175 beats per minute

(Rigorous) (Skill 1.4)

26. Using Cooper's Formula, compute the THR for a 15-year-old student.

    A. 120–153 beats per minute

    B. 123–164 beats per minute

    C. 135–169 beats per minute

    D. 147–176 beats per minute

(Rigorous) (Skill 1.4)

27. Activities to specifically develop cardio-vascular fitness must be:

    A. Performed without developing an oxygen debt

    B. Performed twice daily

    C. Performed every day

    D. Performed for a minimum of 10 minutes

(Average) (Skill 1.6)

28. Which professional organization protects amateur sports from corruption?

    A. AIWA

    B. AAHPERD

    C. NCAA

    D. AAU

(Rigorous) (Skill 1.6)

29. The physical education philosophy that is based on experience is:

    A. Naturalism

    B. Pragmatism

    C. Idealism

    D. Existentialism

(Rigorous) (Skill 1.6)

30. **Idealism is the belief that:**

    A. The laws of nature are ideal

    B. Experience is the key

    C. Practice, practice, practice

    D. The mind is developed through acquisition of knowledge

(Easy) (Skill 1.6)

31. **Which of the following countries did not greatly influence the early development of P.E. in the United States?**

    A. Germany

    B. England

    C. Norway

    D. Sweden

(Average) (Skill 1.6)

32. **What was the first state in the U.S. to require P.E. in its public schools?**

    A. Florida

    B. Massachusetts

    C. New York

    D. California

(Average) (Skill 1.6)

33. **President Eisenhower was alerted to the poor fitness levels of American youths. How was the poor physical conditioning of youths discovered in the Eisenhower Administration?**

    A. By WWII Selective Service Examination

    B. By organizations promoting physical fitness

    C. By the Federal Security Agency

    D. By the Kraus-Weber test

(Rigorous) (Skill 1.6)

34. **In 1956, the AAHPERD Fitness Conferences established:**

    A. The President's Council on Youth Fitness

    B. The President's Citizens' Advisory Committee

    C. The President's Council on Physical Fitness

    D. A and B

(Average) (Skill 1.6)

35. **The Round Hill School (a private school) in Massachusetts was the first school to require P.E. in its curriculum. What year was this?**

    A. 1792

    B. 1823

    C. 1902

    D. 1806

(Average) (Skill 1.6)

36. **What year did California enact a law requiring all public schools to include physical education in its curriculum?**

    A. 1892

    B. 1866

    C. 1901

    D. 1899

(Easy) (Skill 1.6)

37. **Title IX ensured that:**

    A. Boys play baseball while girls play softball

    B. Girls are ensured the same educational and athletic opportunities as boys

    C. Girls and boys have coed physical education classes

    D. All students must dress up for physical education class

(Rigorous) (Skill 1.6)

38. **The affective domain of physical education contributes to all of the following except:**

    A. Knowledge of exercise, health, and disease

    B. Self-actualization

    C. An appreciation of beauty

    D. Good sportsmanship

(Easy) (Skill 1.7)

39. **Two opposing soccer players are trying to gain control of the ball when one player "knees" the other. What is the ruling?**

    A. Direct free kick

    B. Indirect free kick

    C. Fair play

    D. Ejection from a game

(Easy) (Skill 1.7)

40. **A basketball team has an outstanding rebounder. In order to keep this player near the opponent's basket, which strategy should the coach implement?**

    A. Pick-and-roll

    B. Give-and-go

    C. Zone defense

    D. Free-lancing

(Rigorous) (Skill 1.7)

41. **When a defensive tennis player needs more time to return to his position, what strategy should he apply?**

    A. Drop shot

    B. Dink shot

    C. Lob shot

    D. Down-the-line shot

(Average) (Skill 1.7)

42. **A basketball maneuver when an offensive player passes to a teammate and then immediately cuts in toward the basket for a return pass is:**

    A. Charging

    B. Pick

    C. Give-and-go

    D. Switching

(Average) (Skill 1.7)

43. **A soccer pass from the outside of the field near the end line to a position in front of the goal is called:**

    A. Chip

    B. Settle

    C. Through

    D. Cross

(Average) (Skill 1.7)

44. A volleyball that is simultaneously contacted above the net by opponents and momentarily held upon contact is called a(n):

A. Double fault

B. Play over

C. Overlap

D. Held ball

(Average) (Skill 1.7)

45. Volleyball player LB on team A digs a spiked ball. The ball deflects off LB's shoulder. What is the ruling?

A. Fault

B. Legal hit

C. Double foul

D. Play over

(Average) (Skill 1.8)

46. Which of the following pieces of exercise equipment best applies the physiological principles?

A. Rolling machine

B. Electrical muscle stimulator

C. Stationary bicycle

D. Motor-driven rowing machine

(Average) (Skill 1.8)

47. A physical education instructor anticipates and prevents potential injuries, watches for hidden injuries, and takes an injury evaluation of the entire class. Which of the following strategies to prevent injuries is the teacher demonstrating?

A. Maintaining high standards

B. Proper use of equipment

C. Proper procedures for emergencies

D. Participant screening

(Rigorous) (Skill 1.8)

48. Although Mary is a paraplegic, she wants to participate in some capacity in the physical education class. What federal legislative act entitles her to do so?

A. PE 94-142

B. Title IX

C. PL 94-142

D. Title XI

(Easy) (Skill 2.1)

49. Why is it important for physical education instructors to understand physical development in children and adolescents?

A. It helps the instructor to identify early or late maturing individuals

B. Varying levels of development can affect participation in physical activity

C. To better form teams in coeducational classes that accommodate the needs of both genders' changing maturities

D. All of the above

(Rigorous) (Skill 2.2)

50. An instructor used a similar movement from a skill learned in a different activity to teach a skill for a new activity. The technique used to facilitate cognitive learning was:

    A. Conceptual thinking

    B. Transfer of learning

    C. Longer instruction

    D. Appropriate language

(Rigorous) (Skill 2.2)

51. A teacher rewards students for completing tasks. Which method is the teacher using to facilitate psychomotor learning?

    A. Task/reciprocal

    B. Command/direct

    C. Contingency/contract

    D. Physical/reflex

(Average) (Skill 2.2)

52. Teaching methods that facilitate cognitive learning include:

    A. Problem solving, conceptual theory, and guided inquiry

    B. Teacher-centered instruction and progress monitoring

    C. Skill demonstration and learning stations

    D. Instruction, practice, and reward

Management, Motivation, and Communication

(Easy) (Skill 3.1)

53. Which of the following is not a class-management technique?

    A. Explaining procedures for roll call, excuses, and tardiness

    B. Explaining routines for changing and showering

    C. Explaining conditioning

    D. Promoting individual self-discipline

(Average) (Skill 3.1)

54. Which of the following represent the most important element(s) of effective classroom management?

    A. Reminding students of classroom rules and procedures throughout the school year

    B. Fairness and consistency

    C. Addressing negative behaviors first and positive behaviors second

    D. Knowing all of your students by name so they all know they are important to you

(Rigorous) (Skill 3.2)

55. Through physical activities, John has developed self-discipline, fairness, respect for others, and new friends. John has demonstrated which of the following?

   A. Positive cooperation psycho-social influences

   B. Positive group psycho-social influences

   C. Positive individual psycho-social influences

   D. Positive accomplishment psycho-social influences

(Easy) (Skill 3.2)

56. Social skills and values developed by group activity include all of the following except:

   A. Winning at all costs

   B. Making judgments in groups

   C. Communicating and cooperating

   D. Respecting rules and property

(Rigorous) (Skill 3.2)

57. Which of the following psycho-social influences is not considered negative?

   A. Avoidance of problems

   B. Adherence to exercise

   C. Ego-centeredness

   D. Role conflict

(Average) (Skill 3.2)

58. What is the difference between anorexia nervosa and bulimia?

   A. Individuals with bulimia try to abstain from eating. Individuals with anorexia nervosa eat but then purge by inducing themselves to vomit or by taking laxatives.

   B. Individuals with anorexia nervosa try to abstain from eating. Individuals with bulimia eat but then purge by inducing themselves to vomit or by taking laxatives.

   C. There is no difference. Anorexia nervosa and bulimia are two different scientific names for the same disorder.

   D. Anorexia nervosa is a disorder of the nervous system whereas bulimia is a disorder of the digestive system.

(Average) (Skill 3.3)

59. Effective and equitable management of resources such as exercise equipment can be accomplished by:

   A. Ensuring that the advanced students get the first rotation of equipment use so that students of differing capabilities can work at their own pace.

   B. Using sign-up sheets so that all students get a turn to use the equipment

   C. Assigning equipment usage time based strictly on alphabetization of the student's last names

   D. Letting less interested students sit out the activity so that engaged students get more time on the equipment

(Average) (Skill 3.3)

60. **When introducing new skills, what is meant by a tiered plan?**

    A. Practicing intricate skills before addressing less challenging skills

    B. Practicing lower levels of difficulty before the most challenging skills are addressed

    C. Grouping students by ability level, with higher ability students practicing the more challenging skills

    D. A tiered plan involves more than one instructor present

(Easy) (Skill 3.3)

61. **If a class has to be divided into groups because of space or equipment limitations, which of the following must also occur?**

    A. Sign-up sheets should be created so each student is guaranteed equal time with the equipment available

    B. The instructor should allocate sufficient time for the students to change into and out of their P.E. clothing

    C. A tiered instructional plan must be in place

    D. Staffing must also be split so there is an instructor present with each group

(Easy) (Skill 3.4)

62. **What are the advantages of independent activities such as walking, running, and dancing?**

    A. They do not promote unhealthy levels of competitiveness

    B. They are relatively easy fitness activities

    C. They can be done almost anywhere and require few resources

    D. They are widely accepted across different cultures

(Rigorous) (Skill 3.6)

63. **What is the difference between intrinsic and extrinsic positive reinforcement?**

    A. Intrinsic positive reinforcement comes from the outside. Extrinsic positive reinforcement comes from the inside.

    B. Intrinsic positive reinforcement is intricate and detaileExtrinsic positive reinforcement is simple and general.

    C. Intrinsic positive reinforcement can only be communicated verbally. Extrinsic positive reinforcement can only be communicated by example.

    D. Intrinsic positive reinforcement comes from the inside. Extrinsic positive reinforcement comes from the outside.

(Easy) (Skill 3.6)

64. **Which of the following is an example of an intrinsic positive reinforcement?**

    A. The reward given for completing a task correctly

    B. The endorphins released during exercise

    C. An award given to recognize achievement

    D. A disciplinary action taken in response to not following established classroom procedure

(Easy) (Skill 3.6)

65. **Which of the following is an example of an extrinsic positive reinforcement?**

    A. A disciplinary action taken for egregious misbehavior during class time

    B. A disciplinary action taken for a minor infraction

    C. A reward given for completing a task correctly

    D. One's feelings about one's own abilities

(Average) (Skill 4.1)

66. **When addressing poor performance verbally, an instructor should:**

    A. Address the student in front of the group so that other students can learn from the experience

    B. Address the student one-on-one so that the student is not embarrassed in front of his or her peers

    C. Be general in the assessment so the student must deduce the problem, thus deepening the student's learning experience

    D. Stop all group and individual activity to focus on the issues of the poorly performing student

(Average) (Skill 4.1)

67. **Which of the following is not an effective method of nonverbal communication?**

    A. A simple point or motion

    B. A clapped rhythm or whistle

    C. A raised hand, known as "give me five"

    D. A simple stern frown accompanied by physical proximity to the student

(Rigorous) (Skill 4.2)

68. **Which of the following is an effective verbal follow-up to the assessment below?**

    Skill: General pushups

    "You are doing great, Susie. I like that you are using the full range of motion. Just remember to treat your back like a board and try to hold it straight and still from the top to the bottom and back up."

    A. No further verbal follow up is needed because the issue was clearly communicated

    B. "Can I see another one, Susie?"

    C. "If your back isn't straight, then you technically aren't performing a push-up."

    D. "If you don't keep your back straight, you could hurt your back."

(Average) (Skill 4.4)

69. **Which of the following forms of communication can have negative impacts on student learning?**

    A. Connecting student performance to student character

    B. Connecting student performance to student ability

    C. Generalizing student behavior

    D. All of the above

(Average) (Skill 4.4)

70. **An email is similar to/different from a letter in which of the following ways?**

    A. In an email, words and sentences can be abbreviated

    B. An email should be written in the same way as a letter

    C. Emails do not require a salutation or a sign-off

    D. A letter is more formal than an email

(Easy) (Skill 4.4)

71. **Which of the following statements would be most appropriate for an assessment form?**

    A. I just don't see any specific evidence that Jerry can or will meet curriculum goals this quarter

    B. Jerry is not reaching goals

    C. Jerry is performing 2 out of 9 assessment qualifications, and has completed none of the president's physical fitness test

    D. Jerry needs to work on meeting performance goals

Planning, Instruction, and Student Assessment

(Easy) (Skill 5.1)

72. **Using the same foot to take off from a surface and to land is which locomotor skill?**

    A. Jumping

    B. Vaulting

    C. Leaping

    D. Hopping

(Easy) (Skill 5.1)

73. **Which nonlocomotor skill entails movement around a joint where two body parts meet?**

    A. Twisting

    B. Swaying

    C. Bending

    D. Stretching

(Easy) (Skill 5.1)

74. **A sharp change of direction from one's original line of movement is which nonlocomotor skill?**

    A. Twisting

    B. Dodging

    C. Swaying

    D. Swinging

(Easy) (Skill 5.1)

75. **Having students pretend they are playing basketball or trying to catch a bus develops which locomotor skill?**

    A. Galloping

    B. Running

    C. Leaping

    D. Skipping

(Easy) (Skill 5.1)

76. **Having students play Fox and Hound develops:**

    A. Galloping

    B. Hopping

    C. Stepping-hopping

    D. Skipping

(Easy) (Skill 5.1)

77. Having students take off and land with both feet together develops which locomotor skill?

    A. Hopping

    B. Jumping

    C. Leaping

    D. Skipping

(Easy) (Skill 5.1)

78. Activities such as pretending to pick fruit off a tree or reaching for a star develop which nonlocomotor skill?

    A. Bending

    B. Stretching

    C. Turning

    D. Twisting

(Easy) (Skill 5.1)

79. Picking up coins, tying shoes, and petting animals develop which nonlocomotor skill?

    A. Bending

    B. Stretching

    C. Turning

    D. Twisting

(Average) (Skill 5.1)

80. Progressively decreasing the size of a target at which balls are projected develops which manipulative skill?

    A. Throwing

    B. Trapping

    C. Volleying

    D. Kicking

(Average) (Skill 5.1)

81. Hitting a stationary object while in a fixed position, then incorporating movement, develops which manipulative skill?

    A. Bouncing

    B. Trapping

    C. Throwing

    D. Striking

(Easy) (Skill 5.1)

82. Coordinated movements that project a person over an obstacle are known as:

    A. Jumping

    B. Vaulting

    C. Leaping

    D. Hopping

(Rigorous) (Skill 5.1)

83. Which manipulative skill uses the hands to stop the momentum of an object?

    A. Trapping

    B. Catching

    C. Striking

    D. Rolling

(Rigorous) (Skill 5.1)

84. To enhance skill and strategy performance for striking or throwing objects, for catching or collecting objects, and for carrying and propelling objects, students must first learn techniques for:

    A. Offense

    B. Defense

    C. Controlling objects

    D. Continuous play of objects

(Rigorous) (Skill 5.2)

85. What is the proper order of sequential development for the acquisition of locomotor skills?

   A. Creep, crawl, walk, jump, run, slide, gallop, hop, leap, skip, step-hop

   B. Crawl, walk, creep, slide, walk, run, hop, leap, gallop, skip, step-hop

   C. Creep, crawl, walk, slide, run, hop, leap, skip, gallop, jump, step-hop

   D. Crawl, creep, walk, run, jump, hop, gallop, slide, leap, skip, step-hop

(Rigorous) (Skill 5.4)

86. What is the proper sequential order of development for the acquisition of nonlocomotor skills?

   A. Stretch, sit, bend, turn, swing, twist, shake, rock and sway, dodge, fall

   B. Bend, stretch, turn, twist, swing, sit, rock and sway, shake, dodge, fall

   C. Stretch, bend, sit, shake, turn, rock and sway, swing, twist, dodge, fall

   D. Bend, stretch, sit, turn, twist, swing, sway, rock and sway, dodge, fall

(Easy) (Skill 5.4)

87. Having students collapse in their own space or lower themselves as if they are a raindrop or snowflake develops which nonlocomotor skill?

   A. Dodging

   B. Shaking

   C. Swinging

   D. Falling

(Rigorous) (Skill 5.4)

88. Which is the proper sequential order of development for the acquisition of manipulative skills?

   A. Striking, throwing, bouncing, catching, trapping, kicking, ball rolling, volleying

   B. Striking, throwing, kicking, ball rolling, volleying, bouncing, catching, trapping

   C. Striking, throwing, catching, trapping, kicking, ball rolling, bouncing, volleying

   D. Striking, throwing, kicking, ball rolling, bouncing, volleying

(Average) (Skill 5.4)

89. Having students hit a large balloon with both hands develops which manipulative skill?

   A. Bouncing

   B. Striking

   C. Volleying

   D. Trapping

(Easy) (Skill 5.5)

90. If an action results in direct or indirect injury, what is this called under the law?

   A. A tort

   B. A petition

   C. A liability

   D. In loco parentis

(Average) (Skill 5.5)

91. **What is the definition of negligence?**

A. Causing harm or injury through an act of omission

B. Failing to fulfill a legal duty according to common reasoning

C. Causing harm or injury through a direct action

D. The willful intention to cause harm or injury

(Easy) (Skill 5.5)

92. **What is the definition of in loco parentis?**

A. The inability to reason with parents regarding the disciplinary needs of their children

B. The liability of a manufacturer to the person(s) using their products who sustains injury

C. Acting in the place of a parent or guardian in relation to a child

D. Harmful contact of one person by another

(Average) (Skill 5.5)

93. **Grouping students to equalize competitive levels, considering the ability and skill level of participants when planning activities, and properly organizing and supervising classes are concrete actions that can:**

A. Ensure student safety and limit lawsuits due to injury or harm

B. Improve job satisfaction for the physical education instructor

C. Lead to positive teacher-student verbal communication

D. Ensure that the requirements of Title IX are met

(Easy) (Skill 5.6)

94. **Which is an effective method of goal-setting?**

A. Make short-term goals a fixed percentage of the final, long-term goal

B. Set several small, short-term goals as steps to attain one long-term goal

C. Set goals that are slightly out of reach so that students have to strive to achieve them

D. Set the same goals for all students

(Easy) (Skill 5.11)

95. **Which of the following actions does not promote safety?**

A. Allowing students to wear the current style of shoes

B. Presenting organized activities

C. Inspecting equipment and facilities

D. Instructing skill and activities properly

(Easy) (Skill 5.11)

96. **The most important nutrient the body requires, without which life can only be sustained for a few days, is:**

A. Vitamins

B. Minerals

C. Water

D. Carbohydrates

(Average) (Skill 5.11)

97. Which of the following can help prevent Achilles tendon, a common athletic injury?

   A. Stretch dorsiflexion and strengthen plantar flexion (heel raises)

   B. Use high top shoes and tape support

   C. Increase strength and flexibility of calf and thigh muscles

   D. All of the above

(Average) (Skill 6.2)

98. Students are performing trunk extensions. What component of fitness does this activity assess?

   A. Balance

   B. Flexibility

   C. Body composition

   D. Coordination

(Rigorous) (Skill 6.2)

99. Which of the following can be used to assess muscle endurance?

   A. Dynamometers, cable tensiometer, the 1-RM Test

   B. Hydrostatic weighing

   C. Maximal stress test, sub maximal stress test, Bruce Protocol, Cooper 1.5 Mile Run/Walk Fitness Test

   D. Squat-thrust, pull-ups, sit-ups, lateral pull-down, bench press, arm curl, push-ups, and dips

(Average) (Skill 6.3)

100. What is the President's Challenge?

   A. A comprehensive health-related fitness education program developed by physical educators for physical educators

   B. A program that encourages all Americans to make regular physical activity a part of their everyday lives

   C. A program to increase parental awareness of children's fitness levels

   D. A comprehensive nutrition curriculum that public schools can adopt into their curriculum

(Easy) (Skill 6.7)

101. Instructors can encourage students to self-assess their physical education progress by employing:

   A. Reflection

   B. Journal writing

   C. Interdisciplinary study

   D. All of the above

Collaboration, Reflection, and Technology

(Average) (Skill 7.1)

102. What would not be an effective way of tying fitness instruction into social studies instruction?

   A. Teaching how the body processes calories

   B. Teaching how to interpret graphs and charts of performance data

   C. Teaching the mechanics of muscle contraction

   D. Teaching the history of a particular sport

(Easy) (Skill 7.2)

103. Which subject areas have knowledge and skills that can be integrated into physical education instruction?

A. English, math, and social studies

B. Math, science, and social studies

C. History, English, and economics

D. Arts, industrial arts, and social studies

(Easy) (Skill 7.4)

104. What are some ways that P.E. instructors can promote opportunities for physical activity in the community?

A. Send home parks and recreation brochures for parents

B. Facilitate community walks, races, or other volunteer community events

C. All of the above

D. None of the above

(Rigorous) (Skill 8.1)

105. In the reflective cycle, a teacher goes through a constant cycle of learning characterized by:

A. Description, feelings, evaluation, analysis, conclusion, action plan

B. Feelings, description, evaluation, action plan, analysis, conclusion

C. Feelings, evaluation, analysis, conclusion

D. Action plan, analysis, feelings, conclusion

(Average) (Skill 8.1)

106. What is the purpose or point of the reflective cycle?

A. To evaluate the effectiveness of one's teaching

B. To reflect on how to improve team-building exercises in the classroom

C. To share effective teaching strategies with colleagues

D. To practice creating successful action plans

(Average) (Skill 8.1)

107. What type of question should instructors ask themselves during the description phase of the reflective cycle?

A. What occurred?

B. What arc the pros and cons of the occurrence?

C. How would an outsider see this occurrence?

D. What will you do if something similar happens again?

(Rigorous) (Skill 8.1)

108. What type of question should instructors ask themselves during the evaluation phase of the reflective cycle?

A. What could be done with this problem?

B. What are the pros and cons of the occurrence?

C. How would an outsider see this occurrence?

D. What will you do if something similar happens again?

(Average) (Skill 9.1)

109. Which of the following is a movement-driven (rather than joystick-driven) type of game system that can be used to supplement traditional exercise?

   A. Playstation

   B. Atari

   C. Sony Wii

   D. Peertrainer

(Rigorous) (Skill 9.1)

110. Which site is dedicated to voluntary and independent journaling about nutrition and fitness?

   A. *www.aahperd.org*

   B. *www.peertrainer.com*

   C. *www.cooperinstitute.org*

   D. *www.acefitness.org*

(Average) (Skill 9.2)

111. What precaution(s) should be taken when using technology to display online materials during instruction?

   A. Review all online material for appropriateness before using it in instruction

   B. Become familiar with the technology to ensure no difficulties or delays are experienced during the presentation

   C. Verify that the material is consistent with the goals of the President's Challenge

   D. Make sure the material has an interactive learning component

Supplemental Content

(Average) (Domain V)

112. For linear movement, force applied close to the center of gravity requires a _____ magnitude of force to move the object than does force applied farther from the center of gravity.

   A. Larger

   B. Equal

   C. Uneven

   D. Smaller

(Easy) (Domain V)

113. What are the two types of mechanical energy?

   A. Elastic energy and absorption energy

   B. Potential energy and kinetic energy

   C. Gravitational energy and elastic energy

   D. Absorption energy and gravitational energy

(Average) (Domain V)

114. The energy of an object to do work while recoiling is which type of potential energy?

   A. Absorption

   B. Kinetic

   C. Elastic

   D. Torque

(Rigorous) (Domain V)

115. Gradually decelerating a moving mass by utilization of smaller forces over a long period of time is:

   A. Stability

   B. Equilibrium

   C. Angular force

   D. Force absorption

(Average) (Domain V)

116. Equilibrium is maintained as long as:

   A. Body segments are moved independently

   B. The center of gravity is over the base of support

   C. Force is applied to the base of support

   D. The center of gravity is lowered

(Average) (Domain V)

117. Which of the following does not enhance equilibrium?

   A. Shifting the center of gravity away from the direction of movement

   B. Increasing the base of support

   C. Lowering the base of support

   D. Increasing the base of support and lowering the center of support

(Rigorous) (Domain V)

118. How does a first-class lever work?

   A. The force works at a point between the axis and the resistance (the resistance arm is always longer than the force arm)

   B. The axis is between the points of application of the force and the resistance

   C. The force arm is longer than the resistance arm (operator applies resistance between the axis and the point of application of force)

   D. The force arm and the resistance arm are the same length

(Average) (Domain V)

119. Freehand front lunges will help an individual to target muscle endurance in which of the following muscle groups?

   A. Trapezius and lateral muscles

   B. Thighs and hamstrings

   C. Triceps and biceps

   D. Obliques and thighs

(Average) (Domain V)

120. Dumbbell side bends will help an individual to target muscle endurance in which of the following muscle groups?

   A. Trapezius and lateral muscles

   B. Rear deltoids

   C. Triceps and biceps

   D. Obliques

Answer Key

1. B	15. B	29. B	43. D	57. B	71. C	85. D	99. D	113. B
2. C	16. D	30. D	44. D	58. B	72. D	86. C	100. A	114. C
3. A	17. C	31. C	45. B	59. B	73. C	87. D	101. D	115. D
4. C	18. B	32. D	46. C	60. B	74. B	88. B	102. D	116. B
5. D	19. B	33. D	47. D	61. D	75. B	89. C	103. B	117. A
6. C	20. A	34. D	48. C	62. C	76. A	90. A	104. C	118. B
7. A	21. D	35. B	49. D	63. D	77. B	91. B	105. A	119. B
8. B	22. A	36. B	50. B	64. B	78. B	92. C	106. A	120. D
9. A	23. D	37. B	51. C	65. C	79. A	93. A	107. A	
10. C	24. C	38. A	52. A	66. B	80. A	94. B	108. B	
11. B	25. D	39. A	53. C	67. D	81. D	95. A	109. C	
12. D	26. B	40. C	54. B	68. B	82. B	96. C	110. B	
13. A	27. A	41. C	55. B	69. D	83. B	97. A	111. A	
14. C	28. D	42. C	56. A	70. B	84. C	98. B	112. D	

Rigor Table

RIGOR TABLE	
Rigor level	**Questions**
Easy 27%	4, 31, 37, 39, 40, 49, 53, 56, 61, 62, 64, 65, 71, 72, 73, 74, 75, 76, 77, 78, 79, 82, 87, 90, 92, 94, 95, 96, 101, 103, 104, 113
Average 39%	1, 9, 10, 11, 14, 15, 18, 23, 28, 32, 33, 35, 36, 42, 43, 44, 45, 46, 47, 52, 54, 58, 59, 60, 66, 67, 69, 70, 80, 81, 89, 91, 93, 97, 98, 100, 102, 106, 107, 109, 111, 112, 114, 116, 117, 119, 120
Rigorous 34%	2, 3, 5, 6, 7, 8, 12, 13, 16, 17, 19, 20, 21, 22, 24, 25, 26, 27, 29, 30, 34, 38, 41, 48, 50, 51, 55, 57, 63, 68, 83, 84, 85, 86, 88, 99, 105, 108, 110, 115, 118

BONUS Sample Test with Rationales

Content Knowledge and Student Growth and Development

(Average) (Skill 1.1)

1. The ability for a muscle(s) to repeatedly contract over a period of time is:

   A. Cardiovascular endurance

   B. Muscle endurance

   C. Muscle strength

   D. Muscle force

Answer: B. Muscle endurance

Muscle endurance gives the muscle the ability to contract over a period of time. Muscle strength is a prerequisite for muscle endurance. Cardiovascular endurance involves aerobic exercise.

(Rigorous) (Skill 1.1)

2. A 17-year-old male has a body fat composition of 20%. Which is the best interpretation of his obesity level?

   A. Obese

   B. Overweight

   C. Normal

   D. Underweight

Answer: C. Normal

The general chart doctors and insurance companies use to interpret body mass index data is:

Underweight = 18.5

Normal = 18.5–24.9

Overweight = 25–29.9

Obese = 30+

(Rigorous) (Skill 1.1)

3. What is the name of the main chest muscle?

   A. Pectoralis major

   B. Latissimus Dorsi

   C. Deltoids

   D. Rectus Abdominis

Answer: A. Pectoralis major

The pectoralis major is the main chest muscle. It aids in deltoid and latissimus dorsi movement and protects the ribcage and major organs.

(Easy) (Skill 1.1)

4. Which of the following are muscles of the leg?

   A. Hamstrings, gluteus maximus, triceps brachii, rectus abdominis

   B. Quadriceps, gastrocnemius, biceps brachii, hamstrings

   C. Quadriceps, hamstrings, gastrocnemius, gluteus maximus

   D. Pectoralis major, latissimus dorsi, triceps brachii

Answer: C. Quadriceps, hamstrings, gastrocnemius, gluteus maximus

Quadriceps are located in the front of the upper leg. Hamstrings are located in the back of the upper leg. Gastrocnemius are located in the back of the lower leg. Gluteus maximus are located in the buttocks.

(Rigorous) (Skill 1.3)

5. There are two sequential phases to the development of spatial awareness. What is the order of these phases?

 A. Locating more than one object in relation to each other; locating objects in relation to one's own body in space

 B. Locating an object in relation to ones' own body in space; locating more than one object in relation to one's own body

 C. Locating more than one object independent of one's body; locating objects in relation to one's own body

 D. Locating objects in relation to one's own body in space; locating more than one object in relation to each other and independent of one's own body

Answer: D. Locating objects in relation to one's own body in space; locating more than one object in relation to each other and independent of one's own body

These are the two sequential phases to the development of spatial awareness.

(Rigorous) (Skill 1.3)

6. Students that paddle balls against a wall or jump over objects with various heights are demonstrating which quality of movement?

 A. Balance

 B. Time

 C. Force

 D. Inertia

Answer: C. Force

Force is the capacity to do work or create physical change, energy, strength, or active power. It is a classical force that causes a free body with mass to accelerate. A net (or resultant) force that causes such acceleration may be the non-zero additive sum of many different forces acting on a body.

(Rigorous) (Skill 1.3)

7. Which movement concept involves students making decisions about an object's positional changes in space?

 A. Spatial awareness

 B. Effort awareness

 C. Body awareness

 D. Motion awareness

Answer: A. Spatial awareness

Spatial awareness is an organized awareness of objects in the space around us. It is also an awareness of the body's position in space.

(Rigorous) (Skill 1.3)

8. Applying the mechanical principles of balance, time, and force describes which movement concept?

 A. Spatial awareness

 B. Effort awareness

 C. Body awareness

 D. Motion awareness

Answer: B. Effort awareness

Effort awareness is the knowledge of balance, time, and force, and how they relate to athletic movements and activities.

(Average) (Skill 1.3)

9. **Having students move on their hands and knees, move on lines, and/or hold shapes while moving develops which quality of movement?**

   A. Balance

   B. Time

   C. Force

   D. Inertia

Answer: A. Balance

Balance is one of the physiological senses. It allows humans and animals to walk without falling. Some animals are better at this than humans. For example, a cat (a quadruped that also uses its inner ear and tail for balance) can walk on a thin fence.

(Average) (Skill 1.3)

10. **Playing "Simon Says" and having students touch different body parts applies which movement concept?**

   A. Spatial awareness

   B. Effort awareness

   C. Body awareness

   D. Motion awareness

Answer: C. Body awareness

Body awareness is a person's understanding of his or her own body parts and the capability of his or her movements.

(Average) (Skill 1.3)

11. **Having students move in a specific pattern while measuring how long they take to do so develops which quality of movement?**

   A. Balance

   B. Time

   C. Force

   D. Inertia

Answer: B. Time

Time is a sequential arrangement of events or the interval between events in a sequence. Time is the non-spatial continuum in which events occur, in apparently irreversible succession, from the past through the present to the future.

(Rigorous) (Skill 1.4)

12. **Aerobic dance develops or improves each of the following skills or health components except:**

   A. Cardio-respiratory function

   B. Body composition

   C. Coordination

   D. Flexibility

Answer: D. Flexibility

Aerobic dance does not develop flexibility, because flexibility results from stretching and not aerobic exercise. Ballet dancing, however, does develop flexibility. Aerobic dance develops cardio-respiratory function due to the unusual body movements performeIt also improves body composition and coordination due to the movement of various body parts.

(Rigorous) (Skill 1.4)

13. **Rowing develops which health- or skill-related component of fitness?**

    A. Muscle endurance

    B. Flexibility

    C. Balance

    D. Reaction time

Answer: A. Muscle endurance

Rowing helps develop muscle endurance because of the continuous arm movement against the force of the water. Flexibility, balance, and reaction time are not important components of rowing. Rowing also develops the lower abdominal muscles when the individual is in the sitting position when rowing.

(Average) (Skill 1.4)

14. **Calisthenics develops all of the following health- and skill-related components of fitness except:**

    A. Muscle strength

    B. Body composition

    C. Power

    D. Agility

Answer: C. Power

Calisthenics is a sport that actually helps to keep a body fit by combining gymnastic and aerobic activities. Calisthenics develops muscle strength and agility and improves body composition. However, calisthenics does not develop power because it does not involve resistance training or explosiveness.

(Average) (Skill 1.4)

15. **Which health- or skill-related component of fitness is developed by rope jumping?**

    A. Muscle force

    B. Coordination

    C. Flexibility

    D. Muscle strength

Answer: B. Coordination

Rope jumping is a good mental exercise and it improves coordination. Many athletes (e.g., boxers, tennis players) jump rope to improve coordination and quickness. Muscle strength is secondary to this benefit.

(Rigorous) (Skill 1.4)

16. **Working at a level that is above normal is which exercise training principle?**

    A. Intensity

    B. Progression

    C. Specificity

    D. Overload

Answer: D. Overload

Overloading is exercising above-normal capacities. Intensity and progression are supporting principles in the process of overloaOverloading can cause serious issues within the body, either immediately or after some time.

(Rigorous) (Skill 1.4)

17. **Students on a running program to improve cardio-respiratory fitness apply which exercise principle?**

    A. Aerobic

    B. Progression

    C. Specificity

    D. Overload

Answer: C. Specificity

Running to improve cardio-respiratory fitness is an example of specificity. Specificity is the selection of activities that isolate a specific body part or system. Aerobics is also a good option, but it deals with the entire body, including areas not specific to cardio-respiratory fitness.

(Average) (Skill 1.4)

18. **Adding more repetitions to a weightlifting set applies which exercise principle?**

    A. Anaerobic

    B. Progression

    C. Overload

    D. Specificity

Answer: B. Progression

The Progression Principle states that once the body adapts to the original load/stress, no further improvement of a component of fitness will occur without an additional loaAdding more repetitions (reps) to sets when weightlifting is an example of progression. Adding reps can result in overload, but the guiding principle is progression.

(Rigorous) (Skill 1.4)

19. **Which of the following does not modify overload?**

    A. Frequency

    B. Perceived exertion

    C. Time

    D. Intensity

Answer: B. Perceived exertion

One can modify overload by varying frequency, intensity, and time. Frequency is the number of times a training program is implemented in a given period (e.g., three days per week). Intensity is the amount of effort put forth or the amount of stress placed on the body. Time is the duration of each training session. Perceived exertion is not an effective modification, because it is subjective.

(Rigorous) (Skill 1.4)

20. **Overloading for muscle strength includes all of the following except:**

    A. Lifting heart rate to an intense level

    B. Lifting weights every other day

    C. Lifting with high resistance and low reps

    D. Lifting 60% to 90% of assessed muscle strength

Answer: A. Lifting heart rate to an intense level

Overloading muscle strength is possible by lifting the weights every other day or by lifting weights with high resistance and low repetition. Overloading does not cause or require an intense increase in heart rate.

(Rigorous) (Skill 1.4)

21. **Which of the following applies the concept of progression?**

    A. Beginning a stretching program every day

    B. Beginning a stretching program with 3 sets of reps

    C. Beginning a stretching program with ballistic stretching

    D. Beginning a stretching program holding stretches for 15 seconds and working up to holding stretches for 60 seconds

    Answer: D. Beginning a stretching program holding stretches for 15 seconds and working up to holding stretches for 60 seconds

    Progression is the process of starting an exercise program slowly and cautiously before proceeding to more rigorous training. Answer D is the only answer that exemplifies progression.

(Rigorous) (Skill 1.4)

22. **Which of following overload principles does not apply to improving body composition?**

    A. Aerobic exercise three times per week

    B. Aerobic exercise at a low intensity

    C. Aerobic exercise for about an hour

    D. Aerobic exercise with intervals of high intensity

Answer: A. Aerobic exercise three times per week

To improve body composition, a person should engage in aerobic exercise daily, not three times per week. However, an individual can do aerobics for at least half an hour daily, he or she can exercise at a low intensity, or he or she can train with intervals of high intensity.

(Average) (Skill 1.4)

23. **The ability to change the direction of the body rapidly is:**

    A. Coordination

    B. Reaction time

    C. Speed

    D. Agility

Answer: D. Agility

Agility is the ability of the body to change position quickly. Reaction time, coordination, and speed are not the right words to describe the ability to move quickly.

(Rigorous) (Skill 1.4)

24. **Students are performing the vertical jump. What component of fitness does this activity assess?**

    A. Muscle strength

    B. Balance

    C. Power

    D. Muscle endurance

Answer: C. Power

Vertical jumping assesses the power of the entire body. It shows the potential of the legs to hold the upper body and the strength in the joints of the legs. Balance and muscle strength are secondary requirements. Power automatically ensures these secondary requirements.

(Rigorous) (Skill 1.4)

25. **Using the Karvonean Formula, compute the 60% − 80% THR for a 16-year-old student with a RHR of 60.**

    A. 122–163 beats per minute

    B. 130–168 beats per minute

    C. 142–170 beats per minute

    D. 146–175 beats per minute

Answer: D. 146–175 beats per minute

$220 − 16$ (age) $= 204$, $204 − 60$ (RHR) $= 144$, $144 \times .60$ (low end of heart range) $= 86$, $86 + 60$ (RHR) $= 146$ (bottom of THR)

$220 − 16$ (age) $= 204$, $204 − 60$ (RHR) $= 144$, 144×0.80 (high end of heart range) $= 115$, $115 + $ (RHR) $= 175$ (top of THR)

146–175 beats per minute is the 60%-80% THR.

(Rigorous) (Skill 1.4)

26. **Using Cooper's Formula, compute the THR for a 15-year-old student.**

    A. 120–153 beats per minute

    B. 123–164 beats per minute

    C. 135–169 beats per minute

    D. 147–176 beats per minute

Answer: B. 123–164 beats per minute

123-164 beats per minute.

THR $= (200 − $ Age$) \times 0.6$ to $(220 − $ Age$) \times 0.8 = (220 − 15) \times 0.6$ to $(220 − 15) \times 0.8 = 123$ to 164 beats per minute

(Rigorous) (Skill 1.4)

27. **Activities to specifically develop cardiovascular fitness must be:**

    A. Performed without developing an oxygen debt

    B. Performed twice daily

    C. Performed every day

    D. Performed for a minimum of 10 minutes

Answer: A. Performed without developing an oxygen debt

The development of cardiovascular fitness is not dependent on specific time limits or routine schedules. Participants should perform aerobic activities without developing an oxygen debt.

(Average) (Skill 1.6)

28. **Which professional organization protects amateur sports from corruption?**

    A. AIWA

    B. AAHPERD

    C. NCAA

    D. AAU

Answer: D. AAU

The Amateur Athletic Union (AAU) is one of the largest non-profit, volunteer sports organizations in the United States. A multi-sport organization, the AAU dedicates itself exclusively to the promotion and development of amateur sports and physical fitness programs. Answer C may be a tempting choice, but the NCAA deals only with college athletics.

(Rigorous) (Skill 1.6)

29. **The physical education philosophy that is based on experience is:**

   A. Naturalism

   B. Pragmatism

   C. Idealism

   D. Existentialism

Answer: B. Pragmatism

Pragmatism, as a school of philosophy, is a collection of different ways of thinking. Given the diversity of thinkers and the variety of schools of thought that have adopted this term over the years, the term pragmatism has become almost meaningless in the absence of further qualification. Most of the thinkers who describe themselves as pragmatists indicate some connection with practical consequences or real effects as vital components of both meaning and truth.

(Rigorous) (Skill 1.6)

30. **Idealism is the belief that:**

   A. The laws of nature are ideal

   B. Experience is the key

   C. Practice, practice, practice

   D. The mind is developed through acquisition of knowledge

Answer: D. The mind is developed through acquisition of knowledge

Idealism is the belief that the mind continues to develop through the ongoing acquisition of knowledge.

(Easy) (Skill 1.6)

31. **Which of the following countries did not greatly influence the early development of P.E. in the United States?**

   A. Germany

   B. England

   C. Norway

   D. Sweden

Answer: C. Norway

Norway did not have a great influence on the early development of P.E. in the United States.

(Average) (Skill 1.6)

32. **What was the first state in the U.S. to require P.E. in its public schools?**

   A. Florida

   B. Massachusetts

   C. New York

   D. California

Answer: D. California

In 1866, California was the first state in the U.S. to require physical education classes in its public schools curriculum.

(Average) (Skill 1.6)

33. **President Eisenhower was alerted to the poor fitness levels of American youths. How was the poor physical conditioning of youths discovered in the Eisenhower Administration?**

    A. By WWII Selective Service Examination

    B. By organizations promoting physical fitness

    C. By the Federal Security Agency

    D. By the Kraus-Weber test

Answer: D. By the Kraus-Weber test

This is one of the programs that President Dwight Eisenhower implemented during his presidency. Using a test devised by Drs. Hans Kraus and Sonja Weber of New York Presbyterian Hospital, Bonnie began testing children in Europe, Central America, and the United States. The Kraus-Weber test involved six simple movements and took 90 seconds to administer. It compared U.S. children to European children in the areas of strength and flexibility. The fitness emphasis in schools started by Kraus-Weber declined in the 1970s and early 1980s. The President's Council on Physical Fitness and Sports was one result of the Kraus-Weber test results.

(Rigorous) (Skill 1.6)

34. **In 1956, the AAHPERD Fitness Conferences established:**

    A. The President's Council on Youth Fitness

    B. The President's Citizens' Advisory Committee

    C. The President's Council on Physical Fitness

    D. A and B

Answer: D. A and B

The President's Council on Youth Fitness was founded on July 16, 1956 to encourage American children to be healthy and active after a study indicated that American youths were less physically fit than European children. President Eisenhower created the President's Council on Youth Fitness with cabinet-level status. The Executive Order specified "one" objective. The first Council identified itself as a "catalytic agent" concentrated on creating public awareness. A President's Citizens Advisory Committee on Fitness of American Youth was confirmed to give advice to the Council.

(Average) (Skill 1.6)

35. **The Round Hill School (a private school) in Massachusetts was the first school to require P.E. in its curriculum. What year was this?**

    A. 1792

    B. 1823

    C. 1902

    D. 1806

Answer: B. 1823

Requiring physical education in its curriculum in 1823, The Round Hill School paved the way for public schools to follow suit, beginning in 1866 in California.

(Average) (Skill 1.6)

36. **What year did California enact a law requiring all public schools to include physical education in its curriculum?**

   A. 1892

   B. 1866

   C. 1901

   D. 1899

Answer: B. 1866

In 1866, the California legislature became the first state public school system to require physical education in their schools curriculums.

(Easy) (Skill 1.6)

37. **Title IX ensured that:**

   A. Boys play baseball while girls play softball

   B. Girls are ensured the same educational and athletic opportunities as boys

   C. Girls and boys have coed physical education classes

   D. All students must dress up for physical education class

Answer: B. Girls are ensured the same educational and athletic opportunities as boys

In 1972, Title IX was passed, which ensured the same educational and athletic opportunities for both girls and boys. If a male sport was offered, then the same or a similar sport had to be offered for girls, otherwise the girls were allowed to try out for the boys' sport team.

(Rigorous) (Skill 1.6)

38. **The affective domain of physical education contributes to all of the following except:**

   A. Knowledge of exercise, health, and disease

   B. Self-actualization

   C. An appreciation of beauty

   D. Good sportsmanship

Answer: A. Knowledge of exercise, health, and disease

The affective domain encompasses emotions, thoughts, and feelings related to physical education. Knowledge of exercise, health, and disease is part of the cognitive domain.

(Easy) (Skill 1.7)

39. **Two opposing soccer players are trying to gain control of the ball when one player "knees" the other. What is the ruling?**

   A. Direct free kick

   B. Indirect free kick

   C. Fair play

   D. Ejection from a game

Answer: A. Direct free kick

Assuming that the soccer player didn't intentionally hit the other player's knee, the result would be a direct free kick. If the foul was intentional, the referee can give the offender a yellow-card warning or eject the player from the game by giving the player a red carMinor offenses and offenses not involving contact result in indirect free kicks.

(Easy) (Skill 1.7)

40. **A basketball team has an outstanding rebounder. In order to keep this player near the opponent's basket, which strategy should the coach implement?**

    A. Pick-and-roll
    B. Give-and-go
    C. Zone defense
    D. Free-lancing

Answer: C. Zone defense

A zone defense, where each player guards an area of the court rather than an individual player, allows an outstanding rebounder to remain near the basket. Give-and-go, pick-and-roll, and free-lancing are offensive strategies that do not affect rebounding.

(Rigorous) (Skill 1.7)

41. **When a defensive tennis player needs more time to return to his position, what strategy should he apply?**

    A. Drop shot
    B. Dink shot
    C. Lob shot
    D. Down-the-line shot

Answer: C. Lob shot

When a tennis player is off the court and needs time to return to his position, the player should play a lob shot. Down-the-line shots and drop shots are offensive shots and are too risky in this situation. The dink shot would allow the opponent to take control of the point.

(Average) (Skill 1.7)

42. **A basketball maneuver when an offensive player passes to a teammate and then immediately cuts in toward the basket for a return pass is:**

    A. Charging
    B. Pick
    C. Give-and-go
    D. Switching

Answer: C. Give-and-go

In the game of basketball, a give-and-go is an offensive play where a player passes to a teammate and immediately cuts towards the basket for a return pass. Charging is an offensive foul, a pick is a maneuver to free up a teammate for a pass or shot, and switching is a defensive maneuver.

(Average) (Skill 1.7)

43. **A soccer pass from the outside of the field near the end line to a position in front of the goal is called:**

    A. Chip
    B. Settle
    C. Through
    D. Cross

Answer: D. Cross

Any long pass from the side of the field toward the middle is a cross, because the hitter kicks it across the fielA chip is a high touch pass or shot. A through pass travels the length of the field through many players. Finally, settling is the act of controlling the ball after receiving a pass.

(Average) (Skill 1.7)

44. **A volleyball that is simultaneously contacted above the net by opponents and momentarily held upon contact is called a(n):**

   A. Double fault

   B. Play over

   C. Overlap

   D. Held ball

Answer: D. Held ball

In volleyball, if two players simultaneously contact the ball above the net, the ball is a held ball.

(Average) (Skill 1.7)

45. **Volleyball player LB on team A digs a spiked ball. The ball deflects off LB's shoulder. What is the ruling?**

   A. Fault

   B. Legal hit

   C. Double foul

   D. Play over

Answer: B. Legal hit

Since the spiked ball does not touch the ground and instead deflects off LB's shoulder, it is a legal hit. In order for a point to end, the ball must touch the ground. In this instance, it does not.

(Average) (Skill 1.8)

46. **Which of the following pieces of exercise equipment best applies the physiological principles?**

   A. Rolling machine

   B. Electrical muscle stimulator

   C. Stationary bicycle

   D. Motor-driven rowing machine

Answer: C. Stationary bicycle

A stationary bicycle is the best option to support the body physically because it includes all of the operations related to an individual's body (e.g., movement of legs, position of arms, back exercise, stomach movement). Rolling machines, electrical muscle stimulators, and motor-driven rowing machines are all ineffective exercise equipment because they produce passive movement (no voluntary muscle contractions).

(Average) (Skill 1.8)

47. **A physical education instructor antici-pates and prevents potential injuries, watches for hidden injuries, and takes an injury evaluation of the entire class. Which of the following strate-gies to prevent injuries is the teacher demonstrating?**

    A. Maintaining high standards

    B. Proper use of equipment

    C. Proper procedures for emergencies

    D. Participant screening

Answer: D. Participant screening

In order for the instructor to know each student's physical status, she takes an injury evaluation. Such surveys are one way to know the physical status of an individual. It chronicles past injuries, activities, and diseases the individual may have or have haIt helps the instructor to know the limitations of each individual. Participant screening covers all forms of surveying and anticipation of injuries.

(Rigorous) (Skill 1.8)

48. **Although Mary is a paraplegic, she wants to participate in some capacity in the physical education class. What federal legislative act entitles her to do so?**

    A. PE 94-142

    B. Title IX

    C. PL 94-142

    D. Title XI

Answer: C. PL 94-142

It is the purpose of Act PL 94-142 to assure that all handicapped children have available to them, within the time periods specified in section 612(2), (B.), a free, appropriate public education that emphasizes special education and related services designed to meet their unique needs, to assure that the rights of handicapped children and their parents/ guardians are protected, to assist states and localities to provide for the education of all handicapped children, and to assess and assure the effectiveness of efforts to educate handicapped children.

(Easy) (Skill 2.1)

49. **Why is it important for physical education instructors to understand physical development in children and adolescents?**

    A. It helps the instructor to identify early or late maturing individuals

    B. Varying levels of development can affect participation in physical activity

    C. To better form teams in coeducational classes that accommodate the needs of both genders' changing maturities

    D. All of the above

Answer: D. All of the above

Understanding the rate of the devel-opmental growth process that occurs during early childhood and adolescence will help educators understand growth and development norms. Understanding the norms helps to identify individual variations in physical maturities that may affect participation in physical activities or sports.

(Rigorous) (Skill 2.2)

50. An instructor used a similar movement from a skill learned in a different activity to teach a skill for a new activity. The technique used to facilitate cognitive learning was:

    A. Conceptual thinking

    B. Transfer of learning

    C. Longer instruction

    D. Appropriate language

    Answer: B. Transfer of learning

    Using a previously used movement to facilitate a new task is a transfer of learning. The individual relates the past activity to the new one, enabling him or her to learn it more easily. Conceptual thinking is related to the transfer of learning.

(Rigorous) (Skill 2.2)

51. A teacher rewards students for completing tasks. Which method is the teacher using to facilitate psychomotor learning?

    A. Task/reciprocal

    B. Command/direct

    C. Contingency/contract

    D. Physical/reflex

    Answer: C. Contingency/contract

    Because the teacher is rewarding the student, the contingency/contract method is in place. The command/direct method involves the interaction between student and teacher when the student fails to fulfill the requirements.

(Average) (Skill 2.2)

52. Teaching methods that facilitate cognitive learning include:

    A. Problem solving, conceptual theory, and guided inquiry

    B. Teacher-centered instruction and progress monitoring

    C. Skill demonstration and learning stations

    D. Instruction, practice, and reward

    Answer: A. Problem solving, conceptual theory, guided inquiry

    Teaching methods that facilitate cognitive learning include:

    Problem Solving: The instructor presents the initial task and students come to an acceptable solution in unique and divergent ways.

    Conceptual Theory: The instructor's focus is on acquisition of knowledge.

    Guided Inquiry: Stages of instructions strategically guide students through a sequence of experiences

Management, Motivation, and Communication

(Easy) (Skill 3.1)

53. Which of the following is not a class-management technique?

    A. Explaining procedures for roll call, excuses, and tardiness

    B. Explaining routines for changing and showering

    C. Explaining conditioning

    D. Promoting individual self-discipline

Answer: C. Explaining conditioning

Explaining conditioning is not a class management technique. It is an instructional lesson.

(Average) (Skill 3.1)

54. **Which of the following represent the most important element(s) of effective classroom management?**

    A. Reminding students of classroom rules and procedures throughout the school year

    B. Fairness and consistency

    C. Addressing negative behaviors first and positive behaviors second

    D. Knowing all of your students by name so they all know they are important to you

Answer: B. Fairness and consistency

Classroom management requires consistency and fairness. In order to create an effective and positive learning environment, teachers need to make sure that students are aware of classroom rules and procedures and that these rules are applied evenly and consistently with fairness to all students.

(Rigorous) (Skill 3.2)

55. **Through physical activities, John has developed self-discipline, fairness, respect for others, and new friends. John has demonstrated which of the following?**

    A. Positive cooperation psycho-social influences

    B. Positive group psycho-social influences

    C. Positive individual psycho-social influences

    D. Positive accomplishment psycho-social influences

Answer: B. Positive group psycho-social influences

Through physical activities, John developed his social interaction skills. Social interaction is the sequence of social actions between individuals (or groups) that modifies their actions and reactions in response to the actions of their interaction partner(s). In other words, they are events in which people attach meaning to a situation, interpret what others mean, and respond accordingly. Through socialization with other people, John feels the influence of the people around him.

(Easy) (Skill 3.2)

56. **Social skills and values developed by group activity include all of the following except:**

    A. Winning at all costs

    B. Making judgments in groups

    C. Communicating and cooperating

    D. Respecting rules and property

Answer: A. Winning at all costs

Winning at all costs is not a desirable social skill and is considered a potential negative influence of group activity. Instructors and coaches should emphasize fair play and effort more than winning.

(Rigorous) (Skill 3.2)

57. **Which of the following psycho-social influences is not considered negative?**

    A. Avoidance of problems

    B. Adherence to exercise

    C. Ego-centeredness

    D. Role conflict

Answer: B. Adherence to exercise

The ability of an individual to adhere to an exercise routine as a result of his or her excitement, accolades, etis not considered a negative psycho-social influence. Adherence to an exercise routine is healthy and positive.

(Average) (Skill 3.2)

58. **What is the difference between anorexia nervosa and bulimia?**

    A. Individuals with bulimia try to abstain from eating. Individuals with anorexia nervosa eat but then purge by inducing themselves to vomit or by taking laxatives.

    B. Individuals with anorexia nervosa try to abstain from eating. Individuals with bulimia eat but then purge by inducing themselves to vomit or by taking laxatives.

    C. There is no difference. Anorexia nervosa and bulimia are two different scientific names for the same disorder.

    D. Anorexia nervosa is a disorder of the nervous system whereas bulimia is a disorder of the digestive system.

Answer: B. Individuals with anorexia nervosa try to abstain from eating. Individuals with bulimia eat but then purge by inducing themselves to vomit or by taking laxatives.

Both anorexia nervosa and bulimia are serious psychological disorders with high physical stakes if not treateIf a teacher or coach sees signs that a student is not eating, has dropped a lot of weight quickly, or is unusually lethargic, this student could be showing signs of anorexia nervosIf a teacher or coach suspects or is told that a student is vomiting after eating, taking laxatives to induce diarrhea, or exercising to unhealthy limits, this student could be showing signs of bulimia.

(Average) (Skill 3.3)

59. Effective and equitable management of resources such as exercise equipment can be accomplished by:

    A. Ensuring that the advanced students get the first rotation of equipment use so that students of differing capabilities can work at their own pace.

    B. Using sign-up sheets so that all students get a turn to use the equipment

    C. Assigning equipment usage time based strictly on alphabetization of the student's last names

    D. Letting less interested students sit out the activity so that engaged students get more time on the equipment

Answer: B. Using sign-up sheets so that all students get a turn to use the equipment

When equipment is part of the plan, make sure all children get a turn, or have time sign-up lists to use a certain piece of equipment, such as in an independent study class where students have to share cardiovascular equipment.

(Average) (Skill 3.3)

60. When introducing new skills, what is meant by a tiered plan?

    A. Practicing intricate skills before addressing less challenging skills

    B. Practicing lower levels of difficulty before the most challenging skills are addressed

    C. Grouping students by ability level, with higher ability students practicing the more challenging skills

    D. A tiered plan involves more than one instructor present

Answer: B. Practicing lower levels of difficulty before the most challenging skills are addressed

Within the framework of the day, make sure the activities are age-appropriate, time-appropriate, and accessible to all the students of the class. A day that focuses on a difficult skill might be frustrating for students who are not athletes. A tiered plan might work better on these days, where practice of different levels of difficulty are in place before the most challenging moves are addressed.

(Easy) (Skill 3.3)

61. If a class has to be divided into groups because of space or equipment limitations, which of the following must also occur?

    A. Sign-up sheets should be created so each student is guaranteed equal time with the equipment available

    B. The instructor should allocate sufficient time for the students to change into and out of their P.E. clothing

    C. A tiered instructional plan must be in place

    D. Staffing must also be split so there is an instructor present with each group

Answer: D. Staffing must also be split so there is an instructor present with each group

Students should always have an instructor present. If the class needs to be divided into separate groups, the staffing must also be divided so that there is an instructor present with every group of students in the class.

(Easy) (Skill 3.4)

62. **What are the advantages of independent activities such as walking, running, and dancing?**

   A. They do not promote unhealthy levels of competitiveness

   B. They are relatively easy fitness activities

   C. They can be done almost anywhere and require few resources

   D. They are widely accepted across different cultures

Answer: C. They can be done almost anywhere and require few resources

When a person of any age feels successful at something, he or she wants to continue doing it. Simple activities that can be done anywhere make simple lesson plans that work. The child can take that lesson home or to the park and perform well. A dance to a popular song, or an independent sport such as running or jumping rope are easy activities that a child can do on his or her own and feel successful.

(Rigorous) (Skill 3.6)

63. **What is the difference between intrinsic and extrinsic positive reinforcement?**

   A. Intrinsic positive reinforcement comes from the outside. Extrinsic positive reinforcement comes from the inside.

   B. Intrinsic positive reinforcement is intricate and detaileExtrinsic positive reinforcement is simple and general.

   C. Intrinsic positive reinforcement can only be communicated verbally. Extrinsic positive reinforcement can only be communicated by example.

   D. Intrinsic positive reinforcement comes from the inside. Extrinsic positive reinforcement comes from the outside.

Answer: D. Intrinsic positive reinforcement comes from the inside. Extrinsic positive reinforcement comes from the outside.

While the best positive reinforcements are intrinsic and come from within, extrinsic positive reinforcement can be an effective motivator for students.

(Easy) (Skill 3.6)

64. **Which of the following is an example of an intrinsic positive reinforcement?**

   A. The reward given for completing a task correctly

   B. The endorphins released during exercise

   C. An award given to recognize achievement

   D. A disciplinary action taken in response to not following established classroom procedure

Answer: B. The endorphins released during exercise

An intrinsic positive reinforcement comes from inside, whereas an extrinsic positive reinforcement comes from the outside. An example of intrinsic positive reinforcement is the endorphins released during exercise that motivate one to exercise in the future.

(Easy) (Skill 3.6)

65. **Which of the following is an example of an extrinsic positive reinforcement?**

    A. A disciplinary action taken for egregious misbehavior during class time

    B. A disciplinary action taken for a minor infraction

    C. A reward given for completing a task correctly

    D. One's feelings about one's own abilities

Answer: C. A reward given for completing a task correctly

An extrinsic positive reinforcement comes from the outside. Examples of extrinsic positive reinforcement include individual awards or rewards, or letting the students as a group do something they really like as a reward for completing tasks or activities correctly.

(Average) (Skill 4.1)

66. **When addressing poor performance verbally, an instructor should:**

    A. Address the student in front of the group so that other students can learn from the experience

    B. Address the student one-on-one so that the student is not embarrassed in front of his or her peers

    C. Be general in the assessment so the student must deduce the problem, thus deepening the student's learning experience

    D. Stop all group and individual activity to focus on the issues of the poorly performing student

Answer: B. Address the student one-on-one so that the student is not embarrassed in front of his or her peers

Students feel less cornered when addressed in a one-on-one situation, especially when addressing poor performance, a failure in an assessment, or behavioral concerns. When a student is addressed in front of the group, the result can be immediate defensiveness or withdrawal. The lasting impact of embarrassment can cause continuous problems in the current class and even across the curriculum.

(Average) (Skill 4.1)

67. **Which of the following is not an effective method of nonverbal communication?**

    A. A simple point or motion

    B. A clapped rhythm or whistle

    C. A raised hand, known as "give me five"

    D. A simple stern frown accompanied by physical proximity to the student

Answer: D. A simple stern frown accompanied by physical proximity to the student

Although physical proximity to a student can be an effective form of nonverbal communication, it should not be accompanied by disapproving looks. When a teacher needs to get a student back on task, sometimes just standing near her helps the student realize that she needs to make a better choice. Sometimes then, too, the teacher can hear or see what the situation really is, such as student bullying, socialization problems, or problems adhering to general rules.

(Rigorous) (Skill 4.2)

68. Which of the following is an effective verbal follow-up to the assessment below?

Skill: General pushups

"You are doing great, Susie. I like that you are using the full range of motion. Just remember to treat your back like a board and try to hold it straight and still from the top to the bottom and back up."

A. No further verbal follow up is needed because the issue was clearly communicated

B. "Can I see another one, Susie?"

C. "If your back isn't straight, then you technically aren't performing a push-up."

D. "If you don't keep your back straight, you could hurt your back."

Answer: B. "Can I see another one, Susie?"

After the initial positive and specific feedback, the instructor should follow up with asking the child to repeat the task. This would enable the instructor to see whether the feedback was sufficient to correct the student's form. A short demonstration of the exercise will show the teacher whether to modify the exercise again, ask for practice, or teach the child how to develop that level and then move to the next.

(Average) (Skill 4.4)

69. Which of the following forms of communication can have negative impacts on student learning?

A. Connecting student performance to student character

B. Connecting student performance to student ability

C. Generalizing student behavior

D. All of the above

Answer: D. All of the above

Never attack a student's character or generalize his or her behavior. Making statements assuming a child's inability to achieve are also unacceptable. Do not generalize that a child or class of children is "all bad" or assume that an entire class is at fault when a student is acting out. Instead, treat all children like they have potential and ability. It is the responsibility of educators to give children a safe place to learn. No child should feel belittled, humiliated, estranged, or frightened anywhere in school.

(Average) (Skill 4.4)

70. An email is similar to/different from a letter in which of the following ways?

A. In an email, words and sentences can be abbreviated

B. An email should be written in the same way as a letter

C. Emails do not require a salutation or a sign-off

D. A letter is more formal than an email

Answer: B. An email should be written in the same way as a letter

Quick communicating devices that are often used today, such as email and text messaging, should be used in an effective manner. Email should have proper grammar, and texting should always be concise when sent to a colleague. In professional emails, the teacher should treat the colleague as if he is composing a letter, including articles, complete sentences, paragraphs if necessary, and a signature or line for the teacher's name.

(Easy) (Skill 4.4)

71. **Which of the following statements would be most appropriate for an assessment form?**

    A. I just don't see any specific evidence that Jerry can or will meet curriculum goals this quarter

    B. Jerry is not reaching goals

    C. Jerry is performing 2 out of 9 assessment qualifications, and has completed none of the president's physical fitness test

    D. Jerry needs to work on meeting performance goals

Answer: C. Jerry is performing 2 out of 9 assessment qualifications, and has completed none of the president's physical fitness test

In a discipline referral, include only specific facts. Remember that administration and parents will have access to this form. In assessments, remember to quantify data specifically, not generally. A statement like "Jerry is not reaching goals" is not specific enough to help the student, teachers, or parents address the situation. "Jerry is performing 2 out of 9 assessment qualifications, and has completed none of the president's physical fitness test" helps the parents understand why he has his current grade, and helps them see where their child needs to apply himself.

Planning, Instruction, and Student Assessment

(Easy) (Skill 5.1)

72. **Using the same foot to take off from a surface and to land is which locomotor skill?**

    A. Jumping

    B. Vaulting

    C. Leaping

    D. Hopping

Answer: D. Hopping

Hopping is a move with light, bounding skips or leaps. Basically, it is the ability to jump on one foot.

(Easy) (Skill 5.1)

73. **Which nonlocomotor skill entails movement around a joint where two body parts meet?**

    A. Twisting

    B. Swaying

    C. Bending

    D. Stretching

Answer: C. Bending

Bending is a deviation from a straight-line position. It also means to assume a curved, crooked, or angular form or direction, or to incline the body.

(Easy) (Skill 5.1)

74. **A sharp change of direction from one's original line of movement is which nonlocomotor skill?**

    A. Twisting

    B. Dodging

    C. Swaying

    D. Swinging

Answer: B. Dodging

Dodging is the ability to avoid something by moving or shifting aside quickly.

(Easy) (Skill 5.1)

75. **Having students pretend they are playing basketball or trying to catch a bus develops which locomotor skill?**

    A. Galloping

    B. Running

    C. Leaping

    D. Skipping

Answer: B. Running

Playing basketball involves nearly constant running up and down the court. In addition, chasing is a good example to use with children to illustrate the concept of running.

(Easy) (Skill 5.1)

76. **Having students play Fox and Hound develops:**

    A. Galloping

    B. Hopping

    C. Stepping-hopping

    D. Skipping

Answer: A. Galloping

Fox and Hound is an activity that emphasizes rapid running. The form of the exercise most closely resembles a gallop, especially in rhythm and rapidity. It can develop or progress at an accelerated rate.

(Easy) (Skill 5.1)

77. **Having students take off and land with both feet together develops which locomotor skill?**

    A. Hopping

    B. Jumping

    C. Leaping

    D. Skipping

Answer: B. Jumping

Jumping is a skill that most humans and many animals share. It is the process of getting one's body off of the ground for a short time using one's own power, usually by propelling oneself upward via contraction and then forceful extension of the legs. One can jump up to reach something high, jump over a fence or ditch, or jump down from a higher point to a lower one. One can also jump while dancing and as a sport in track and field.

(Easy) (Skill 5.1)

78. **Activities such as pretending to pick fruit off a tree or reaching for a star develop which nonlocomotor skill?**

    A. Bending

    B. Stretching

    C. Turning

    D. Twisting

Answer: B. Stretching

Stretching is the activity of gradually applying tensile force to lengthen, strengthen, and lubricate muscles, often performed in anticipation of physical exertion and to increase the range of motion within a joint. Stretching is an especially important accompaniment to activities that emphasize controlled muscular strength and flexibility. These include ballet, acrobatics, and martial arts. Stretching may also help prevent injury to tendons, ligaments, and muscles by improving muscular elasticity and reducing the stretch reflex in greater ranges of motion that might cause injury to tissue.

(Easy) (Skill 5.1)

79. **Picking up coins, tying shoes, and petting animals develop which nonlocomotor skill?**

    A. Bending

    B. Stretching

    C. Turning

    D. Twisting

Answer: A. Bending

Bending is the action of moving the body across a skeletal joint. In each of the sample activities, one must bend from the waist or knees to reach a low object.

(Average) (Skill 5.1)

80. **Progressively decreasing the size of a target at which balls are projected develops which manipulative skill?**

    A. Throwing

    B. Trapping

    C. Volleying

    D. Kicking

Answer: A. Throwing

Children develop throwing skills (the ability to propel an object through the air with a rapid movement of the arm and wrist) by projecting balls at progressively smaller targets.

(Average) (Skill 5.1)

81. **Hitting a stationary object while in a fixed position, then incorporating movement, develops which manipulative skill?**

   A. Bouncing

   B. Trapping

   C. Throwing

   D. Striking

Answer: D. Striking

Striking is giving impetus to an object with the use of the hands or another object.

(Easy) (Skill 5.1)

82. **Coordinated movements that project a person over an obstacle are known as:**

   A. Jumping

   B. Vaulting

   C. Leaping

   D. Hopping

Answer: B. Vaulting

Vaulting is defined as coordinated movements that project a person over an obstacle. Jumping involves projectile movements that momentarily suspend the body in midair. Leaping is similar to running but has greater height, flight, and distance. Hopping uses the same foot to take off from a surface and to land.

(Rigorous) (Skill 5.1)

83. **Which manipulative skill uses the hands to stop the momentum of an object?**

   A. Trapping

   B. Catching

   C. Striking

   D. Rolling

Answer: B. Catching

The ability to use the hands to catch an object is a manipulative skill. A successful catch harnesses the force of the oncoming object to stop the object's momentum.

(Rigorous) (Skill 5.1)

84. **To enhance skill and strategy performance for striking or throwing objects, for catching or collecting objects, and for carrying and propelling objects, students must first learn techniques for:**

   A. Offense

   B. Defense

   C. Controlling objects

   D. Continuous play of objects

Answer: C. Controlling objects

For enhancing the catching, throwing, carrying, or propelling of objects, a student must learn how to control the objects. The control gives the player a sense of the object. Thus, offense, defense, and continuous play come naturally, as they are part of the controlling process.

(Rigorous) (Skill 5.2)

85. What is the proper order of sequential development for the acquisition of locomotor skills?

    A. Creep, crawl, walk, jump, run, slide, gallop, hop, leap, skip, step-hop

    B. Crawl, walk, creep, slide, walk, run, hop, leap, gallop, skip, step-hop

    C. Creep, crawl, walk, slide, run, hop, leap, skip, gallop, jump, step-hop

    D. Crawl, creep, walk, run, jump, hop, gallop, slide, leap, skip, step-hop

    Answer: D. Crawl, creep, walk, run, jump, hop, gallop, slide, leap, skip, step-hop

    Each skill in the progression builds on the previous skills.

(Rigorous) (Skill 5.4)

86. What is the proper sequential order of development for the acquisition of nonlocomotor skills?

    A. Stretch, sit, bend, turn, swing, twist, shake, rock and sway, dodge, fall

    B. Bend, stretch, turn, twist, swing, sit, rock and sway, shake, dodge, fall

    C. Stretch, bend, sit, shake, turn, rock and sway, swing, twist, dodge, fall

    D. Bend, stretch, sit, turn, twist, swing, sway, rock and sway, dodge, fall

    Answer: C. Stretch, bend, sit, shake, turn, rock and sway, swing, twist, dodge, fall

    Each skill in the progression builds on the previous skills.

(Easy) (Skill 5.4)

87. Having students collapse in their own space or lower themselves as if they are a raindrop or snowflake develops which nonlocomotor skill?

    A. Dodging

    B. Shaking

    C. Swinging

    D. Falling

    Answer: D. Falling

    Falling is a major cause of personal injury in athletics. Athletic participants must learn how to fall in such a way as to limit the possibility of injury.

(Rigorous) (Skill 5.4)

88. Which is the proper sequential order of development for the acquisition of manipulative skills?

    A. Striking, throwing, bouncing, catching, trapping, kicking, ball rolling, volleying

    B. Striking, throwing, kicking, ball rolling, volleying, bouncing, catching, trapping

    C. Striking, throwing, catching, trapping, kicking, ball rolling, bouncing, volleying

    D. Striking, throwing, kicking, ball rolling, bouncing, volleying

    Answer: B. Striking, throwing, kicking, ball rolling, volleying, bouncing, catching, trapping

    Each skill in this progression builds on the previous skill.

(Average) (Skill 5.4)

89. **Having students hit a large balloon with both hands develops which manipulative skill?**

    A. Bouncing

    B. Striking

    C. Volleying

    D. Trapping

    Answer: C. Volleying

    In a number of ball games, a volley is the ball that a player receives and delivers without touching the grounThe ability to volley a ball back and forth requires great body control and spatial awareness.

(Easy) (Skill 5.5)

90. **If an action results in direct or indirect injury, what is this called under the law?**

    A. A tort

    B. A petition

    C. A liability

    D. In loco parentis

    Answer: A. A tort

    A tort is a legal wrong resulting in a direct or indirect injury; torts include omissions and acts intended or unintended to cause harm.

(Average) (Skill 5.5)

91. **What is the definition of negligence?**

    A. Causing harm or injury through an act of omission

    B. Failing to fulfill a legal duty according to common reasoning

    C. Causing harm or injury through a direct action

    D. The willful intention to cause harm or injury

    Answer: B. Failing to fulfill a legal duty according to common reasoning

    Negligence is failing to fulfill a legal duty according to common reasoning; negligence can apply to instruction and facility maintenance. Instructors must consider sex, size, and skill of participants when planning activities and grouping students.

(Easy) (Skill 5.5)

92. **What is the definition of in loco parentis?**

    A. The inability to reason with parents regarding the disciplinary needs of their children

    B. The liability of a manufacturer to the person(s) using their products who sustains injury

    C. Acting in the place of a parent or guardian in relation to a child

    D. Harmful contact of one person by another

Answer: C. Acting in the place of a parent or guardian in relation to a child

When students are at school, teachers are acting in a capacity of in loco parentis and have a responsibility to ensure the safety and welfare of the students on behalf of the parents.

(Average) (Skill 5.5)

93. **Grouping students to equalize competitive levels, considering the ability and skill level of participants when planning activities, and properly organizing and supervising classes are concrete actions that can:**

    A. Ensure student safety and limit lawsuits due to injury or harm

    B. Improve job satisfaction for the physical education instructor

    C. Lead to positive teacher-student verbal communication

    D. Ensure that the requirements of Title IX are met

Answer: A. Ensure student safety and limit lawsuits due to injury or harm

The above actions, as well as knowing the health status of each student, using safe equipment and facilities, never leaving a classroom unattended, knowing first aid, and giving instruction prior to dangerous activities (and other actions) can directly limit the likelihood of student injury and resulting lawsuits.

(Easy) (Skill 5.6)

94. **Which is an effective method of goal-setting?**

    A. Make short-term goals a fixed percentage of the final, long-term goal

    B. Set several small, short-term goals as steps to attain one long-term goal

    C. Set goals that are slightly out of reach so that students have to strive to achieve them

    D. Set the same goals for all students

Answer: B. Set several small, short-term goals as steps to attain one long-term goal

Goal-setting is an effective way of achieving progress. In order to preserve and increase self-confidence, you and your students must set goals that are consistently reachable. One such way of achieving this is to set several small, short-term goals to attain one long-term goal. Be realistic in goal-setting to increase fitness levels gradually. As students reach their goals, set new goals in order to continue performance improvement.

(Easy) (Skill 5.11)

95. **Which of the following actions does not promote safety?**

    A. Allowing students to wear the current style of shoes

    B. Presenting organized activities

    C. Inspecting equipment and facilities

    D. Instructing skill and activities properly

Answer: A. Allowing students to wear the current style of shoes

Shoes are very important in physical education and the emphasis on current shoe styles does not promote safety, because it focuses more on the look of the clothing rather than its functionality.

(Easy) (Skill 5.11)

96. The most important nutrient the body requires, without which life can only be sustained for a few days, is:

    A. Vitamins

    B. Minerals

    C. Water

    D. Carbohydrates

Answer: C. Water

Although the body requires vitamins, minerals, and carbohydrates to achieve proper growth and shape, water is essential. Without it, the body gets dehydrated and death is a possibility. Water should be pure and desalinated, because seawater can cause kidney failure and death.

(Average) (Skill 5.11)

97. **Which of the following can help prevent Achilles tendon, a common athletic injury?**

    A. Stretch dorsiflexion and strengthen plantar flexion (heel raises)

    B. Use high top shoes and tape support

    C. Increase strength and flexibility of calf and thigh muscles

    D. All of the above

Answer: A. Stretch dorsiflexion and strengthen plantar flexion (heel raises)

Stretching dorsiflexion and strengthening plantar flexion can help prevent Achilles tendon. Using high top shoes and tape support will help prevent ankle injuries. Increasing the strength and flexibility of calf and thigh muscles will help prevent knee injuries.

(Average) (Skill 6.2)

98. **Students are performing trunk extensions. What component of fitness does this activity assess?**

    A. Balance

    B. Flexibility

    C. Body composition

    D. Coordination

Answer: B. Flexibility

The core component of trunk extensions is flexibility. Trunk extension also indicates the body's capacity for full expansion and emphasizes areas such as the stomach, arms, and shoulder joints.

(Rigorous) (Skill 6.2)

99. **Which of the following can be used to assess muscle endurance?**

    A. Dynamometers, cable tensiometer, the 1-RM Test

    B. Hydrostatic weighing

    C. Maximal stress test, sub maximal stress test, Bruce Protocol, Cooper 1.5 Mile Run/Walk Fitness Test

    D. Squat-thrust, pull-ups, sit-ups, lateral pull-down, bench press, arm curl, push-ups, and dips

Answer: D. Squat-thrust, pull-ups, sit-ups, lateral pull-down, bench press, arm curl, push-ups, and dips

Squat-thrust, pulls-ups, sit-ups, lateral pull-downs, bench press, arm curls, push-ups, and dips are good activities for assessing muscle endurance.

(Average) (Skill 6.3)
100. **What is the President's Challenge?**

A. A comprehensive health-related fitness education program developed by physical educators for physical educators

B. A program that encourages all Americans to make regular physical activity a part of their everyday lives

C. A program to increase parental awareness of children's fitness levels

D. A comprehensive nutrition curriculum that public schools can adopt into their curriculum

Answer: A. A program that encourages all Americans to make regular physical activity a part of their everyday lives

The President's Challenge is a program that encourages all Americans to make regular physical activity a part of their everyday lives. No matter what your activity and fitness level, the President's Challenge can help motivate you to improve. *http://www.presidentschallenge.org/.*

(Easy) (Skill 6.7)
101. **Instructors can encourage students to self-assess their physical education progress by employing:**

A. Reflection

B. Journal writing

C. Interdisciplinary study

D. All of the above

Answer: D. All of the above

Reflection and questioning, journal writing, and relating physical education topics to other content areas through interdisciplinary study are just some of the ways teachers can promote students' ability to assess their own physical fitness.

Collaboration, Reflection, and Technology

(Average) (Skill 7.1)
102. **What would not be an effective way of tying fitness instruction into social studies instruction?**

A. Teaching how the body processes calories

B. Teaching how to interpret graphs and charts of performance data

C. Teaching the mechanics of muscle contraction

D. Teaching the history of a particular sport

Answer: D. Teaching the history of a particular sport

Teaching the history of a particular sport would be a good way to tie fitness instruction into social studies or history instruction. Teaching the science behind body processes or how to interpret performance data when it is presented in charts or graphs would be a good exercise in P.E.-Science cross-curricular study.

(Easy) (Skill 7.2)

103. **Which subject areas have knowledge and skills that can be integrated into physical education instruction?**

    A. English, math, and social studies

    B. Math, science, and social studies

    C. History, English, and economics

    D. Arts, industrial arts, and social studies

Answer: B. Math, science, and social studies

Science: Anatomy, study of forces, biology, and nutrition are all health and fitness-related subjects.

Mathematics: Statistics, graphs, charts, formulas, and ratios are all health- and fitness-related subjects.

Social Studies: Histories of sports or activities, such as the Olympics, are health-and fitness-related subjects.

When teaching students about any of these topics, coordinate with other teachers, and check sources. Study and cross-curricular workshops can also help.

(Easy) (Skill 7.4)

104. **What are some ways that P.E. instructors can promote opportunities for physical activity in the community?**

    A. Send home parks and recreation brochures for parents

    B. Facilitate community walks, races, or other volunteer community events

    C. All of the above

    D. None of the above

Answer: C. All of the above

The physical education teacher is sometimes the parents' resource for what is going on in the community and the resource for getting involveThe instructor can facilitate healthy community activities or send home information about public community resources.

(Rigorous) (Skill 8.1)

105. **In the reflective cycle, a teacher goes through a constant cycle of learning characterized by:**

    A. Description, feelings, evaluation, analysis, conclusion, action plan

    B. Feelings, description, evaluation, action plan, analysis, conclusion

    C. Feelings, evaluation, analysis, conclusion

    D. Action plan, analysis, feelings, conclusion

Answer: A. Description, feelings, evaluation, analysis, conclusion, action plan

This list represents the correct order of the stages of the reflective cycle.

(Average) (Skill 8.1)

106. **What is the purpose or point of the reflective cycle?**

    A. To evaluate the effectiveness of one's teaching

    B. To reflect on how to improve team-building exercises in the classroom

    C. To share effective teaching strategies with colleagues

    D. To practice creating successful action plans

Answer: A. To evaluate the effectiveness of one's teaching

The point of this cycle is that we as teachers must constantly reevaluate our own teaching. What works and what doesn't? How can the lesson be tweaked to get the same message across? How can we reach all of the students? How can we avoid pitfalls and hiccoughs in our plans?

(Average) (Skill 8.1)

107. **What type of question should instructors ask themselves during the description phase of the reflective cycle?**

    A. What occurred?

    B. What are the pros and cons of the occurrence?

    C. How would an outsider see this occurrence?

    D. What will you do if something similar happens again?

Answer: A. What occurred?

The questions of the description phase help the instructor to define what occurred.

(Rigorous) (Skill 8.1)

108. **What type of question should instructors ask themselves during the evaluation phase of the reflective cycle?**

    A. What could be done with this problem?

    B. What are the pros and cons of the occurrence?

    C. How would an outsider see this occurrence?

    D. What will you do if something similar happens again?

Answer: B. What are the pros and cons of the occurrence?

The questions of the evaluation phase help the instructor to evaluate what worked and didn't work.

(Average) (Skill 9.1)

109. **Which of the following is a movement-driven (rather than joystick-driven) type of game system that can be used to supplement traditional exercise?**

    A. Playstation

    B. Atari

    C. Sony Wii

    D. Peertrainer

Answer: C. Sony Wii

Many technological game systems are movement-driven, instead of joystick-driven. The Sony Wii is the first marketed system that reads the player's body rather than signals from buttons. Many others are following suit. By using a remote signal, the game player can move like the joystick controller, making movement important to the outcome of the game. This is not to say that the Wii can replace sports and games, but that it is an alternative to sitting and playing.

(Rigorous) (Skill 9.1)

110. **Which site is dedicated to voluntary and independent journaling about nutrition and fitness?**

    A. *www.aahperd.org*

    B. *www.peertrainer.com*

    C. *www.cooperinstitute.org*

    D. *www.acefitness.org*

Answer: B. *www.peertrainer.com*

In an independent fitness class, students can journal about their nutrition and movement. One site that is dedicated to voluntary and independent journaling is *www.peertrainer.com*. A person can join a group or team with similar goals or create one with similar goals and make notes. A teacher could have a peer trainer team for each class and motivate students through a social network by reviewing exercise and nutritional trends for the students.

(Average) (Skill 9.2)

111. **What precaution(s) should be taken when using technology to display online materials during instruction?**

    A. Review all online material for appropriateness before using it in instruction

    B. Become familiar with the technology to ensure no difficulties or delays are experienced during the presentation

    C. Verify that the material is consistent with the goals of the President's Challenge

    D. Make sure the material has an interactive learning component

Answer: A. Review all online material for appropriateness before using it in instruction

Most schools now have a setup allowing teachers to use technology to present material. Document cameras with computer access can display documents, presentations, or online content on a large screen for the class, or even an auditorium full of people, to see. With this comes the responsibility for reviewing all online data first and only using data for student learning and learning enhancement.

Supplemental Content

(Average) (Domain V)

112. **For linear movement, force applied close to the center of gravity requires a _____ magnitude of force to move the object than does force applied farther from the center of gravity.**

    A. Larger

    B. Equal

    C. Uneven

    D. Smaller

    Answer: D. Smaller

    For movement to occur, force must overcome the inertia of the object and any other resisting forces. For linear movement, force applied close to the center of gravity requires a smaller magnitude of force to move the object than does force applied farther from the center of gravity.

(Easy) (Domain V)

113. **What are the two types of mechanical energy?**

    A. Elastic energy and absorption energy

    B. Potential energy and kinetic energy

    C. Gravitational energy and elastic energy

    D. Absorption energy and gravitational energy

Answer: B. Potential and kinetic energy

The two major types of mechanical energy are potential energy and kinetic energy. Potential energy is the energy possessed by virtue of position, absolute location in space, or change in shape. Kinetic energy is the energy possessed by virtue of motion. Elastic and gravitational energy are types of potential energy.

(Average) (Domain V)

114. **The energy of an object to do work while recoiling is which type of potential energy?**

    A. Absorption

    B. Kinetic

    C. Elastic

    D. Torque

Answer: C. Elastic

In materials science, the word elastomer refers to a material that is very elastic (like rubber). The word elastic is often used colloquially to refer to an elastomeric material such as rubber or cloth/rubber combinations. An elastomer is capable of withstanding stress without injury. Elastic potential energy describes the energy inherent in flexible objects or the energy potential of an object to do work while recoiling (or reforming) after stretching, compressing, or twisting.

(Rigorous) (Domain V)

115. **Gradually decelerating a moving mass by utilization of smaller forces over a long period of time is:**

    A. Stability

    B. Equilibrium

    C. Angular force

    D. Force absorption

Answer: D. Force absorption

Force absorption is the gradual deceleration of a moving mass by utilization of smaller forces over a long period of time.

(Average) (Domain V)

116. **Equilibrium is maintained as long as:**

    A. Body segments are moved independently

    B. The center of gravity is over the base of support

    C. Force is applied to the base of support

    D. The center of gravity is lowered

Answer: B. The center of gravity is over the base of support

Equilibrium is a state in which all acting influences are canceled by others, resulting in a stable, balanced, or unchanging system. An object maintains equilibrium as long as its center of gravity is over its base of support.

(Average) (Domain V)

117. **Which of the following does not enhance equilibrium?**

    A. Shifting the center of gravity away from the direction of movement

    B. Increasing the base of support

    C. Lowering the base of support

    D. Increasing the base of support and lowering the center of support

Answer: A. Shifting the center of gravity away from the direction of movement

The entire center of gravity of the body shifts in the same direction as the movement of the body's segments. As long as the center of gravity remains over the base of support, the body will remain in a state of equilibrium. The more the center of gravity is situated over the base, the greater the stability. A wider base of support and/or a lower center of gravity enhances stability. To be effective, the base of support must widen in the direction of the force produced or opposed by the body. Shifting weight in the direction of the force in conjunction with widening the base of support further enhances stability.

(Rigorous) (Domain V)

118. How does a first-class lever work?

A. The force works at a point between the axis and the resistance (the resistance arm is always longer than the force arm)

B. The axis is between the points of application of the force and the resistance

C. The force arm is longer than the resistance arm (operator applies resistance between the axis and the point of application of force)

D. The force arm and the resistance arm are the same length

Answer: B. The axis is between the points of application of the force and the resistance

The definition of a first-class lever is that the axis is between the points of application of the force and the resistance. An example is a pair of pliers.

(Average) (Domain V)

119. Freehand front lunges will help an individual to target muscle endurance in which of the following muscle groups?

A. Trapezius and lateral muscles

B. Thighs and hamstrings

C. Triceps and biceps

D. Obliques and thighs

Answer: B. Thighs and hamstrings

Freehand front lunges work large muscle groups in the lower body, especially the legs. These muscles are the thighs and hamstrings.

(Average) (Domain V)

120. Dumbbell side bends will help an individual to target muscle endurance in which of the following muscle groups?

A. Trapezius and lateral muscles

B. Rear deltoids

C. Triceps and biceps

D. Obliques

Answer: D. Obliques

Dumbbell side bends work large muscle groups in the midsection. These muscles are the obliques.

CPSIA information can be obtained at www.ICGtesting.com
Printed in the USA
LVOW031616200412

278500LV00002B/83/P

WITHDRAWAL